Examining the Aging Workforce and Its Impact on Economic and Social Development

Bruno de Sousa Lopes
University of Aveiro, Portugal

Maria Céu Lamas
School of Health, Polytechnic of Porto, Portugal

Vanessa Amorim
University of Aveiro, Portugal

Orlando Lima Rua
Porto Accounting and Business School, Polytechnic of Porto, Portugal

A volume in the Advances in Human Resources Management and Organizational Development (AHRMOD) Book Series

IGI Global
PUBLISHER of TIMELY KNOWLEDGE

Published in the United States of America by
IGI Global
Business Science Reference (an imprint of IGI Global)
701 E. Chocolate Avenue
Hershey PA, USA 17033
Tel: 717-533-8845
Fax: 717-533-8661
E-mail: cust@igi-global.com
Web site: http://www.igi-global.com

Library of Congress Cataloging-in-Publication Data

Names: Lopes, Bruno, 1996- editor. | Lamas, Maria, 1968- editor. | Amorim, Vanessa, 1992- editor.
Title: Examining the aging workforce and its impact on economic and social development / edited by Bruno Lopes, Maria Lamas, Vanessa Amorim, Orlando Rua.
Description: Hershey, PA : Business Science Reference, [2023] | Includes bibliographical references and index. | Summary: "This comprehensive and timely publication aims to be an essential reference source, building on existing literature in the field of the aging workforce for the economic and social development of countries while providing additional research opportunities in this dynamic and growing field. Thus, the book aims to reflect on this critical issue, increasing the understanding of the importance of the Aging Workforce in the context of the Business and Management Area, and providing relevant academic work, empirical research findings, and an overview of this relevant field of study. It is hoped that this book will provide the resources necessary for policymakers, academicians, interdisciplinary researchers, advanced-level students, technology developers, managers, and government officials to adopt and implement solutions for a new social and economic reality with a direct impact on the workforce derived from the aging population"-- Provided by publisher.
Identifiers: LCCN 2022043697 (print) | LCCN 2022043698 (ebook) | ISBN 9781668463512 (hardcover) | ISBN 9781668463529 (paperback) | ISBN 9781668463536 (ebook)
Subjects: LCSH: Age and employment. | Older people--Employment. | Personnel management. | Organizational change. | Economic development.
Classification: LCC HD6279 .E93 2023 (print) | LCC HD6279 (ebook) | DDC 331.3/98--dc23/eng/20220908
LC record available at https://lccn.loc.gov/2022043697
LC ebook record available at https://lccn.loc.gov/2022043698

This book is published in the IGI Global book series Advances in Human Resources Management and Organizational Development (AHRMOD) (ISSN: 2327-3372; eISSN: 2327-3380)

British Cataloguing in Publication Data
A Cataloguing in Publication record for this book is available from the British Library.

All work contributed to this book is new, previously-unpublished material.
The views expressed in this book are those of the authors, but not necessarily of the publisher.

For electronic access to this publication, please contact: eresources@igi-global.com.

Advances in Human Resources Management and Organizational Development (AHRMOD) Book Series

Patricia Ordóñez de Pablos
Universidad de Oviedo, Spain

ISSN:2327-3372
EISSN:2327-3380

MISSION

A solid foundation is essential to the development and success of any organization and can be accomplished through the effective and careful management of an organization's human capital. Research in human resources management and organizational development is necessary in providing business leaders with the tools and methodologies which will assist in the development and maintenance of their organizational structure.

The **Advances in Human Resources Management and Organizational Development (AHRMOD) Book Series** aims to publish the latest research on all aspects of human resources as well as the latest methodologies, tools, and theories regarding organizational development and sustainability. The **AHRMOD Book Series** intends to provide business professionals, managers, researchers, and students with the necessary resources to effectively develop and implement organizational strategies.

COVERAGE

- Succession Planning
- Training and Development
- Personnel Retention
- Employment and Labor Laws
- Human Relations Movement
- Organizational Development
- Employee Evaluation
- Corporate Governance
- Skills Management
- Coaching and Mentoring

IGI Global is currently accepting manuscripts for publication within this series. To submit a proposal for a volume in this series, please contact our Acquisition Editors at Acquisitions@igi-global.com or visit: http://www.igi-global.com/publish/.

The Advances in Human Resources Management and Organizational Development (AHRMOD) Book Series (ISSN 2327-3372) is published by IGI Global, 701 E. Chocolate Avenue, Hershey, PA 17033-1240, USA, www.igi-global.com. This series is composed of titles available for purchase individually; each title is edited to be contextually exclusive from any other title within the series. For pricing and ordering information please visit http://www.igi-global.com/book-series/advances-human-resources-management-organizational/73670. Postmaster: Send all address changes to above address.

Titles in this Series

For a list of additional titles in this series, please visit: http://www.igi-global.com/book-series/

The Experiences of Black Women Diversity Practitioners in Historically White Institutions
Tristen Brenaé Johnson (Moffitt Cancer Center, USA)
Information Science Reference • © 2023 • 330pp • H/C (ISBN: 9781668435649) • US $215.00

Handbook of Research on Acceleration Programs for SMEs
Inês Lisboa (Politechnic Institute of Leiria, Portugal) Nuno Teixeira (Politechnic Institute of Setúbal, Portugal) Liliane Segura (Presbiteriano Mackenzie Institute, Brazil) Tomáš Krulický (Institute of Technology and Business, České Budějovice, Czech Republic) and Veronika Machová (Institute of Technology and Business, České Budějovice, Czech Republic)
Business Science Reference • © 2023 • 575pp • H/C (ISBN: 9781668456668) • US $360.00

Leadership Perspectives on Effective Intergenerational Communication and Management
Fatma Ince (Mersin University, Turkey)
Business Science Reference • © 2023 • 320pp • H/C (ISBN: 9781668461402) • US $230.00

Developing Diversity, Equity, and Inclusion Policies for Promoting Employee Sustainability and Well-Being
Sónia P. Gonçalves (ISCSP-ULisboa, Portugal) Paula Cristina Nunes Figueiredo (Universidade Lusófona, Portugal) Eduardo Luis Soares Tomé (ULHT - Universidade Lusófona, Portugal) and José Baptista (ISCSP-ULisboa, Portugal)
Business Science Reference • © 2023 • 330pp • H/C (ISBN: 9781668441817) • US $240.00

Global Citizenship and Its Impact on Multiculturalism in the Workplace
Randa Diab-Bahman (Kuwait College of Science and Technology, Kuwait) and Abrar Al-Enzi (Gulf University for Science and Technology, Kuwait)
Business Science Reference • © 2023 • 300pp • H/C (ISBN: 9781668454367) • US $240.00

Socio-Economic Disparities, Vulnerable Communities, and the Future of Work and Entrepreneurship
JoAnn Denise Rolle (Medgar Evers College, City University of New York, USA) and Micah Crump (Medgar Evers College, City University of New York, USA)
Business Science Reference • © 2023 • 335pp • H/C (ISBN: 9781668469903) • US $240.00

IGI Global
PUBLISHER of TIMELY KNOWLEDGE

701 East Chocolate Avenue, Hershey, PA 17033, USA
Tel: 717-533-8845 x100 • Fax: 717-533-8661
E-Mail: cust@igi-global.com • www.igi-global.com

Editorial Advisory Board

Table of Contents

Preface xii

Chapter 1
Engaging the Aging Process: Unlock the Fountain of Youth 1
Abeni El-Amin, Fort Hays State University, USA & Shenyang Normal University, China

Chapter 2
Understanding the Evolution of Sensory Aging in the Workforce 19
Maria Céu Lamas, School of Health, Polytechnic of Porto, Portugal
Orlando Lima Rua, Porto Accounting and Business School, Polytechnic of Porto, Portugal
Bruno de Sousa Lopes, University of Aveiro, Portugal
Vanessa Amorim, Porto Accounting and Business School, Polytechnic of Porto, Portugal

Chapter 3
Aging in Portugal: The Social Development Point of View 45
Maria Inês Sousa, ISCTE, University Institute of Lisbon, Portugal

Chapter 4
The Aging Workforce in Indonesia and Its Impact on Economic and Social Development 73
Elni Jeini Usoh, Universitas Negeri Manado, Indonesia
Linda Lambey, University of Sam Ratulangii, Indonesia
John Burgess, Torrens University, Australia

Chapter 5
The Importance of Aging in the Innovation Process of Organizations................93
Bruno de Sousa Lopes, University of Aveiro, Portugal
Vanessa Amorim, Porto Accounting and Business School, Polytechnic of Porto, Portugal
Orlando Lima Rua, Porto Accounting and Business School, Polytechnic of Porto, Portugal
Maria Céu Lamas, School of Health, Polytechnic of Porto, Portugal

Chapter 6
Restructuring the Workforce Through Non-Ageist Hiring and Retention Practices That Value Aging Workers' Expertise: Recognizing the Need for Workplace Age Diversity...107
Nadine E. Franz, Baylor University, USA

Chapter 7
The Journey Between the Final Stage of Career and the Adaptation to Retirement...129
Bruno de Sousa Lopes, University of Aveiro, Portugal

Chapter 8
Enterprise Architecture Solutions for an Aging Workforce..............................161
Raja Saravanan, University of Aveiro, Portugal

Glossary 176

Compilation of References 182

About the Contributors 210

Index 213

Detailed Table of Contents

Preface...xii

Chapter 1
Engaging the Aging Process: Unlock the Fountain of Youth 1
Abeni El-Amin, Fort Hays State University, USA & Shenyang Normal University, China

Employment for aging is a significant aspect shaping the aging processes during formative years. Therefore, work opportunities combined and consequential impacts later in life merit special consideration. Given that population aging has become a global pattern with ensuing changes in labor markets far and wide, there is increased concern about the impacts of retirement around the globe and the macroeconomic advantages frequently connected with delaying retirement. It is fundamental for nations with aging populations to maintain profitability, given an aging workforce. Governments must make it simpler for individuals to maintain a significant presence in the workforce. This contribution focuses on improving the quality of life for aging individuals instead of only focusing on adding years to their lives.

Chapter 2
Understanding the Evolution of Sensory Aging in the Workforce 19
Maria Céu Lamas, School of Health, Polytechnic of Porto, Portugal
Orlando Lima Rua, Porto Accounting and Business School, Polytechnic of Porto, Portugal
Bruno de Sousa Lopes, University of Aveiro, Portugal
Vanessa Amorim, Porto Accounting and Business School, Polytechnic of Porto, Portugal

The aging workforce is a growing reality, given demographic changes and socioeconomic trends. Therefore, it is crucial to understand, accept, and respect the issues of an aging workforce regarding health and safety in the workplace, especially when aiming to keep the individual longer in the labor market. It is also essential to consider the potential sensory disabilities of each individual so that they can overcome them and fully perform their functions in the workplace. From this perspective, the sensory capabilities of individuals must be assured through different means to guarantee that the organic and functional changes arising from aging are successfully overcome. In this follow-up, a bibliometric analysis between 2001 and 2022 was conducted to explore the most relevant authors, journals, countries, institutions, and publications in sensory aging and the workforce.

Chapter 3
Aging in Portugal: The Social Development Point of View 45
Maria Inês Sousa, ISCTE, University Institute of Lisbon, Portugal

The chapter explores demographic aging data in Europe and the world, but more precisely in Portugal. A gradual increase in seniors and a reduction in youth characterize demographic evolution. In the chapter, the factors leading to these phenomena will be identified and duly explained, as well as the responses developed for their effect. One of the objectives is to identify solutions and answers for healthy and stimulated aging at institutions and professional areas, such as sociocultural animation. Despite several designations worldwide, its purpose is the same: to provide moments of leisure, stimulation, and learning to the entire population. In this sense, lifelong learning is a concept to be explored.

Chapter 4
The Aging Workforce in Indonesia and Its Impact on Economic and Social Development 73
Elni Jeini Usoh, Universitas Negeri Manado, Indonesia
Linda Lambey, University of Sam Ratulangii, Indonesia
John Burgess, Torrens University, Australia

Indonesia is an emerging economy that has undergone structural change and achieved sustained growth rates that have lifted average living standards over the past three decades. Compared to advanced economies, the Indonesian population and workforce are relatively young. However, the population will age over the coming decades, and the profile will resemble that of advanced economies. Poverty and inequality are extensive, and the challenge of an aging population is that only a minority of the workforce has access to a secure post-retirement income and services that support quality aging. The challenges of an aging population and workforce are discussed in the chapter. These include the large share of workers in the informal sector and the growth of contingent work arrangements in the formal sector. Many continue to work into old age as they cannot afford to retire. Despite an increase in schooling and post-secondary education participation, the quality of education and the low investment in training has limited productivity growth.

Chapter 5
The Importance of Aging in the Innovation Process of Organizations................93
Bruno de Sousa Lopes, University of Aveiro, Portugal
Vanessa Amorim, Porto Accounting and Business School, Polytechnic of Porto, Portugal
Orlando Lima Rua, Porto Accounting and Business School, Polytechnic of Porto, Portugal
Maria Céu Lamas, School of Health, Polytechnic of Porto, Portugal

The authors of this chapter aim to present the links between an aging workforce, innovation, and creativity. They address each of these themes individually, and then analyze the interconnection between the central theme (i.e., the aging workforce with creativity and innovation), and in the last point, analyze the innovative work behavior as a conclusive way of using the knowledge and skills of the aging workforce as a competitive advantage for an organization. Thus, this chapter demonstrates that the aging workforce, contrary to popular belief, is one of the age segments of organizations that contributes most to the innovation process since there is a symbiotic process between older and younger workers, and this is also evident in the creative process since innovation and creativity are intrinsic processes.

Chapter 6
Restructuring the Workforce Through Non-Ageist Hiring and Retention Practices That Value Aging Workers' Expertise: Recognizing the Need for Workplace Age Diversity...107
Nadine E. Franz, Baylor University, USA

The aging workforce faces obstacles in a youth-obsessed society. Ageist assumptions dominate the airwaves, where society celebrates youth while undervaluing older people. These stereotypes permeate as companies marginalize older people while sending veiled messages that diminish their worth. Older people endure barriers, whether seeking new opportunities or promotions. Ageism is widespread, and hiring and retention practices often neglect older workers. The disregard for more senior talent results from ageist stereotypes. These biases ignore older employees' worth. Employer mistreatment of older employees signals their lack of commitment to diversity. Employers must implement non-ageist HR initiatives while continuously holding themselves accountable for executing fair employment policies. This chapter explores ageist issues, controversies, problems, and steps employers must take to create and implement non-ageist hiring and retention policies to safeguard a diverse workforce.

Chapter 7
The Journey Between the Final Stage of Career and the Adaptation to Retirement 129
Bruno de Sousa Lopes, University of Aveiro, Portugal

This chapter aims to understand the organizational practices of disengagement of senior employees, focusing primarily on the final phase of the careers of this class of employees and their entry into retirement. It analyzed the challenges of adaptation to retirement, as well as the disengagement practices used by organizations, and characterized the individual career management of seniors. The methodology used was qualitative, using a semi-structured interview complemented by a socio-demographic survey for data collection. The results of the study point to the fact that the whole process of end-of-career and retirement has a significant impact on both individuals and organizations. The evidence shows that factors such as aging and the importance of health and family are some of the main concerns of individuals. At the same time, organizations focus mainly on career management, succession processes, and employee satisfaction at the end of their careers and, consequently, on acceptable entry into retirement.

Chapter 8
Enterprise Architecture Solutions for an Aging Workforce 161
Raja Saravanan, University of Aveiro, Portugal

The aging workforce has been a topic of discussion for many years, and as we enter the fourth industrial revolution, it is clear that the issue will only become more pressing. In the past, it was believed that the older population would be unable to adapt to the increasingly technological world. However, as technology advances, many older workers are adapting and finding ways to remain competitive in the workplace. In this chapter, the authors examine how the aging workforce impacts economic and social development, and they discuss how Industry 4.0 and enterprise architecture can help address these challenges.

Glossary 176

Compilation of References 182

About the Contributors 210

Index 213

Preface

Overall, the reduction in the number of births and the decrease in mortality in the first years of life, in association with the increase in the average life expectancy at birth and at 65 years of age, have contributed to the increase in population aging and longevity. These two concepts, although correlated, have different interpretations or meanings. If longevity presupposes an organism's life duration, longer than normal but with a limit related to the species, aging refers to the effect of becoming old. In a more simplistic reading, we can say that the longer an individual lives, the older he will be. However, aging is a more complex and constant process that begins while individuals are still active. Both phenomena - aging and longevity - are determined by physiological pathways under the influence of multiple factors, namely genetic, environmental, behavioral, dietary, and stochastic.

Aging can be defined as a dynamic, progressive process characterized by functional, morphological, and psychological changes. It results from molecular and cellular changes in all types of cells in the body, regardless of the specific characteristics of the various organs and systems. It leads to greater vulnerability and aging-related pathophysiological mechanisms, such as genetic information, oxidative stress, telomerase activity, and the activity of the mTOR (mammalian target of rampamycin) axis, are determinant, despite the difficulty in assessing its real effect, and the process through which these mechanisms play their role.

When we approach aging, the first impulse is to situate ourselves in the number of years lived. This is not always a positive aspect, especially in societies that value the myth of eternal youth and contribute to perpetuating stereotypes. Thus, along with psychological and social age comes functional age, as a result of a process throughout life in which functions may diminish but be compensated for by the stabilization or development of others. This concept allows us to look at aging from an optimization perspective, thus counteracting the devaluation of older people. This aspect is essential because it influences behavior toward them. From a negative perspective, terms such as incompetence, frail, incapable, slow, and forgetful are often used about older people. However, positively they are perceived as wise, mature, sagacious, trustworthy, and kind.

Following this, Miguel (2014) identified three dimensions associated with aging in a representative study of the Portuguese population. The first relates to relational and cognitive incompetence, in which older people are boring, stubborn, and little interactive. On the other hand, cognitively, they are uncreative, and their accumulated knowledge is of no interest to the younger generations. The second dimension is related to physical and emotional dependence, based on the idea that older people need more rest, attention, and patience. The third dimension is associated with a positive image characterized by maturity, adaptability, and well-being.

Thus, one can see how deeply ingrained the stereotypes associated with older people are. It is necessary to break the prejudices referring to older ages because they are barriers to individuals' development of active and successful aging. Thus, subjective age is a fundamental determinant in the relationship of the self with others, to the extent that interpersonal phenomena are intrinsically linked to social phenomena. This is why age, as a number, is fundamental to investigating and understanding the aging process, but it does not explain nor is it the basis for everything that occurs in this process. Aging is a lifelong process that is intrinsically different from individual to individual.

According to the United Nations, the world population will reach 10.9 billion by the end of this century (Roser & Rodés-Guirão, 2019), which will have a very significant impact. To lessen the impact of population aging and postpone situations of frailty, several approaches focusing on the potential of older people have been advocated. Europe puts forward the models of Healthy Aging and Active Aging. At the same time, the United States of America advocates the model of Successful Aging based on a more holistic life course concept, with a greater focus on individual responsibility. Despite the differences, these conceptual models are a positive alternative in the fight against ageism and the vision focused on the decline that accompanies aging.

On the other hand, the changes observed in demographic indicators worldwide are signs of structural solid and dimensional transformations. They must be considered individually, socially, and economically because they impose profound changes in the most diverse sectors. Although this is not a new problem, as it has been gradually addressed since industrialization, today, a wide variety of organizations will encounter issues related to aging their workforce.

It will be necessary to consider and implement new strategies that believe that age management can positively contribute to society at various stages of life. To increase the employment rate of older workers, a set of actors - the State, Social Partners, Companies, and Workers - must actively intervene in structural reform of the way the workforce is thought of (Barroca et al., 2014).

Thus, it will be the State's responsibility to create the necessary conditions for sustainable employment and thus encourage organizations to retain and attract more older workers. Among the most appropriate measures, we can emphasize benefits applied to employers of older people and incentives for workers to stay in the labor market for as long as possible while discouraging older workers from leaving the labor market early for early retirement. In turn, the Social Partners must assist in planning at the structural level, moving from how the management of the labor force is currently thought of to how it will have to be considered in the future, anticipating and acting on these changes. Finally, companies must reverse the prejudice that older workers represent lower productivity and a greater aversion to change. They should view them as an additional talent because they have skills consolidated by their experience. This encourages creating an organizational career management plan (Barroca et al., 2014).

This comprehensive publication on the universal phenomenon of population aging, focusing on its implications for the workforce, crosses several original contributions and interdisciplinary methods in various fields and areas. For this reason, it is timely due to its topicality and the need for responses to the various transformations that occur in the most diverse scenarios. The existing literature provides information from research conducted in several countries. The present book intends to reflect on this pressing issue, increasing the understanding of the importance of the topics and providing relevant academic work, empirical research results, fieldwork, and an overview of this relevant field of study. In this way, it is estimated that this book will provide the resources necessary for academics, interdisciplinary researchers, advanced-level students, managers, and government officials to adopt and implement solutions for a more economically and socially balanced world, privileging intergenerational dynamics. The book comprises eight chapters, each addressing the importance of reflecting on population aging in various contexts, particularly its impact on the workforce.

The first chapter, "Engaging the Aging Process: Unlock the Fountain of Youth," addresses employment as a modulating criterion for the aging process over the life course. Populationally aging nations must maintain profitability as the working population is also aging. This global trend introduces global labor market changes, so work opportunities and the consequent impacts later in life deserve special consideration. In this wake, governments must make it simpler to maintain a meaningful presence in the workforce and parallel lessen retirement impacts by providing increased quality-of-life years.

Successful aging implies an adaptive response capacity to the most diverse endogenous and exogenous challenges associated with the aging process. Inherently, aging represents the gradual, variable, continuous, and irreversible deterioration of cellular functions and physiological processes, promoting the individual's vulnerability (Bernardes & Pinheiro, 2014). With aging, there is a gradual decline in all senses that make up the sensory system. Although some changes go unnoticed, vision and hearing are greatly affected. Thus, considering that the sensory organs permeate the individual's relationship with the environment, a series of changes occur in the individual's behavior that condition his or her behavior pattern. Given the importance of the subject in the theme of the book, Chapter 2, "Understanding the Evolution of Sensory Aging in the Workforce," through a bibliometric analysis between 2001 and 2022, it was investigated the most pressing and explored clusters, focusing on the most relevant authors, journals, countries, institutions, and documents in the area of sensory aging and the workforce.

As the European continent is one of the geographical areas with the most developed socio-economic structures, population aging is expected to be progressive. This reveals a tendency for the number of inhabitants to stabilize. Interestingly, demographic aging in the United States of America has been slower. This is probably due to the fertility rate being much higher than in other developed countries. In Europe, despite the global trend, it is up to each country to characterize its demographic aging and reflect on the negative and positive impacts. In this context, Chapter 3, "Aging in Portugal: The Social Development Point of View," analyzes the data on demographic aging in Europe, focusing on Portugal. The chapter is developed by identifying the factors contributing to the gradual increase in the number of older people and the decrease in the youth population, the respective rationale, and the main responses developed. One of the main objectives is to identify solutions that contribute to healthy aging, even if many times already sustained in institutional responses and/or specific areas such as Sociocultural Animation. Lifelong learning is also a concept explored and underlying the chapter.

As in Europe, this is a concern in other countries with emerging economies. Chapter 4, "The Aging Workforce in Indonesia and Its Impact on Economic and Social Development," analyzes the Indonesian population and workforce. The past thirty years have seen an increase in the average standard of living due to structural changes that have been introduced and have allowed for sustained growth. Moreover, compared to other advanced economies, the coming decades will see demographic aging similar to those economies despite the current youthfulness of the population and labor force. This is challenging and disturbing, especially when only a minority of the workforce will have access to a secure income upon retirement and quality geriatric services. Indeed, poverty and inequality are extensive, with many people working into old age because they cannot afford to lose that income. Following this, the challenges of an aging population and workforce are discussed, highlighting the large proportion of workers in the informal sector and the growth of contingent work arrangements in the formal sector.

Based on the realization that, in general, the world's population is living longer lives, consequently, they are also working longer. However, age is crucial in some companies or organizations, especially in recruitment. Often older people are not valued, and are even discriminated against because they are too qualified for the job or position. Meanwhile, they lose an experienced and diverse workforce. Greater productivity can be achieved with multigenerational work teams because they are equipped with broader and more diverse ideas and knowledge, which can mobilize a wider range of people. However, intergenerational inclusion is often not a priority in creating a diverse culture, but to achieve a high-performing workforce, diversity and inclusion policies, including age, are needed. Following this, Chapter 5, "The Importance of Aging in the Innovation Process of Organizations," looks at the aging workforce, innovation, and creativity in isolation and then explores the links between the aging workforce and others. As the last focus, it examines how the knowledge and skills of the aging workforce are a competitive advantage for organizations; and how it is assumed to be the age segment in an organization that contributes most to creative and innovation processes arising from intergenerational cooperation links.

In turn, Chapter 6, "Restructuring the Workforce Through Non-Ageist Hiring and Retention Practices That Value Aging Workers' Expertise: Recognizing the Need for Workplace Age Diversity," explores the problems facing the aging workforce and measures employers should review and respect when implementing hiring and retention policies for non-aging workers to safeguard a diverse workforce. On the other hand, the importance of co-responsibility for implementing fair employment policies is emphasized. The increasingly globalized labor market is not keeping pace with attitudes toward age in the workplace, despite the inherent benefits of age-diverse teams. Thus, older workers are more likely to be laid off compared to their colleagues and are more likely to remain unemployed for a long time. Defining strategies in which diversity and inclusion are catalysts for more productivity and innovation is not yet a transversal reality in the business world. However, it is a reality in some and a reference to good practices.

In the context of the successive transitions and consequent adaptations that the individual makes throughout life, in the most diverse domains, retirement is an important event. It requires an effort of personal and social reorganization, which can be more strongly felt the longer the professional activity is. The transition to retirement is experienced by individuals in different ways, although there may be common feelings. To control the constraints associated with the lack of preparation for this new stage, we must ask ourselves: "How will the transition from working life to retirement be experienced?" Following this, Chapter 7, "The Journey Between the Final Stage of Career and the Adaptation to Retirement," aims to understand the organizational practices of disengagement of senior employees, focusing on the transition from the final stage of their careers to retirement. To this end, the challenges of adaptation to retirement and the disengagement practices used by organizations were analyzed using the semi-structured interview technique complemented by a sociodemographic survey for data collection. The results show that this transition is impactful at both the individual and organizational levels, regardless of the reasons not being coincidental. Suppose that on the individual side, there are family and health concerns. In that case, the organizations focus mainly on career management, succession processes, and employee satisfaction at the end of their careers and, consequently, on moving on to retirement.

Considering that work organizes human activity, its importance throughout life is unquestionable. Extending working life implies reflecting on a panoply of complex issues to implement policies and programs that allow older people to remain in the labor market for longer. It is, therefore, necessary to develop knowledge about the nature and effectiveness of working conditions for older people. The eighth chapter, "Enterprise Architecture Solutions for an Aging Workforce," focuses on the fourth industrial revolution and the vital importance of discussing and including an aging workforce. Despite the stereotype that older people would be unable to adapt to technology, it has been seen that as technology advances, many older workers are adapting and finding ways to remain competitive in the workplace. This chapter has examined how the aging workforce impacts economic and social development and how Industry 4.0 and Enterprise Architecture can help address these challenges.

The demographic aging of the countries covered in this book is not very different from the world panorama. Thus, as life expectancy increases, there are several challenges in various sectors: health, social support structures, and the economy, with important implications for government policies. Therefore, more holistic approaches are needed to promote healthy aging with quality of life and participation. Providing organizations with a diverse and intergenerational workforce can be advantageous from several perspectives. Hence, age diversity should be considered in recruitment and promotion processes. This can result in significant benefits for both employees and employers. The former achieves higher levels of job satisfaction and motivation, better work-life balance, and the ability to maintain workability and employability throughout a career. While the latter benefit from the ability to keep experienced workers in their organizations while controlling hiring, integration, and training costs. An individual's work capacity results from the balance between his or her resources and work. Several factors can affect this capacity, including health and functional abilities, educational level and competence, values and motivation, work environment, and work requirements and organization. Therefore, the workplace plays a crucial role in maintaining work capacity if it promotes activities that moderate physical decline and a healthy lifestyle. For many people, work is the most meaningful activity of their lives. Therefore, another point of central importance is preparation for retirement. This constitutes a significant turning point, as it launches the individual into realities that can provide a set of expectations, feelings, and behaviors that may result in several consequences in various areas: satisfaction, well-being, psychological, relational, lifestyle habits, and eventually personality.

We hope that this book provides an enjoyable reading experience.

Bruno de Sousa Lopes
University of Aveiro, Portugal

Maria Céu Lamas
School of Health, Polytechnic of Porto, Portugal

Vanessa Amorim
Porto Accounting and Business School, Polytechnic of Porto, Portugal

Orlando Lima Rua
Porto Accounting and Business School, Polytechnic of Porto, Portugal

REFERENCES

Barroca, A., Meireles, G., & Neto, C. (2014). *Estudo sobre Boas Práticas: Para o Aumento da Força de Trabalho Disponível em Portugal através da Manutenção e Reinserção de Seniores no Mercado de Trabalho* [Study on Best Practices: Towards Increasing the Available Workforce in Portugal by Retaining and Reintegrating Seniors into the Labor Market]. Advancis Business Services.

Bernardes, A., & Pinheiro, S. (2014). Anatomia do Envelhecimento [Anatomy of Aging]. In M. T. Veríssimo (Ed.), *Geriatria Fundamental, Saber e Praticar* [Fundamental Geriatrics, Know & Practice]. LIDEL, Edições Técnicas, Lda.

Miguel, I. (2014). Envelhecimento e Desenvolvimento Psicológico: Entre Mitos e Factos [Aging and psychological development: Between myths and facts]. In H. R. Amaro da Luz & I. Miguel (Eds.), Gerontologia Social: Perspetivas de Análise e Intervenção [Social Gerontology: Perspectives of Analysis and Intervention] (pp. 53-67). Center for Research in Social and Organizational Innovation - Instituto Superior Bissaya Barreto.

Roser, M., & Rodés-Guirão, L. (2019). *Future Population Growth*. Retrieved from https://ourworldindata.org/future-population-growth

Chapter 1
Engaging the Aging Process:
Unlock the Fountain of Youth

Abeni El-Amin
https://orcid.org/0000-0001-7506-1658
Fort Hays State University, USA & Shenyang Normal University, China

ABSTRACT

Employment for aging is a significant aspect shaping the aging processes during formative years. Therefore, work opportunities combined and consequential impacts later in life merit special consideration. Given that population aging has become a global pattern with ensuing changes in labor markets far and wide, there is increased concern about the impacts of retirement around the globe and the macroeconomic advantages frequently connected with delaying retirement. It is fundamental for nations with aging populations to maintain profitability, given an aging workforce. Governments must make it simpler for individuals to maintain a significant presence in the workforce. This contribution focuses on improving the quality of life for aging individuals instead of only focusing on adding years to their lives.

INTRODUCTION

Several myths about aging exist, and society often conjures negative images of older adults (Robnett & Chop, 2013). This conceptual research analysis discusses two blanket assumptions often made about older adults, which are refutable. For instance, psychologically, older adults are set in their ways. Consequently, older adults can learn if they choose and often learn new hobbies, take community college courses, and volunteer to share their insights (Deller & Walwei, 2022). Second, older adults do not have the physical capability or desire for physical fitness to coincide with

DOI: 10.4018/978-1-6684-6351-2.ch001

an active lifestyle or enhanced careers (Hekmat-Panah, 2019). Many older adults participate in fitness classes, walk, golf, play tennis, and other physical modalities to stay healthy. Likewise, employment is an aspect of life that must be fundamentally reconsidered regarding expanding global health care (El-Amin, 2022a). Despite the challenges of aging, the opportunity to live a long, productive, and fully engaged life is greater now than ever before (Fried, 2000).

Older people have many more opportunities to live long and productive lives (Fried, 2000). Some reasons for this are improvements in medical and application technologies. These improvements allow people to live longer, have more security, and be independent. Notwithstanding, the aging process is universal, but institutions and laws around health, working, and welfare differ. The economic, social, and political context of the aging link to the economic and social challenges of the aging workforce.

BACKGROUND

Gerontology Vs. Geriatrics

Gerontology and geriatrics differ in their core functions. There are critical differences between gerontology and geriatrics, yet they work in concert to mitigate issues involving older adults (Robnett & Chop, 2013). Gerontology is the scientific analysis of aging that assesses the biological, psychological, and sociological factors correlated with aging (Kleineidam et al., 2019). The elements that affect how we age are extensive in range and varied. For instance, biological aspects include genetic background and physical health; psychological influences incorporate levels of cognition, mental health status, and overall well-being; sociological factors extend from interpersonal relationships to society's cultures, policies, and infrastructure (Gilles et al., 2022). In comparison, geriatrics is a medical expression for analyzing, diagnosing, and treating diseases and health problems pertinent to older adults (Huot et al., 2022). Gerontology and geriatrics work to mitigate issues involving older adults by challenging how older adults are perceived in society.

A Sense of Independence

Older adults value their independence and like to be in control of their own lives. There are four challenges that caregivers and older adults face as the older adult's role evolves (Schumacher et al., 2006). For example, cultural perspectives on caregiving and older adults include the fact that older adults value their independence; family members are not always prepared to take on the role of the caregiver; caregivers are typically the eldest daughter or daughter-in-law of the family, yet, other family members are more capable or have the desire to assume the role of the caregiver; older adults tend to maintain their autonomy until they can no longer do so, and financial challenges of being a caregiver to older adults dictate how finances are managed so that older adults who are often on fixed incomes live with other family members.

Quality of Life (QoL)

The definition of Quality of Life (QoL) is subjective. Schalock discussed the core principles that compose quality of life (Vanleerberghe et al., 2017). These principles are understood from the individual's perspective: well-being, meeting basic needs, opportunities to achieve personal goals and challenges, autonomy, a sense of community, and multidimensionality (Ranzijn, 2002). The most crucial aspect of gauging the quality of life is determining their needs, as each individual's quality of life varies.

Strategies of intervention and prescription employed to alleviate some of the challenges that a person with dementia experiences ensure the client is provided with respect and compassion by not communicating as if they were not present (Vanleerberghe et al., 2017). Utilizing emotional intelligence by being self-aware, creating an atmosphere of relaxation, and creating a diversion to provide the client with a sense of well-being is optimal.

Aging in Place

Aging in place means *"the individual's ability to continue to live in his or her abode safely, as independently as possible, and comfortably, regardless of age, income, or ability level"* is observed so that older people can continue their lives with family and friends (Stones & Gullifer, 2016). The primary factors contributing to the older adult's continued ability to age in place are if the home is structurally able to support the person's safety (Robnett & Chop, 2013). Challenges of universal design, adaptation, and compensation are factors of aging in place. Additionally, family members, friends, and caregivers must support this decision to assist the person where necessary.

Living situations can influence an older adult's overall abilities and quality of life. As a health care practitioner, the primary concern when talking with older adults living arrangements is to respect their decision and collaborate with them to achieve their goals and objectives in this vein. Older people may decide to live alone, in an independent living center, with family or friends, share a home with others, or live in a long-term facility. Whatever their choice, a healthcare provider's role is to help them achieve the best environment for them.

Long-term care is an array of long-term services and provisions utilized by older people who require assistance to function daily (Barken & Lowndes, 2018). Long-term care includes providing personal care, rehabilitation, social services, assistive technology, health care, home modifications, care coordination, and assisted transportation, to name a few (El-Amin, 2022b). The need for a long-term option is defined as the period in which a person needs these services. According to Paterson and Warburton (2010) that 60% of individuals aged 75 and older have no functional limitations requiring assistance from another person. Likewise, Fried (2000) indicated that preventive care permits aging individuals to thrive regardless of the aging stage.

Physiological Factors

Chronological age is a convenient and often excellent indicator of aging adults' health status, yet disease issues and physical capacity naturally decline (Jakovljevic, 2018). There is individual variability, with some older individuals generally having excellent well-being and others showing the quickened onset of weakness, inability to function, and frailty. As a result, frailty is a clinical geriatric disorder that emerges from different body structures due to a lack of activity. The authors found that older adults experienced well-being challenges connected with frailty rates and cardiovascular aging. As a result, mature individuals experience greater hypertension levels, elevated cholesterol, type-2 diabetes, and joint issues than moderate-weight individuals in the height range. Research indicated that while no particular practices can alter weight management, a combined strategy of factors helps weight management. This study is critical because it highlights the importance of considering the societal impacts that influence cardiovascular aging. Programs and initiatives that target more vulnerable populations are a tremendous strategy to encourage individuals to reduce calorie utilization and increase physical activity.

Moreover, smoking leads to strokes, cardiovascular ailments, and, eventually, mortality (Jakovljevic, 2018). Not surprisingly, it was found that stroke survivors who smoke have an expanded danger of premature death. Low-income people experienced even greater cardiovascular aging mortality connected with poor health practices.

Physical Aging Factors

Traditionally, physical activity helps older people improve physical and mental functions and reduce the impacts of chronic disease to keep older individuals active and independent (McPhee et al., 2016). Further, as the capacity of dynamic cognition declines, this prevalence influences memory and learning. Also, musculoskeletal degeneration develops frailty (known as sarcopenia) and age-related bone mineral density decline, leading to osteoporosis (Robnett & Chop, 2013). Likewise, musculoskeletal dysfunction is a primary cause of incapacity in older adults.

Musculoskeletal dysfunction affects older adults and occurs through osteoporosis (loss of bone mass and density), osteoarthritis (a degenerative joint disease, which is very common in older adults), and skeletal muscle loss (often causing muscle atrophy, an increase in adipose tissue, and loss of motor neuron connectivity). Some older people experience extreme limitations in physical and mental functions. This limits their capacity to incorporate fundamental exercises into everyday living (Puvill, 2016). Frailty is generally analyzed according to the ability and will of individuals. There is evidence that routine physical activity is reasonable for healthy and for fragile older individuals, and the dangers of developing cardiovascular and metabolic infections, obesity, falls, cognitive hindrances, osteoporosis, and weakness are diminished by consistently achieving exercises ranging from low-intensity walking to more enthusiastic games and weight-bearing exercises. However, participation in physical exercises remains relatively low amongst older adults. Musculoskeletal dysfunction is a significant cause of disability in older adults. Fighting musculoskeletal dysfunction includes taking vitamin supplements, exercising, and stretching.

Unfortunately, several stereotypes are associated with aging (Robnett & Chop, 2013). Aging stereotypes may become self-fulfilling prophecies that lead to the decline of some older adults. Some older adults indicated that dying by degrees is linked to aging because of a decline in mental and physical health. Stereotypes linked to aging exacerbate the challenges some older adults experience. Negative stereotypes create bias and keep older adults from economic and social opportunities.

Physical Mobility Factors

Physical activity and psychological well-being practice programs for older adults are intentionally created to help healthcare professionals make informed healthcare services (Netz et al., 2005). Physical activity and psychological well-being practice programs are utilized to reduce poor fitness outcomes and advance the delivery of appropriate medicinal services. Likewise, physical activity and psychological well-being practice programs give a tool by which healthcare professionals are held accountable for clients or participants. Albeit much of the development and evaluation of physical activity and psychological well-being programs for older people has occurred in geriatrics, other healthcare professionals are intrigued by the utilization of programs as one method for encouraging confirmation-based practices. A healthcare professional can create physical activity and psychological well-being practice programs internally or externally (Delle Fave et al., 2018). Although internal programs may require fewer resources and might be better executed, physical activity and psychological well-being practices are needed where older people exist.

Moreover, healthcare professionals should look to external or federal entities for direction on physical activity and psychological well-being programs. Physical activity and psychological well-being practice programs are utilized in geriatrics to improve quality and delivery, and prescription of fitness activities preceded client analysis. Likewise, Range of Motion (ROM) refers to the joint's ability to move through its natural movement pattern. Various ways to maintain or improve current ROM for older adults include exercise through weight-bearing exercises, cardio, and stretching. To ensure older adults remain healthy, they should not extend past their ROM as the probability of short-term pain and long-term injury increase.

Additionally, various sensory changes occur with aging. Loss or decline of visual skills may result in becoming dependent on others and unable to do everyday activities with the ease they once performed (Rogers & Peelle, 2022). The specific visual skills that decline with aging are visual processing speed, sensitivity to light, ability to see well in dim light, near vision, especially problematic for reading small print, upward gaze without moving head, contrast sensitivity, color sensitivity, especially along with the blue-yellow axis of color, and dynamic vision. The strategies employed to address impaired vision challenges are providing correct vision tools, i.e., glasses (prescription or reading), ensuring written material is legible and readable by increasing the font size, and electronic devices are programmed to show more extensive and enhanced font and light adjustment.

There is a stigma regarding older adults in the workforce. However, the benefits of hiring older workers for both employers and older adults are more dependability, fewer issues of absenteeism, and more productivity because of increased emotional intelligence (self-aware, controlled emotions, and enhanced ability to focus) (Robnett & Chop, 2013). Older adults gain a sense of independence and purpose in the workforce, increasing their quality of life.

Physiologic Change Factors

Physiologic changes in both men and women may preclude sexual activity due to chemical changes in the body and other general physical changes in appearance and function. Decreasing amounts of estrogen and testosterone may contribute to a decline in sexual activity (Robnett & Chop, 2013). Chemical changes in the body due to a lack of estrogen in women cause menopause, an uncomfortable phase of the aging process. Women experience reduced libido, weight gain, thinning of vaginal walls, sweating, and incontinence. Men lose libido, experience weight gain, and a loss of testosterone, leading to muscle atrophy, and may have lessened arousal, issues with orgasm, post-orgasm, and extragenital issues.

Societal perceptions often indicate that sex and sexuality are issues and are thought of only concerning the young. The perception of more vitality in youth is an exciting perspective as youth tend to have more energy, are fitter, see themselves as attractive, and have more virility. In contrast, older adults face psychological, physiological, and physical changes and find having sex less appealing. They may have a lessened desire for sex, body awareness issues, no longer psychically attracted to their partner, or have physical limitations such as arthritis and joint or muscular degeneration that make it harder to sustain sex.

Healthcare providers should tactfully and respectfully approach the sexual function of aging patients by demystifying the idea that older adults do not have or enjoy sex. As a healthcare provider, one might improve safe sex practices among this population by holding discussion groups about the subject via health promotion programming, having one-on-one discussions about the subject, host socials to encourage older adults to mingle while also providing health promotion materials available such as pamphlets, playing games, and condoms.

Aging Women's Care

With regards to women's care for aging, physically active women have lower resting mean arterial pressure (MAP) and higher cerebrovascular conductance (CVC) than sedentary women (Brown et al., 2010). Overall cognition was adversely correlated with age and categorically correlated with VO2max. VO2max was a predictor of resting CVC and MAP, CVC, and MAP when end-tidal gases were held persistent at near-resting values. MAP and CVC were predictors of cognition (Brown et al., 2010). Further, older women's health status is based on lifestyle behaviors, well-being practices, and overall health. Well-being status is measured by the development of health and well-being initiated by older women. For instance, the relationship between the aggregate volume of leisure-time physical action (LTPA) and obesity among older women demonstrated that the relationship between LTPA and weight for older women is persistent.

Notwithstanding, older women who engage in increased frequency of LTPA increase cardiorespiratory fitness and cerebral blood flow on cognitive outcomes in older women. As a result, older women need to participate for 300 minutes or more weekly (Brown et al., 2010). This way, older women are less inclined to experience cerebral blood flow on cognitive degeneration. Likewise, when older women experience well-being, they are more likely to attain greater vigor levels. Further, a systematic review of physical activity interventions among older women indicated that positive behavioral interventions occur within group settings.

A Comparative Analysis: The Social Context of Aging in the United States of America, Japan, and Sweden

The ways that the older adult population of the future (the baby boomers) will be different from their predecessors are that they are more educated and liberated; their family size is smaller, they have more companionship and better health, and are economically better positioned (Staudinger et al., 2016). This will affect older people's health care and other care required in future years because of the expense of providing quality health care. This results from the healthcare industry and politicians controlling costs, particularly in the US.

The age composition and abilities to address aging problems in the United States (US), Japan, and Sweden are similar because longevity has increased in developing countries. This is because more people are educated, eat healthier, and have access to healthcare. In the US, social security via Medicare and Medicaid assumes much healthcare. Conversely, 80% of healthcare in Japan is provided by the private sector for older persons. Consequently, in both the US and Japan, Sweden has universal healthcare. Sweden passed its Social Services Act, which provided municipal social services to all persons who needed them regardless of age. In the passage of this act, access to social services was established as a right of all Swedish citizens. Sweden's older residents enjoy one of the most extended lifespans globally and live independently for most of their lives. Their pension system is well-funded to provide financial support for its citizens. However, challenges persist for those who want to work (Berg & Piszczek, 2022).

Age-Related Illnesses

The three general categories of illness intertwined with the age-related decline of the immune system functioning are infections, cancer, and autoimmune disease (Robnett & Chop, 2013). These diseases preferentially affect older adults because their immune system is weaker. As a result, infectious disease occurs. In older adults, infectious diseases are mainly in the following categories: influenza, pneumonia, Covid-19, tuberculosis, meningitis, and urinary tract infections (Savioli et al., 2022). One of the biological aging theories is Telomere Erosion Theory (TET) (Libertini et al., 2017). This perspective of biological aging suggests that *"age and cell mortality are caused by the gradual loss of the protective telomere nucleotide sequences at the ends of the DNA strands within chromosomes with each new cell division and the resultant inability of those cells to continue to divide"* (Libertini et al., 2017). This theory is critical because it helps to describe how stress plays a factor in the aging process.

Pharmacokinetics

The concept of pharmacokinetics is the study of how drugs travel through the body over time (van den Anker et al., 2018). It indicates various aspects of drug disposition in the body, involving absorption from the administration site, distribution into various body compartments, and clearance from the body. Pharmacokinetics attempts to accomplish and understand how drugs flow through the body to heal or eliminate pain. Addressed in pharmacokinetics is the inability of the body to absorb drugs properly. Polypharmacy indicates the prevalence of more than one drug administered to an individual.

Societal perceptions indicate that many people believe we have an over-medicated population (Robnett & Chop, 2013). Polypharmacy is the use of multiple medications in one individual. The prevalence of pharmacokinetics may occur more often in older adults. Some strategies for reducing polypharmacy are tracking medication, ensuring no adverse drug interaction occurs, communicating with older adults to gauge to determine if medication is still needed based on their symptoms and biometrics, and working cross-functionally with healthcare providers to ensure older adults are not abusing drugs.

A personal philosophy regarding medication management for older adults is that older adults should not take any medication or supplements they do not need to prevent gastrointestinal disorders, adverse drug reactions, drug addiction, and drug abuse. An effective management program entails a periodic review of a patient's medications (prescription, nonprescription, vitamin supplements, herbal remedies, and nutritional products) to assess whether they are medically necessary and customize prescriptions (van den Anker et al., 2018).

Accordingly, factors that need to be considered to ensure an optimal program are enacting or obtaining necessary assessments of the medical client's health status, developing a medication treatment plan, identifying, initiating, adapting, or administering medication therapy, and monitoring and assessing the client's response to therapy, including safety and effectiveness, providing an encompassing medication review to identify, resolve, and prevent adverse medication issues, including drug interactions, documenting the care delivered and communicating vital information to the client's collaborating primary care providers, providing health education, promotion, and training designed to enhance patient understanding and appropriate use of their medications.

Nutrition

Multiple factors can affect the nutrition status of aging. Four nutrition status factors are changes in social, economic, psychological, and physical well-being (Robnett &

Chop, 2013). Older adults often change their nutrition habits due to a loss of friends or family, personal finances, changes in medication or emotional state (they may eat too much or not enough), and are physically unable to purchase food supplies. As a healthcare professional, there are strategies to mitigate nutrition status factors, which are ensuring older adults have social meals by eating with others, follow a nutrient-rich diet consisting of vitamins and minerals, and tracking their consumption to ensure they get the preferable mix of calories in fats, carbs, protein, and fiber.

One of the nutrition challenges is converting practical knowledge into a daily plan on and meal-by-meal basis. Important concepts to remember when planning meals for older adults are ensuring older adults get adequacy, balance, calorie control, moderation, and variety (ABCMV) (Hollis et al., 2020). For instance, adequacy, a diet that provides enough of the essential nutrients, fiber, and energy; balance, a diet that does not overemphasize one food at the expense of another; calorie control, a diet that has just enough calories to maintain a healthy weight; moderation, a diet that does not contain excessive amounts of unwanted items such as sugar, salt, and fat; and variety, a diet that has many different nutrient-rich foods.

The six classes of nutrients required for optimum health for older adults are protein, healthy fats, water consumption, vitamins, minerals, and fiber. Older adults need to have an adequate daily intake of nutrients to maintain bodily function, reduce disease, reduce the effects of aging due to degeneration, and weight management. Water, in particular, is vital for excellent bodily and organ functions.

Health practitioners have widely determined that experiencing longevity, food restriction, cognitive exercise, sustained social engagement, positive interactions, and physical exercise are crucial (Miller et al., 2012). Additionally, the aspects mentioned above significantly reduce the prevalence of depression in older people. Physical exercise and mental wellness have been considered conceivable factors in advancing cognitive aging advancements. As a result, the information ascertained indicated a cross-sectional, longitudinal, and intervention analysis. Miller et al. (2012) concluded that many methodological challenges limit older people's quality of life.

Further, health practitioners do not always agree on the most proficient method to promote exercise and fitness programs for older people. Significant challenges persist for older people concerning actionable activities that make a lifelong impact on exercisers. Likewise, cognitive performance in older people requires involvement. Intervention methods develop an improved ability to improve connections between physical and psychological factors. Often older people experience the ill effects of issues emerging from inadequate care and decisions about the cognitive measures needed to improve daily living. The relationship between exercise and fortified cognition during aging proves that physical exercise is the likelihood for healthy cognitive aging presently cannot seem to be approved. Older people suffer unnecessarily from disease and the natural effects of aging without physical fitness, appropriate nutrition, and cognitive exercise.

SOLUTIONS AND RECOMMENDATIONS

Legal Protections of Aging Adults

As a person ages or no longer becomes mentally coherent, the involuntary approach to decision-making usually results in the probate court appointing a person to make personal and financial decisions for the incapacitated person (Robnett & Chop, 2013). Sometimes it is necessary to administer an involuntary civil assurance to protect people (Ambrosini et al., 2018). An appointee makes personal decisions and makes financial decisions. These individuals are appointed and perform the alleged incapacitated person (AIP) duties until the probate court can permanently assign a person to care for one's estate. There are protections for the rights of individuals after an AIP is appointed. For instance, individuals may secure an attorney and agree to a guardian or conservator's appointment but wish a specific person appointed with expressly limited powers. Hence, they protect and make decisions for their personage and estate.

The primary function of a Geriatric Care Manager (GCMs) is to help older persons or clients and their families access quality care (Kapp, 2020). They support the individual's and the family's economic security by providing access to information to make informed care decisions. Typically, GCMs are nurses or social workers. They provide recommendations based on a person's specific needs. As it relates to gerontology, the legal standards involved with executing a will are the sufficient ability and capacity to decide or sign a legal document usually depends on state law and sometimes on federal law (Kapp, 2020). The legal standard to execute a will is that the person must want to sign the will, know what property they own, and name their relatives to inherit one's estate. A requirement for witnesses is to understand their employers' policies and the laws concerning being a witness as a healthcare provider. The witnesses' functions are to assist the client/patient by signing the will, but if a healthcare provider thinks signing the will is against their desire, they can choose not to be a witness and intervene. It is the lawyer's duty to determine whether the person has sufficient capacity to sign a will.

The Professional Gerontologist

A gerontology healthcare professional can engage in lifelong learning in the field to remain current on the most efficacious healthcare practices is to taking college, certification, and industry courses (Spitzer & Davidson, 2013). Nevertheless, continuing education is a requirement in most healthcare occupations to work in the field. The primary focus areas of occupational therapists are healthcare practitioners who work with people of all ages to help them gain or regain daily living activities (ADLs). Occupational therapy is client-centered, whereas the client's objectives are considered and respected as part of the habilitation or rehabilitation process (Reitz & Scaffa, 2020). Physical therapists (PTs) are skilled healthcare workers who have completed an entry-level master's or doctorate program attested by the Commission on Accreditation in Physical Therapy Education (CAPTE). These professionals help people regain physical mobility. Their primary philosophy and belief are to do what they can as healthcare professionals to resume activities. The primary differences in their functions to assist older adults as occupational therapists are cerebral, and physical therapists' role is to help people obtain physical normality.

Healthcare Providers: The Circle of Care

Healthcare is often provided most effectively in the framework of a team. An interdisciplinary team of healthcare workers aims to get the person back to a state where they can enjoy a standard or better quality of life (Robnett & Chop, 2013). Healthcare teams consist of physicians and their assistants, nurses and their assistants, occupational, physical, respiratory, and speech therapists (assistants and aides as well), case managers, psychologists and psychiatrists, nutritionists or dieticians, laboratory/medical technicians, medical equipment vendors, therapeutic recreation specialists, and social workers to name a few. The three basic types of teams in today's healthcare arena are multidisciplinary, interdisciplinary, and transdisciplinary (Fraher & Brandt, 2019). The common traits of healthcare providers that work with older adults are that they all seek to promote caring and respect for older people.

FUTURE RESEARCH DIRECTIONS

Gerontology Health Promotion

Health literacy is the degree to which a person can obtain, process, and understand necessary health information and services to make appropriate health decisions (Robnett & Chop, 2013). Health literacy challenges requires mitigation so that older adults understand the health education and information provided. As some older people tend to have vision or hearing loss, these challenges present unique problems for older adults regarding their rights. Additionally, an increasing amount of health information is located online, yet written in a confusing manner, which is not easy to decipher or translate into the person's language.

The minimum requirements for explicit language standards for print and web-based information and applicable for older adults include: content, structure/organization, writing style, and print material. For instance, content: information is accurate, up-to-date, and limited; structure/organization: structure and organize information from the user's perspective; writing style: as noted earlier, most adults best understand everyday language; and appearance and appeal: print materials and websites must be attractive, inviting, and appear easy to read (Robnett & Chop, 2013).

Indeed, the six verbal communication tips that are recommended by the American Medical Association (AMA) and how they can apply to older adults include slowing down, using plain, non-technical language, showing or drawing pictures, limiting the amount of information or repeating it, use the teach-back technique, and creating a shame-free environment (Robnett & Chop, 2013). These techniques help healthcare professionals communicate better with older people and provide a comfortable environment.

CONCLUSION

Presently, aging people live longer than before (Staudinger et al., 2016). The prevalence of formal or informal employment supports older adults' working well into their lifetimes. Likewise, work engagement after the age of 65 is predicated on the social insurance provided within a country (Robnett & Chop, 2013). Notwithstanding, developed countries aim to support programs to encourage older adults in the workforce, especially those capable of working for the more significant part of their lives. Future studies must convey the particular challenges of promoting work or health programs for older adults past the period of qualification for benefits. Facing this challenge requires multiplicate strategies that encourage older adults willing to work and companies willing to hire them.

REFERENCES

Ambrosini, D. L., Hirsch, C. H., & Hategan, A. (2018). Ethics, Mental Health Law, and Aging. In A. Hategan, J. Bourgeois, C. Hirsch, & C. Giroux (Eds.), *Geriatric Psychiatry* (pp. 201–216). Springer. doi:10.1007/978-3-319-67555-8_9

Barken, R., & Lowndes, R. (2018). Supporting Family Involvement in Long-Term Residential Care: Promising Practices for Relational Care. *Qualitative Health Research, 28*(1), 60–72. doi:10.1177/1049732317730568 PMID:28918701

Berg, P., & Piszczek, M. M. (2022). Organizational Response to Workforce Aging: Tensions in Human Capital Perspectives. *Work, Aging and Retirement, 8*(1), 7–24. doi:10.1093/workar/waab026

Brown, A. D., McMorris, C. A., Longman, R. S., Leigh, R., Hill, M. D., Friedenreich, C. M., & Poulin, M. J. (2010). Effects of Cardiorespiratory Fitness and Cerebral Blood Flow on Cognitive Outcomes in Older Women. *Neurobiology of Aging, 31*(12), 2047–2057. doi:10.1016/j.neurobiolaging.2008.11.002 PMID:19111937

Delle Fave, A., Bassi, M., Boccaletti, E. S., Roncaglione, C., Bernardelli, G., & Mari, D. (2018). Promoting Well-Being in Old Age: The Psychological Benefits of Two Training Programs of Adapted Physical Activity. *Frontiers in Psychology, 9*, 828. doi:10.3389/fpsyg.2018.00828 PMID:29910755

Deller, J., & Walwei, U. (2022). Workforce Age Trends and Projections 1. In H. Zacher & C. W. Rudolph (Eds.), *Age and Work: Advances in Theory, Methods, and Practice*. Routledge. doi:10.4324/9781003089674-3

El-Amin, A. (2022a). Organizational Climate Change: Diversity, Equity, Inclusion, and Belonging. In A. El-Amin (Ed.), *Implementing Diversity, Equity, Inclusion, and Belonging Management in Organizational Change Initiatives* (pp. 1–23). IGI Global. doi:10.4018/978-1-6684-4023-0.ch001

El-Amin, A. (2022b). Do Board Member Duties of Care, Loyalty, and Obedience Matter in a Disaster? *Progress in Industrial Ecology, 15*(2-4), 268–276. doi:10.1504/PIE.2022.125577

Fraher, E., & Brandt, B. (2019). Toward a System where Workforce Planning and Interprofessional Practice and Education are Designed around Patients and Populations not Professions. *Journal of Interprofessional Care, 33*(4), 389–397. doi:10.1080/13561820.2018.1564252 PMID:30669922

Fried, L. P. (2000). Epidemiology of Aging. *Epidemiologic Reviews, 22*(1), 95–106. doi:10.1093/oxfordjournals.epirev.a018031 PMID:10939013

Gilles, M. A., Gaudez, C., Savin, J., Remy, A., Remy, O., & Wild, P. (2022). Do Age and Work Pace Affect Variability when Performing a Repetitive Light Assembly Task? *Applied Ergonomics, 98*, 103601. doi:10.1016/j.apergo.2021.103601 PMID:34634583

Hekmat-Panah, J. (2019). The "Elderly" in Medicine: Ethical Issues Surrounding This Outdated and Discriminatory Term. *Inquiry: A Journal of Medical Care Organization. Provision and Financing, 56*, 46958019856975. doi:10.1177/0046958019856975 PMID:31189387

Hollis, J. L., Collins, C. E., DeClerck, F., Chai, L. K., McColl, K., & Demaio, A. R. (2020). Defining Healthy and Sustainable Diets for Infants, Children and Adolescents. *Global Food Security, 27*, 100401. doi:10.1016/j.gfs.2020.100401

Huot, C., Cruz-Knight, W., Jester, D. J., Wenders, A., Andel, R., & Hyer, K. (2022). Impact of Establishing a Geriatrics Workforce Enhancement Program Clinic on Preventive Health and Medicare Annual Wellness Visits. *Gerontology & Geriatrics Education, 43*(2), 285–294. doi:10.1080/02701960.2020.1854247 PMID:33272147

Jakovljevic, D. G. (2018). Physical Activity and Cardiovascular Aging: Physiological and Molecular Insights. *Experimental Gerontology, 109*, 67–74. doi:10.1016/j.exger.2017.05.016 PMID:28546086

Kapp, M. B. (2020). Legal Issues in Older Adults. In R. Rosenthal, M. Zenilman, & M. Katlic (Eds.), *Principles and Practice of Geriatric Surgery* (pp. 313–338). Springer. doi:10.1007/978-3-319-47771-8_20

Kleineidam, L., Thoma, M. V., Maercker, A., Bickel, H., Mösch, E., Hajek, A., König, H. H., Eisele, M., Mallon, T., Luck, T., Röhr, S., Weyerer, S., Werle, J., Pentzek, M., Fuchs, A., Wiese, B., Mamone, S., Scherer, M., Maier, W., ... Wagner, M. (2019). What Is Successful Aging? A Psychometric Validation Study of Different Construct Definitions. *The Gerontologist, 59*(4), 738–748. doi:10.1093/geront/gny083 PMID:30016435

Libertini, G., Rengo, G., & Ferrara, N. (2017). Aging and Aging Theories. *Journal of Gerontology and Geriatrics, 65*(1), 59–77.

McPhee, J. S., French, D. P., Jackson, D., Nazroo, J., Pendleton, N., & Degens, H. (2016). Physical Activity in Older Age: Perspectives for Healthy Ageing and Frailty. *Biogerontology, 17*(3), 567–580. doi:10.100710522-016-9641-0 PMID:26936444

Meléndez, J. C., Deholm, I., & Satorres, E. (2022). Emotions and Emotional Intelligence in the Field of Gerontology. In Promoting Good Care of Older People in Institutions (pp. 67-82). doi:10.2307/j.ctv2gz3tp3.9

Miller, D. I., Taler, V., Davidson, P. S., & Messier, C. (2012). Measuring the Impact of Exercise on Cognitive Aging: Methodological Issues. *Neurobiology of Aging, 33*(3). doi:10.1016/j.neurobiolaging.2011.02.020

Netz, Y., Wu, M. J., Becker, B. J., & Tenenbaum, G. (2005). Physical Activity and Psychological Well-being in Advanced Age: A Meta-analysis of Intervention Studies. *Psychology and Aging*, *20*(2), 272–284. doi:10.1037/0882-7974.20.2.272 PMID:16029091

Ortiz-Barrios, M., Silvera-Natera, E., Petrillo, A., Gul, M., & Yucesan, M. (2022). A Multicriteria Approach to Integrating Occupational Safety & Health Performance and Industry Systems Productivity in the Context of Aging Workforce: A Case Study. *Safety Science*, *152*, 105764. doi:10.1016/j.ssci.2022.105764

Paterson, D. H., & Warburton, D. E. (2010). Physical Activity and Functional Limitations in Older Adults: A Systematic Review Related to Canada's Physical Activity Guidelines. *The International Journal of Behavioral Nutrition and Physical Activity*, *7*(38), 1–22. doi:10.1186/1479-5868-7-38 PMID:20459782

Puvill, T., Lindenberg, J., de Craen, A. J., Slaets, J. P., & Westendorp, R. G. (2016). Impact of Physical and Mental Health on Life Satisfaction in Old Age: A Population based Observational Study. *BMC Geriatrics*, *16*(1), 194. doi:10.118612877-016-0365-4 PMID:27887583

Qualls, K. E. (2022). Pharmacokinetics and Pharmacodynamics. In P. C. Bollu (Ed.), *Neurochemistry in Clinical Practice* (pp. 313–316). Springer. doi:10.1007/978-3-031-07897-2_16

Ranzijn, R. (2002). The Potential of Older Adults to Enhance Community Quality of Life: Links between Positive Psychology and Productive Aging. *Ageing International*, *27*(2), 30–55. doi:10.100712126-002-1001-5

Reitz, S. M., Scaffa, M. E., & Dorsey, J. (2020). Occupational Therapy in the Promotion of Health and Well-Being. *The American Journal of Occupational Therapy*, *74*(3). doi:10.5014/ajot.2020.743003

Robnett, R. H., & Chop, W. C. (2013). *Gerontology for the Health Care Professional*. Jones & Bartlett Publishers.

Rogers, C. S., & Peelle, J. E. (2022). Interactions Between Audition and Cognition in Hearing Loss and Aging. In L. L. Holt, J. E. Peelle, A. B. Coffin, A. N. Popper, & R. R. Fay (Eds.), *Speech Perception* (pp. 227–252). Springer. doi:10.1007/978-3-030-81542-4_9

Savioli, G., Ceresa, I. F., Novelli, V., Ricevuti, G., Bressan, M. A., & Oddone, E. (2022). How the coronavirus disease 2019 pandemic changed the patterns of healthcare utilization by geriatric patients and the crowding: A call to action for effective solutions to the access block. *Internal and Emergency Medicine*, *17*(2), 503–514. doi:10.100711739-021-02732-w PMID:34106397

Schumacher, K., Beck, C. A., & Marren, J. M. (2006). Family Caregivers: Caring for Older Adults, Working with their Families. *The American Journal of Nursing*, *106*(8), 40–50. doi:10.1097/00000446-200608000-00020 PMID:16905931

Spitzer, W. J., & Davidson, K. W. (2013). Future Trends in Health and Health care: Implications for Social Work Practice in an Aging Society. *Social Work in Health Care*, *52*(10), 959–986. doi:10.1080/00981389.2013.834028 PMID:24255978

Staudinger, U. M., Finkelstein, R., Calvo, E., & Sivaramakrishnan, K. (2016). A Global View on the Effects of Work on Health in Later Life. *The Gerontologist*, *56*(Supplement 2), S281–S292. doi:10.1093/geront/gnw032 PMID:26994267

Stones, D., & Gullifer, J. (2016). 'At home it's just so much easier to be yourself': Older adults' perceptions of ageing in place. *Ageing and Society*, *36*(3), 449–481. doi:10.1017/S0144686X14001214

van den Anker, J., Reed, M. D., Allegaert, K., & Kearns, G. L. (2018). Developmental Changes in Pharmacokinetics and Pharmacodynamics. *Journal of Clinical Pharmacology*, *58*, S10–S25. doi:10.1002/jcph.1284 PMID:30248190

Vanleerberghe, P., De Witte, N., Claes, C., Schalock, R. L., & Verté, D. (2017). The Quality of Life of Older People Aging in Place: A Literature Review. *Quality of Life Research: An International Journal of Quality of Life Aspects of Treatment, Care and Rehabilitation*, *26*(11), 2899–2907. doi:10.100711136-017-1651-0 PMID:28707047

KEY TERMS AND DEFINITIONS

Aging in Place: Means *"the individual's ability to continue to live in his or her abode safely, as independently as possible, and comfortably, regardless of age, income, or ability level"* is observed so that older people can continue their lives with family and friends (Ortiz-Barrios et al., 2022; Stones & Gullifer, 2016).

Geriatric: A medical expression for analyzing, diagnosing, and treating diseases and health problems pertinent to older adults. Gerontology and geriatrics work to mitigate issues involving older adults by challenging how older adults are perceived in society (Huot et al., 2022).

Gerontology: Is the scientific analysis of aging that assesses the biological, psychological, and sociological factors correlated with aging (Meléndez et al., 2022; Kleineidam et al., 2019).

Pharmacodynamics: A drug's existent effect on the body (Qualls, 2022).

Pharmacokinetics: The study of how drugs travel through the body over time (Qualls, 2022; van den Anker et al., 2018).

Quality of Life (QoL): This principle is understood from the individual's perspective and embodies feelings of well-being, basic needs are met, opportunities to achieve personal goals and challenges, autonomy, a sense of community, and multidimensionality (Ranzijn, 2002).

Telomere Erosion Theory (TET): Age and cell mortality are caused by the gradual loss of the protective telomere nucleotide sequences at the ends of the DNA strands within chromosomes with each new cell division and the resultant inability of those cells to continue to divide (Libertini et al., 2017).

Chapter 2
Understanding the Evolution of Sensory Aging in the Workforce

Maria Céu Lamas
School of Health, Polytechnic of Porto, Portugal

Orlando Lima Rua
Porto Accounting and Business School, Polytechnic of Porto, Portugal

Bruno de Sousa Lopes
University of Aveiro, Portugal

Vanessa Amorim
https://orcid.org/0000-0001-9738-5485
Porto Accounting and Business School, Polytechnic of Porto, Portugal

ABSTRACT

The aging workforce is a growing reality, given demographic changes and socioeconomic trends. Therefore, it is crucial to understand, accept, and respect the issues of an aging workforce regarding health and safety in the workplace, especially when aiming to keep the individual longer in the labor market. It is also essential to consider the potential sensory disabilities of each individual so that they can overcome them and fully perform their functions in the workplace. From this perspective, the sensory capabilities of individuals must be assured through different means to guarantee that the organic and functional changes arising from aging are successfully overcome. In this follow-up, a bibliometric analysis between 2001 and 2022 was conducted to explore the most relevant authors, journals, countries, institutions, and publications in sensory aging and the workforce.

DOI: 10.4018/978-1-6684-6351-2.ch002

INTRODUCTION

The working population worldwide is aging due to the birth rate. This phenomenon compromises the availability of labor, a situation that in some countries may have severe consequences in the future; there may not be enough young people to meet current organizational needs (Santos & Almeida, 2017).

There is still no universally accepted definition for the category of older workers. However, some institutions - the European Commission, Eurostat, and the International Labor Organization - have defined it conceptually for those between 55 and 64 (EU-OSHA et al., 2017). Nevertheless, due to demographic aging, its productive capacity will be fundamental for the functioning and sustainability of the most diverse countries in the short and medium term.

As workers age, changes occur that may affect their ability to work, such as a decrease in muscular, aerobic, cognitive, and sensory capacities that make it more or less difficult for them to perform tasks and interact socially in the workplace (EU-OSHA et al., 2017; Santos & Almeida, 2017). However, such changes must be analyzed individually because aging is a very heterogeneous process, varying from individual to individual, and work performance is not exclusively and directly associated with age. Thus, it is possible to observe older employees with higher skills in the workplace than younger ones (Santos & Almeida, 2017). In the general framework of changes resulting from aging, a gradual decline occurs in all senses that make up the sensory system. Nevertheless, some sensory modalities, such as vision and hearing, are more affected. These changes imply decreased autonomy, low relational levels, increased physical and psychological vulnerability, and loss of well-being and quality of life.

The aging workforce is an opportunity, provided that investments are made in improving working conditions, and organizing work to meet the needs of workers and organizations in order to make work more sustainable and ensure healthier working lives (Santos & Almeida, 2017). This chapter addresses the main changes in each direction and their implications for older workers' functionality and quality of life from a sensory aging perspective. In order to better understand the research being done in this area, a bibliometric analysis was conducted between 2001 and 2022, focusing on the most relevant authors, journals, countries, institutions, and other documents in the area of sensory aging and the workforce.

BACKGROUND

The normal aging process, common to all individuals and characterized by the decrease in physiological reserves and the increase in pathologies, assumes variable expressions that determine, with greater or lesser intensity, an individual physical, mental and functional decline (Kirkwood, 2005; Ermida, 2014). Despite having a genetic basis, this process is influenced by the environment in which the individual is inserted and affects the individual's social performance and quality of life (Kirkwood, 2005). The individual's adaptive capacity to deal with the aggressions to which he/she is subjected throughout life changes as a result of a complex interaction between the aging processes at the level of cells, organs, and systems with environmental, physical, psychological, and social factors (Oliveira & Pinto, 2014). This assumes that aging should be an individual life project and an inclusive, integrated and articulated collective responsibility (Gomes, 2011). The individual and collective contribution to healthy aging, as opposed to senescence, will allow for better adequacy of economic and financial resources in this age group (Oliveira & Pinto, 2014). It is considered that the biological decline causes consequences of economic character, family integration, and the social network in which the individual is inserted, which in themselves may constitute a more serious problem than those related to health or other physical problems that may exist (Ermida, 2014).

The aging process entails organic changes, in which the various systems age at different rates. With an undetermined onset, despite its variability, it can be divided into primary (considered normal) and secondary, determined by a greater predisposition to the development of diseases (Bernardes & Pinheiro, 2014). Senescence directly influences the sensory system. The decrease in vision, hearing, smell, taste, and touch, although gradual, often result in functional, psychological, social, and cognitive impairments with an impacting effect on productivity and quality of life, adding high costs to the health sector (Schlicht, 2008; Damasceno et al., 2015).

Main Changes in the Sensory System Due to Aging

For a better understanding of the age-related sensory changes that occur, the main changes in the five general senses, and their relation to functional implications, are summarized in Table 1.

The eye is one of the organs most affected by aging. In general, changes in the structure of the eye and visual function appear after the age of 40 (Hooper & Bello-Haas, 2009; Cypel et al., 2017). As we can see from the analysis of Table 1, there are several causes of decreased visual acuity resulting in narrowing of the visual field, sensitivity to bright light, poor night vision, confusing dark colors, and dry eyes (Lopes et al., 2020).

Table 1. Sensory changes associated with aging and their implications on functionality

Sensory System	Main Age-related Changes	Functional Implications
Vision	Loss of subcutaneous fat around the eye.	Reduced near vision.
	Decreased tissue elasticity and tonus.	Weak eye coordination.
	Decreased strength of the eye muscles.	Image distortion.
	Decreased transparency of the cornea.	Blurry vision.
	Degeneration of sclera, pupil, and iris.	Night vision compromised.
	Increased density and rigidity of the lens.	Loss of color sensitivity.
	Increased frequency of intrinsic diseases of the eye - glaucoma, cataract, macular degeneration, and retinopathy.	Blurred vision; loss of peripheral vision; difficulty recognizing moving targets and complex figures (due to difficulty perceiving details).
	The central nervous system slows down in processing information.	
Audition	Loss or damage to the ciliated cells of the cochlea.	Difficulty in hearing higher frequencies, tinnitus. Decreased ability for height discrimination and balance.
	Degeneration of central auditory pathways and loss of neurotransmitters.	Altered discrimination for phonemes and in understanding rapid speech or in noisy environments.
Smell	Decrease of the olfactory neuroepithelium, receptors, and neurons. Loss of fibers of the olfactory bulb. Modification of neurotransmitters.	Decline in sensitivity to detect and identify odors.
Palate	Decreased number of sensory receptors. Decreased ability of the brain to interpret taste sensations.	Higher thresholds for substance identification. Loss in detecting salty, bitter, sweet, and sour.
Touch	Slowing of nerve conduction. Decreased skin receptors.	Decreased response to tactile stimuli. Changes in pain perception and temperature.

Source: Adapted from Hooper and Bello-Haas, 2009

Age-related deafness - presbycusis - is characterized by decreased hearing acuity in the frequencies of high sounds and difficulty in oral perception. It is a multifactorial pathology caused by genetic and environmental factors, the latter being widely studied: exposure to noise and chemicals, ototoxic medication, and diseases such as diabetes mellitus, renal failure, and cardiovascular diseases (Paiva & Paiva, 2014).

Changes in olfaction are rarely considered serious problems for individual life (Saraiva, 2011) and work life. Unless, as a result of their profession, they can put their lives or the lives of others at risk.

Taste is based on the perception of four basic tastes: sweet, salty, sour, and bitter. The tongue has different taste zones with different sensitivity to tastes. Nevertheless, with age, taste perception deteriorates, and the individual loses the ability to detect salty, sweet, and sour tastes (Lalwani & Snow, 2002).

Touch is the sense responsible for perceiving different sensations in the skin, assuming an essential role in body positioning, physical protection, and affectivity. This is because through the various receptors distributed among the different layers of the skin, pressure, pain, temperature, and movement are perceived. Due to sensory aging, tactile thresholds increase; consequently, the discriminative sensitivity through touch to heat sources, presence, and identification of objects decrease (Lamas & Paúl, 2013).

Main Implications of Sensory Aging at Work

Deficits in visual acuity may be more noticeable in jobs that require more attention and precision, such as reading printed materials, driving at night, and others. From this perspective, appropriate lighting conditions should be created to reduce the risk of accidents caused by visual impairments and to make it easier for older workers to perform their professional duties. Here are some examples of simplified applicability: avoid using blue colors in offices or combined with green or black; have clearly visible and easily intelligible signage for older workers (Whillans et al., 2016). One can also opt for visual correction and technological assistance, such as using larger screens/monitors, changing the font size of letters, adjusting contrast, and using magnifying media, among others (Crawford et al., 2010; Yeomans, 2011; Weyman et al., 2013).

Degenerative changes at the level of sensory cells and receptors responsible for the sense of balance are common. When present, certain workers are at risk of falling, notably emergency service workers, construction workers, firefighters, and all those who work at heights. To protect the health and lives of older employees, it is advisable to adjust task times, illuminate passages, and mark stairways and uneven areas with highly contrasting signs (EU-OSHA et al., 2017).

Regardless of age, hearing loss increases the risk of injury and accidents at work for all people. However, presbycusis is related to more significant safety risks, such as increased accidents and falls in the context of noise exposure. It can also mask noise-induced hearing loss by making it difficult to hear warnings or work instructions (Powell & Bonito, 2015). Nevertheless, accumulated work experience allows the worker to compensate for these limitations. However, from an accountability and safety perspective, its importance cannot be overlooked, especially in motor vehicle contexts, as it contributes to increased accidents and traffic violations. Contrary to what one might think, older workers have fewer accidents, by compensation with more moderate driving and work experience. On the other hand, related to hearing, loss of balance is a concern for people who perform activities at heights or control vehicles with rapid head movements, although balance training can help mitigate this (Crawford et al., 2010; Beers & Butler, 2012). Another aspect to consider is the difficulty in communication between workers due to tinnitus. This can be limiting in contexts of intense teamwork. It is essential to manage noise levels and reduce or even cancel the echo in workspaces (Lu et al., 2016).

Although the problems related to the loss of smell are not as relevant as the previous sense organs, they can cause enormous suffering by losing the quality of life. The dangers that can occur from this are related when the olfactory capacity is an integral part of the individual's professional activity. They are also related to safety issues due to the decreased ability to detect danger signals such as gas smell, smoke/fire, and spoiled food (Saraiva, 2011). In this sense, the implementation or reinforcement of safety conditions - application of smoke detectors and enforcement of food storage and refrigeration rules, help to minimize these risks.

With age, taste perception deteriorates. The individual first loses the ability to detect salty, then sweet and sour tastes. The bitter taste lasts the longest (Dharmarajan, 2021). Consequently, it tends to cook saltier and sweeter food because all food seems tasteless and bitter to it, often leading to other types of consequences - poorly controlled diabetes or hypertension, on an individual level, but with repercussions on collective health if the work activity is developed in the hotel industry. In addition, there are the costs of rejecting cooked food.

As a result of the aging of touch, the sensation of heat, cold, pressure, and vibration diminishes. Thus, increased pain tolerance makes low-intensity pain stimuli imperceptible, which is assumed to be a risk for burns and other skin injuries, for example. Skin becoming less elastic, drier, thinner, and more susceptible to irritation can be a risk factor for workers handling chemicals. In this regard, specific precautions should be implemented because wounds in older people take four times longer to heal compared to younger people (Saraiva, 2011).

METHODOLOGY

Bibliometrix and Biblioshiny (present in RStudio) were used to conduct the bibliometric analysis. These kinds of software can statistically and graphically analyze the data present in the literature, namely: 1) citation information (such as authors, years of publication, citation count, sources, and types of documents, among others); 2) bibliographical information; 3) abstract and keywords, and 4) other information. Since the collection of information is parameterizable, it is possible to obtain specific data depending on the data users intend to analyze. According to Hackenberger (2020), RStudio stands out from other software by having several packages available on CRAN (Comprehensive R Archive Network) servers, which contain functions, algorithms, and distinct procedures, allowing various types of data processing and analysis.

The research was conducted in November 2022 through the Scopus database, applying the terms "sens* ag*" and "workforce." To analyze only those articles aligned with the study's objective, the following inclusion and exclusion criteria were applied in Scopus: 1) keywords contained in the title, abstract, and keywords; 2) in the period between 2001 and 2022; 3) keywords only present in articles type documents and journals; and 4) published in the Medicine, Social Sciences, Nursing, Business, Management and Accounting, Psychology and Health Professions. After applying the inclusion and exclusion criteria, 732 articles were obtained. The query applied in Scopus is as follows: (TITLE-ABS-KEY (sens*) AND TITLE-ABS-KEY (ag*) AND TITLE-ABS-KEY (workforce)) AND (LIMIT-TO (SRCTYPE,"j")) AND (LIMIT-TO (DOCTYPE,"ar")) AND (LIMIT-TO (SUBJAREA,"MEDI") OR LIMIT-TO (SUBJAREA,"SOCI") OR LIMIT-TO (SUBJAREA,"NURS") OR LIMIT-TO (SUBJAREA,"BUSI") OR LIMIT-TO (SUBJAREA,"PSYC") OR LIMIT-TO (SUBJAREA,"HEAL")) AND (LIMIT-TO (PUBYEAR,2022) OR LIMIT-TO (PUBYEAR,2021) OR LIMIT-TO (PUBYEAR,2020) OR LIMIT-TO (PUBYEAR,2019) OR LIMIT-TO (PUBYEAR,2018) OR LIMIT-TO (PUBYEAR,2017) OR LIMIT-TO (PUBYEAR,2016) OR LIMIT-TO (PUBYEAR,2015) OR LIMIT-TO (PUBYEAR,2014) OR LIMIT-TO (PUBYEAR,2013) OR LIMIT-TO (PUBYEAR,2012) OR LIMIT-TO (PUBYEAR,2011) OR LIMIT-TO (PUBYEAR,2010) OR LIMIT-TO (PUBYEAR,2009) OR LIMIT-TO (PUBYEAR,2008) OR LIMIT-TO (PUBYEAR,2007) OR LIMIT-TO (PUBYEAR,2006) OR LIMIT-TO (PUBYEAR,2005) OR LIMIT-TO (PUBYEAR,2004) OR LIMIT-TO (PUBYEAR,2003) OR LIMIT-TO (PUBYEAR,2002) OR LIMIT-TO (PUBYEAR,2001)).

RESULTS

Scientific Production

Between 2001 and 2022, 732 articles were produced, accessed through 528 different sources, using 30603 references. An average of 6.12 articles were published per year, with an average citation rate of 18.23 per document and an average of 2.459 citations per document per year. The literature on the topic totals 3047 authors, of which 94 were single-authors of articles and 2953 were multi-authored. From this perspective, the collaboration index presents a significant value (4.63). Table 2 below contains the information regarding the main data collected.

Table 2. Main information about articles collected

Description	Results
Timespan	2001:2022
Sources	528
Documents	732
Average years from publication	6.12
Average citations per document	18.23
Average citations per year per doc	2.459
References	30603
Articles	732
Keywords Plus	4050
Author's Keywords	2404
Authors	3047
Authors of single-authored documents	94
Authors of multi-authored documents	2953
Single-authored documents	94
Documents per Author	0.24
Authors per Document	4.16
Co-Authors per Documents	4.33
Collaboration Index	4.63

Source: Own elaboration, 2022

Figure 1 represents the annual scientific production between 2001 and 2022. During the period under analysis, 732 articles were produced, with the scientific production of the last five years corresponding to 48.5% (355 articles) and the last ten years corresponding to 75.8% (555 articles). From this perspective, it can be considered that the years 2022 (84 articles), 2021 (85 articles), 2020 (65 articles), 2019 (68 articles), and 2018 (53 articles) were the most significant. On the other hand, the years with the lowest scientific production on the topic were 2001 (5 published articles), 2002 (4 published articles), 2003 (4 published articles), and lastly, 2005 (9 published articles). Currently, there is an annual growth rate of 14.8%.

As seen in Figure 2, the number of articles (N) has been increasing yearly. The average number of citations per article (MeanTCperArt) was most significant in 2003 (95.8 citations). However, over the last five years, there has been a decline in this indicator, as shown by the following results 2018 (18.9 citations), 2019 (10.7 citations), 2020 (8.51 citations), 2021 (4.25 citations) and 2022 (0.85 citations per article). The average total citations per year (MeanTCperYear) was also found and the most significant year was 2003 (5.04 citations). The average total citations per year have increased in the last five years, as can be seen through the following results: 2018 (4.72 citations), 2019 (3.56 citations), 2020, and 2021 (4.25 citations).

Figure 1. Annual scientific production between 2001 and 2022
Source: Own elaboration, 2022

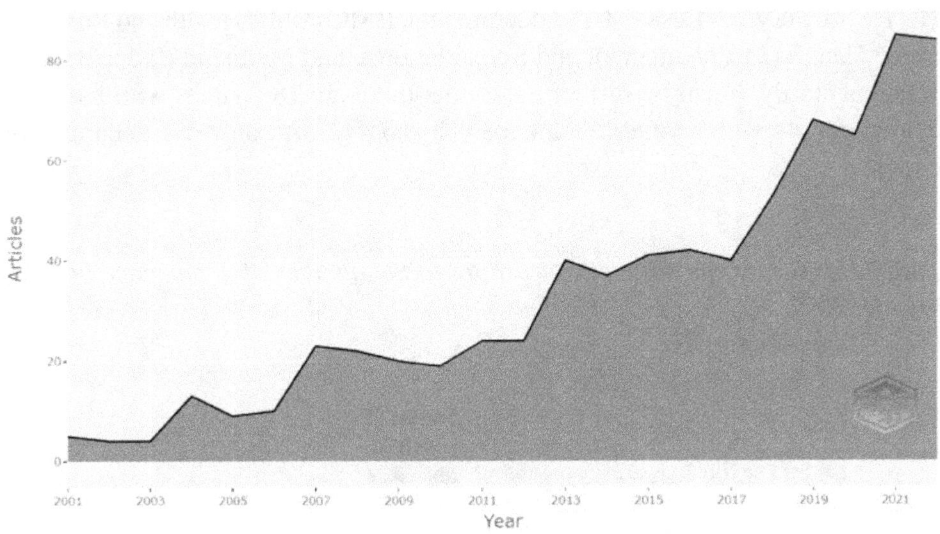

Figure 2. Average of total citations per article and year between 2001 and 2022
Source: Own elaboration, 2022

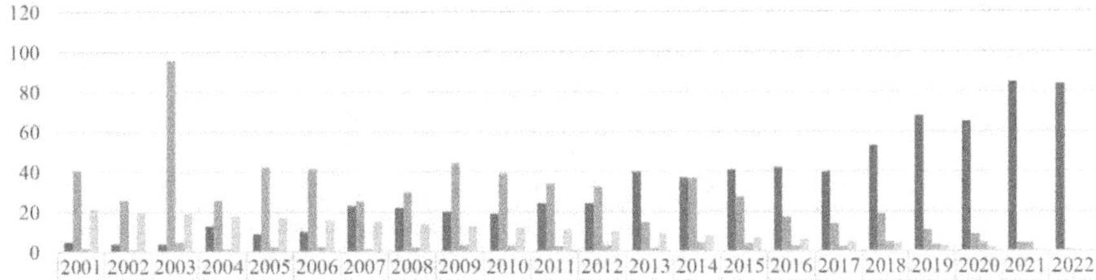

	2001	2002	2003	2004	2005	2006	2007	2008	2009	2010	2011	2012	2013	2014	2015	2016	2017	2018	2019	2020	2021	2022
N	5	4	4	13	9	10	23	22	20	19	24	24	40	37	41	42	40	53	68	65	85	84
MeanTCperArt	40,6	25,8	95,8	25,6	42,1	41,4	25,4	30	44,2	39,1	34,1	32,5	14,6	36,9	27,2	17,2	14	18,9	10,7	8,51	4,25	0,85
MeanTCperYear	1,93	1,29	5,04	1,42	2,48	2,59	1,69	2,14	3,4	3,25	3,1	3,25	1,62	4,61	3,89	2,87	2,8	4,72	3,56	4,25	4,25	
CitableYears	21	20	19	18	17	16	15	14	13	12	11	10	9	8	7	6	5	4	3	2	1	0

Sources

Most relevant sources

The analysis showed 528 sources with publications in sensory aging and the workforce. However, for data analysis purposes, all sources with a total number of published documents equal to or greater than four were considered (Figure 3). From this perspective, the sources with the most significant number of documents are BMC Health Services Research (14 documents), BMC Public Health and Rural and Remote Health (11 documents), and Social Science and Medicine (9 documents). Complementarily, it can be further noted that there are 18 sources with a total of 3 documents, 44 with a total of 2 documents, and 442 with only one document on the topic.

Figure 3. Most relevant sources, according to the number of documents, between 2001 and 2022
Source: Own elaboration, 2022

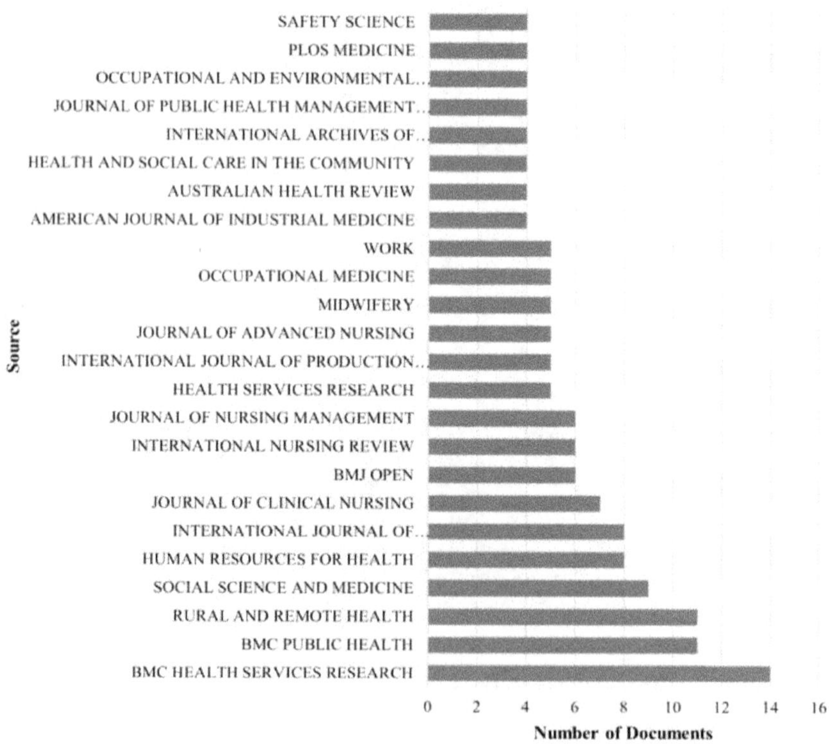

Most Local Cited Sources

The analysis of the most local cited sources comprised the graphical analysis of the cited sources and the number of local citations. Only cited sources with a total number of local citations equal to or greater than sixty were considered (Figure 4). The most cited local sources, in the context of the study, are the Lancet (159 citations), the Journal of Advanced Nursing (153 citations), JAMA (134 citations), and the Journal of Applied Psychology (131 citations). The most cited local sources indicated represent only 6.5% of the total local citations.

Figure 4. Most local cited sources, according to the number of local citations, between 2001 and 2022
Source: Own elaboration, 2022

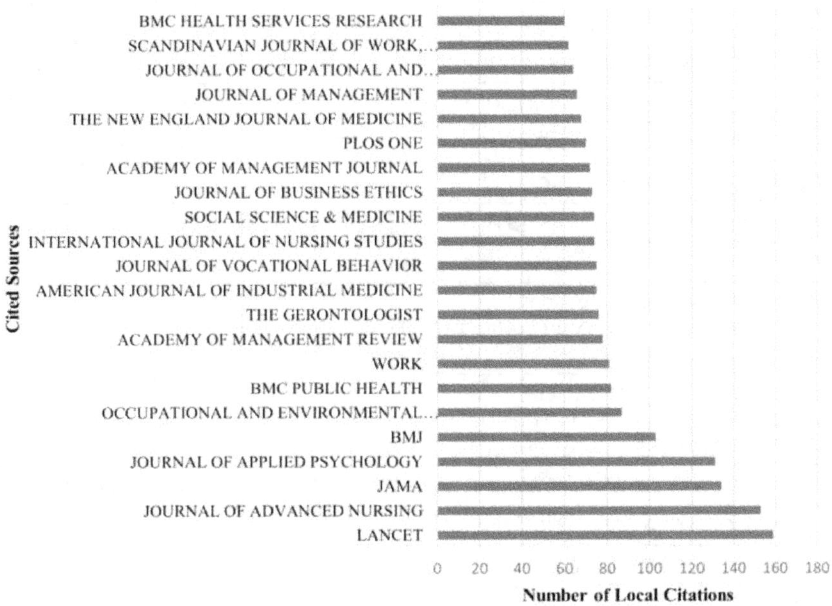

Impact

Some indicators, such as the H-index, the G-index, the M-index, or the number of total citations, can measure the impact of sources. In the analysis of the source's impact (Table 3), H-index was used because it is an indicator that reflects the performance of a journal, which is reflected in its relevance (Silva & Moreira,

2022). In this perspective, the authors considered sources with an H-index equal to or greater than four. Thus, the most relevant sources in the scope of sensory aging and workforce are BMC Public Health (9), Journal of Clinical Nursing (7), BMC Health Services Research (6), Journal of Nursing Management (6), Rural and Remote Health (6), Social Science and Medicine (6), Human Resources for Health (5), Midwifery (5), International Archives of Occupational and Environmental Health (4), Environmental Research and Public Health (4), International Nursing Review (4), Journal of Advanced Nursing (4), Occupational Medicine (4), PLOS Medicine (4), Safety Science (4), and Work (4).

Table 3. Source impact between 2001 and 2022

R	Source	H	G	M	TC	NP	Year
1	BMC PUBLIC HEALTH	9	11	0,56	304	11	2007
2	JOURNAL OF CLINICAL NURSING	7	7	0,44	156	7	2007
3	BMC HEALTH SERVICES RESEARCH	6	12	0,40	257	12	2008
4	JOURNAL OF NURSING MANAGEMENT	6	6	0,38	168	6	2007
5	RURAL AND REMOTE HEALTH	6	10	0,38	148	10	2007
6	SOCIAL SCIENCE AND MEDICINE	6	8	0,43	511	8	2009
7	HUMAN RESOURCES FOR HEALTH	5	8	0,33	257	8	2008
8	MIDWIFERY	5	5	0,38	196	5	2010
9	INTERNATIONAL ARCHIVES OF OCCUPATIONAL AND ENVIRONMENTAL HEALTH	4	4	0,29	127	4	2009
10	INTERNATIONAL JOURNAL OF ENVIRONMENTAL RESEARCH AND PUBLIC HEALTH	4	7	1,00	102	7	2019
11	INTERNATIONAL NURSING REVIEW	4	6	0,25	60	6	2007
12	JOURNAL OF ADVANCED NURSING	4	4	0,24	35	4	2006
13	OCCUPATIONAL MEDICINE	4	4	0,27	114	4	2008
14	PLOS MEDICINE	4	4	0,50	45	4	2015
15	SAFETY SCIENCE	4	4	0,57	69	4	2016
16	WORK	4	5	0,19	57	5	2002
Abbreviations: R: Ranking; H: H-index; G: G-index; M: M-index; TC: Total citation; NP: Number of publications							

Source: Own elaboration, 2022

Source growth

From the analysis of Figure 5, it can be stated that BMC Health Services Research is one of the journals with the highest cumulative occurrences (14) and has been growing since 2017. This is followed by Rural and Remote Health (with 11 cumulative occurrences) and the International Journal of Environmental Research and Public Health (with 9 cumulative occurrences). On the other hand, BMC Public Health and Human Resources for Health have remained without growth and stable since 2019 and 2020, respectively.

Figure 5. Source growth, according to cumulate occurrences, between 2001 and 2022
Source: Own elaboration, 2022

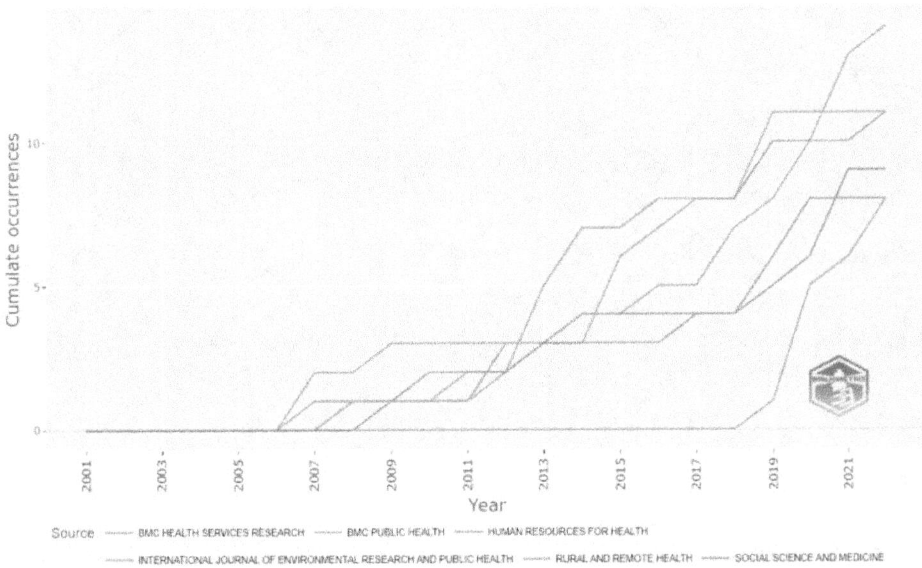

Authors

Authors' Production over Time

An analysis of the twenty authors with the highest scientific production was performed. The analysis and interpretation of Figure 6 allow for establishing the authors who gather the most significant number of publications and the number of total citations. The author's Chang C-H., Fenwick J., Goodman D.C., Nair S., Sidebotham M., Taylor-Phillips S., Tuckett A., Wang H., and Wang J. produced three total articles with 141, 99, 199, 27, 56, 7, 42, 32, and 53 total citations respectively. On the other hand, the following authors produced two articles over the period under review, namely: Ball J., Barnard A., Bauer G., Berridge C., Bloor K., Boughton M., Brown P., Butler S.S. and Ahmed F., whose citations total 9, 9, 40, 24, 29, 31, 82, 45 and 1, respectively. Finally, author Bag S. produced 1 article, which has ten citations.

Figure 6. Authors' production between 2001 and 2022
Source: Own elaboration, 2022

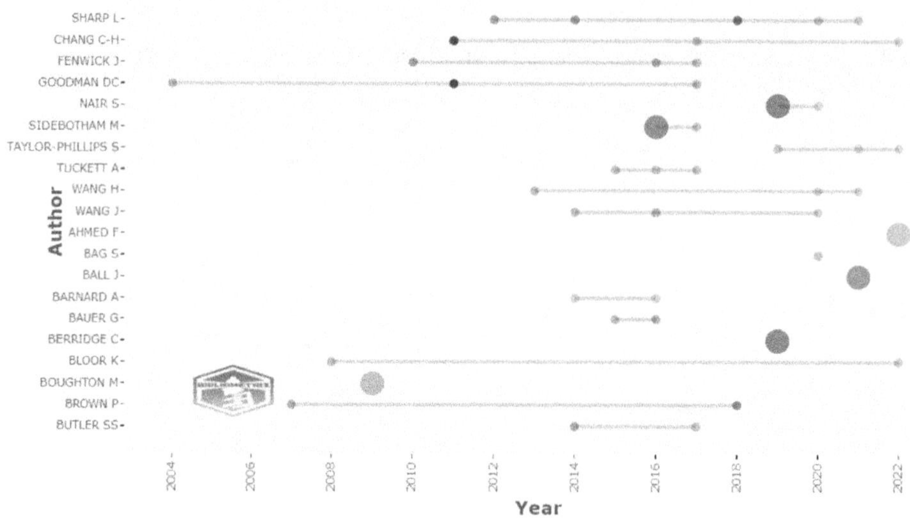

Impact

In order to analyze the author's impact on the scope of sensory aging and workforce, only the inclusion of authors with an H-index equal to or greater than two was considered, as shown in Table 4. The following authors have the highest impact on this field: Sharp, L. (H-index of 4); Fenwick, J. (H-index of 3); Goodman, D.C. (H-index of 3); Sidebotham, M. (H-index of 3); Tuckett, A. (H-index of 3); and Wang, J. (H-index of 3).

Table 4. Author impact between 2001 and 2022

R	Author	H	G	M	TC	NP
1	SHARP L	4	5	0,36	141	5
2	FENWICK J	3	3	0,23	99	3
3	GOODMAN DC	3	3	0,16	199	3
4	SIDEBOTHAM M	3	3	0,43	56	3
5	TUCKETT A	3	3	0,38	42	3
6	WANG J	3	3	0,33	53	3
7	BAG S	2	2	0,67	10	2
8	BARNARD A	2	2	0,22	9	2
9	BAUER G	2	2	0,25	40	2
10	BERRIDGE C	2	2	0,50	24	2
11	BOUGHTON M	2	2	0,14	31	2
12	BROWN P	2	2	0,13	82	2
13	BUTLER SS	2	2	0,22	45	2
14	CADILHAC DA	2	2	0,17	75	2
15	CALVERT M	2	2	0,20	10	2
16	CARTER R	2	2	0,17	75	2
17	CHANG C-H	2	2	0,17	141	2
18	CHEN Y-C	2	2	0,67	4	2
19	CHOI NG	2	2	0,17	47	2
20	CRANE L	2	2	0,15	37	2
21	CREEDY DK	2	2	0,29	43	2
22	CUMMING TB	2	2	0,17	75	2
23	DEUBNER DC	2	2	0,09	70	2
24	DUFFIELD C	2	2	0,29	45	2
25	EISEN EA	2	2	0,11	78	2
26	FLANAGAN WM	2	2	0,29	65	2
27	GALLAGHER R	2	2	0,20	16	2
28	GAO F	2	2	0,25	32	2
29	GARNER R	2	2	0,29	65	2
30	GREENFIELD S	2	2	0,14	172	2
31	GUPTA P	2	2	0,22	42	2
32	HANLY P	2	2	0,18	88	2
33	HANSEN V	2	2	0,20	39	2
34	HENNESSY D	2	2	0,29	65	2

continues on following page

Table 4. Continued

R	Author	H	G	M	TC	NP
35	JEFFERS L	2	2	0,13	84	2
36	KARUNANITHI M	2	2	0,50	7	2
37	KIM K	2	2	0,33	19	2
38	LEE S	2	2	0,18	79	2
39	MAGNUS A	2	2	0,17	75	2
40	MARSHALL DA	2	2	0,29	65	2
41	NAIR S	2	3	0,50	27	3
42	NEAL-BOYLAN L	2	2	0,17	26	2
43	NELSON S	2	2	0,13	28	2
44	NEWCOMBE P	2	2	0,25	32	2
45	OPRESCU F	2	2	0,22	105	2
46	OSTASZKIEWICZ J	2	2	0,25	34	2
47	PEARCE DC	2	2	0,17	75	2
48	PEISAH C	2	2	0,13	62	2
49	PIT SW	2	2	0,20	39	2
50	RAMOS R	2	2	0,25	40	2
51	RUSSELL A	2	2	0,13	58	2
52	SANMARTIN C	2	2	0,29	65	2
53	SHARIF B	2	2	0,29	65	2
54	SHEPPARD L	2	2	0,17	75	2
55	SINGH A	2	2	0,29	5	2
56	TARLO SM	2	2	0,17	90	2
57	TILSE C	2	2	0,25	32	2
58	VAN DER BEEK AJ	2	2	0,22	53	2
59	VECCHIO N	2	2	0,14	12	2
60	WANG H	2	3	0,20	32	3
61	WANG Y	2	2	0,15	24	2
62	WILSON J	2	2	0,25	32	2
63	YANG J	2	2	0,20	33	2
Abbreviations: R: Ranking; H: H-index; G: G-index; M: M-index; TC: Total citation; NP: Number of publications						

Source: Own elaboration, 2022

Affiliations and Countries

Tekles and Bornmann (2020, p. 1510) state that *"adequately disambiguating author names in bibliometric databases is a precondition for conducting reliable analyses at the author level."* The respective parameterization was made in the software to analyze the most relevant affiliations. For the analysis, all affiliations with several articles equal to or greater than ten were considered (Figure 7). Thus, the ten most relevant affiliations are as follows: Monash University – Australia (44 articles), Griffith University – Australia (24 articles), University of Toronto – Canada (24 articles), Deakin University – Australia (22 articles), The University of Queensland – Australia (22 articles), University of Washington – United States of America (22 articles), University of Manchester – United Kingdom (21 articles), University of Melbourne – Australia (21 articles), University of York – United Kingdom (18 articles), and Queensland University of Technology – Australia (17 articles).

Figure 7. Most relevant affiliations, according to the number of articles, between 2001 and 2022
Source: Own elaboration, 2022

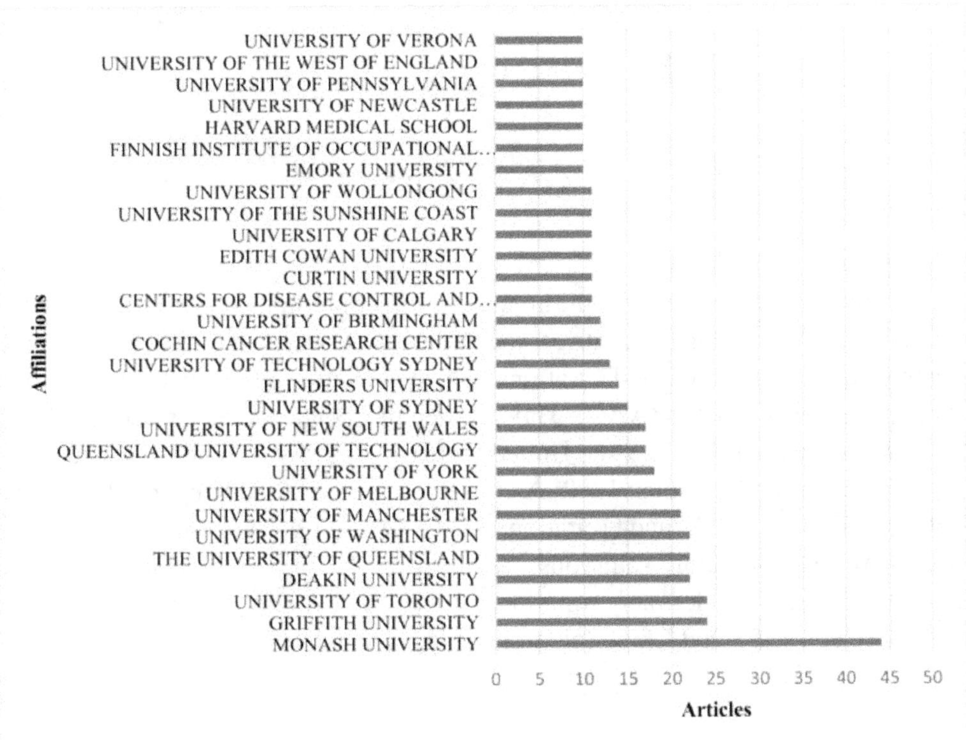

The indicator for the scientific production of each country results from the analysis of the country of affiliation of each author and co-author in each article, grouping them into their respective countries (Figure 8). The ten countries representing the highest scientific production are the United States of America (888), Australia (523), the United Kingdom (358), Canada (196), Germany (112), Italy (97), India (95), China (78), Netherlands (67), and Finland (39).

Figure 8. Country scientific production between 2001 and 2022
Source: Own elaboration, 2022

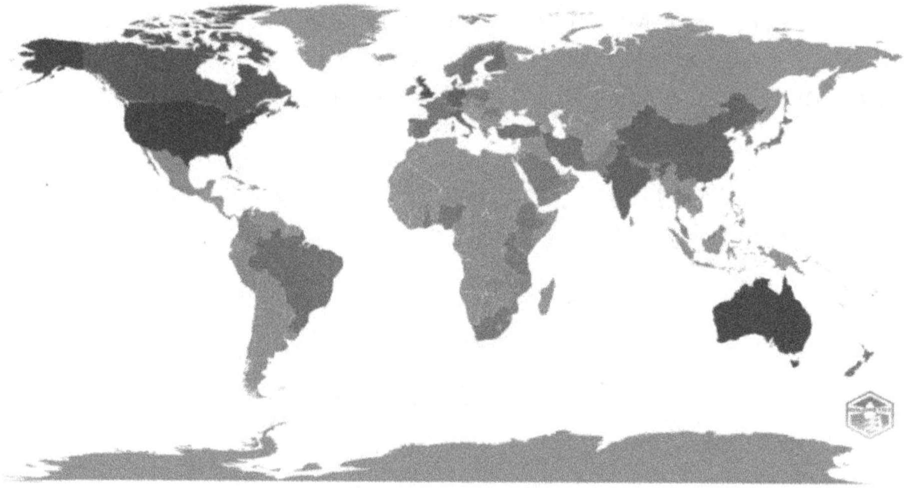

Following the countries with the highest scientific production, the authors wanted to analyze the most cited countries, using Figure 9, where the indicator defined for this purpose was the Total Citations, which also allowed the calculation of the Average Article Citations (AAC). Thus, the ten most cited countries between 2001 and 2022 were the following: the United States of America (citations: 3547; AAC: 22.449), Australia (citations: 1982; AAC: 19.243), the United Kingdom (citations: 1500; AAC: 18.293), Canada (citations: 784; AAC: 21.778), Denmark (citations: 412; AAC: 82.400), Italy (citations: 294; AAC: 24.500), Netherlands (citations: 274; AAC: 19.571), Germany (citations: 204; AAC: 10.200), Sweden (citations: 161; AAC: 20.125), and China (citations: 155; AAC: 9.118).

Figure 9. Most cited countries between 2001 and 2022
Source: Own elaboration, 2022

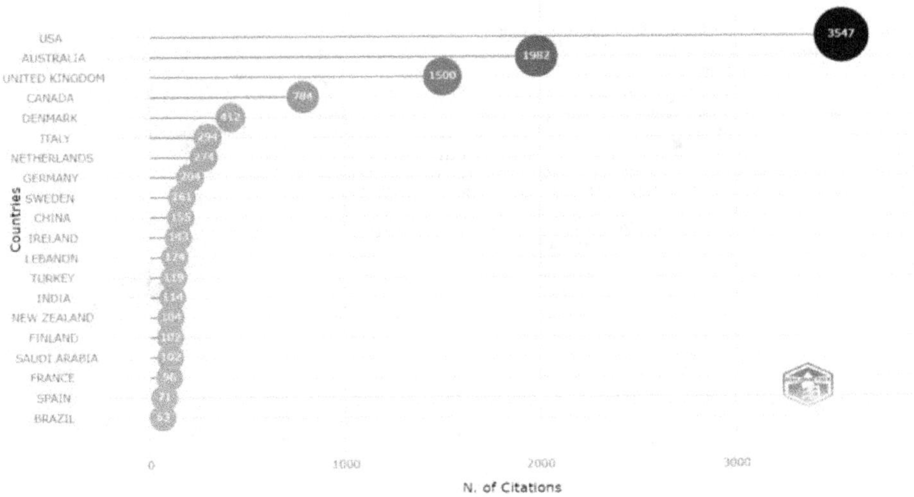

Regarding the collaboration between authors, it was found that in sensory aging research and workforce, 732 articles were produced by 3047 authors, of which only 94 produced their research independently. In this sense, the collaboration index is quite significant (4.63), which makes it pertinent to evaluate the interconnections between authors from different countries. As can be seen in Figure 10, there are 328 collaborations between different countries. However, in the present analysis, the authors will highlight the most significant collaborations, namely between the United States and Canada (13), between the United States and the United Kingdom (8), between Australia and the United Kingdom (6), between the United States and the Netherlands (6), between Canada and the Netherlands (5), between Germany and the Netherlands (5), and lastly, between the United States and Australia (5).

Documents and Words

The most cited documents were obtained according to the total number of citations they gathered, as shown in Figure 11, representing the 20 most relevant articles on the topic. In this follow-up, the five most cited papers are the following: Kurtz et al. (2014) with 642 citations; Schor (2003) with 319 citations; Pedersen et al. (2012) with 299 citations; Correa-Velez et al. (2010) with 274 citations; and Duffy and Hund (2015) with 238 citations.

Figure 10. Collaboration world map
Source: Own elaboration, 2022

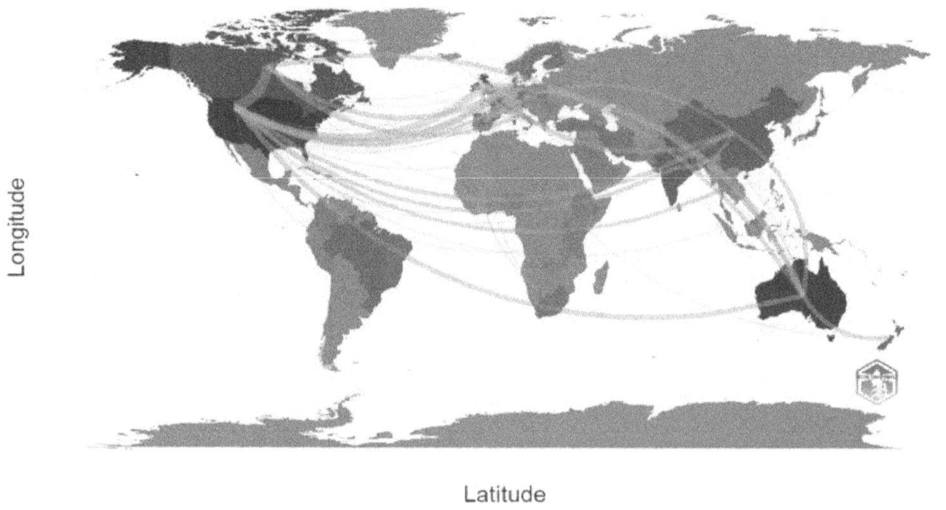

Figure 11. Most cited documents between 2001 and 2022
Source: Own elaboration, 2022

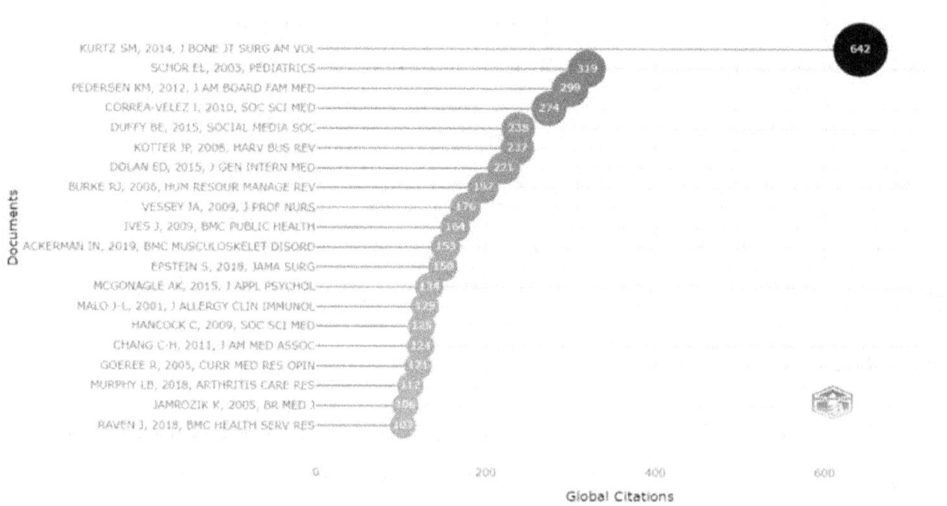

Next, the 20 most relevant words were analyzed according to the authors' keywords, using the number of occurrences as a criterion. Thus, the most frequent keywords are represented by workforce (38 occurrences), covid-19 (19 occurrences), Australia (18 occurrences), occupational health and qualitative research (15 occurrences), gender and nursing (14 occurrences), health workforce and mental health (13 occurrences), employment, job satisfaction and primary care (11 occurrences), burnout, education, nurses and training (10 occurrences), retention (9 occurrences) and, lastly, dementia, diversity, and work (8 occurrences).

The trend topics can be obtained according to the period one wants to analyze. For this purpose, the authors defined that the trend topics would be obtained through the authors' keywords between 2011 and 2022. As for the graphic criteria, a word minimum frequency and several words per year of 10 were set. After applying the parameterization shown above, Figure 12 was obtained. In this figure, the following words stand out according to the following frequencies: workforce (37), covid-19 (19), occupational health (15), qualitative research (15), gender (14), nursing (14), mental health (13), health workforce (13), job satisfaction (11), burnout (10) and education (10).

Figure 12. Trend topics between 2011 and 2022
Source: Own elaboration, 2022

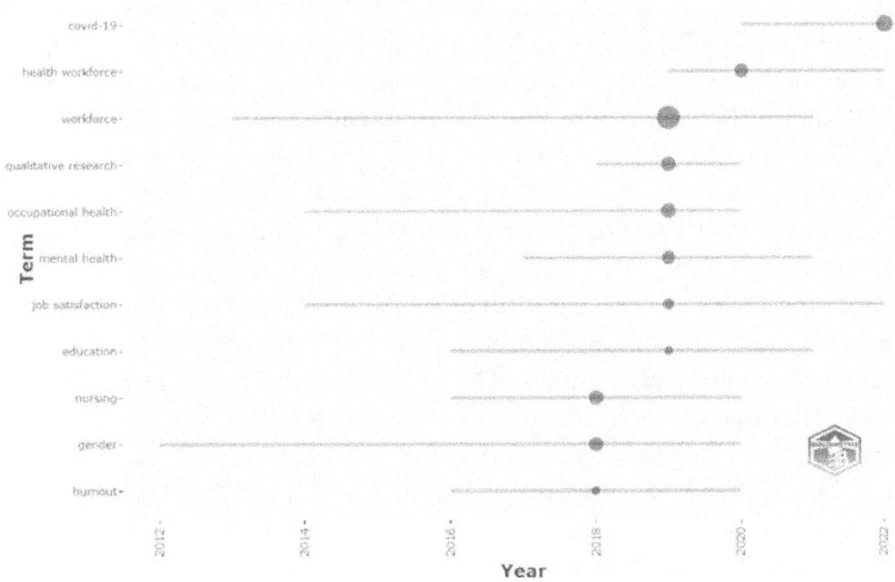

CONCLUSION

The health of individuals stems from the balanced functioning of certain functional domains: cognition, mobility, communication, and mood. Nevertheless, biological, cognitive, functional, and sensory changes occur with aging. Sensory decline, although differentiated, can affect safety, quality of life, and the ability to work with older workers to a greater or lesser degree. However, because of their experience, wisdom, and expertise, these workers can better face real-world problems or difficulties. In order to respect their professional usefulness and to enable them to work for a long and productive period under conditions of health and safety, workplaces must be adapted to the needs of these workers.

Researchers in the area of sensory aging and the workforce produced 732 articles in the period between 2001 and 2022. Over the last five years, there has been an increase in interest in the topic, which can be justified by the fact that 48.5% of the total scientific production was produced in this period. This study also concluded that the most significant scientific production corresponds to 2021 and 2022; the current growth rate is 14.8%.

Regarding the number of global citations, the average indicator of total citations per article has declined in the last five years. On the other hand, the average total citations per year indicator has shown an inverse behavior, having increased in the last five years.

In the present analysis, the authors used the H-index to analyze the relevance of sources and authors in sensory aging and workforce research. In this sense, BMC Public Health (H-index of 9), Journal of Clinical Nursing (H-index of 7), BMC Health Services Research (H-index of 6), Journal of Nursing Management (H-index of 6), Rural and Remote Health (H-index of 6) and Social Science and Medicine (H-index of 6) are the most relevant sources. From the perspective of the authors, the following stand out as having the most significant impact Sharp, L. (H-index of 4); Fenwick, J. (H-index of 3); Goodman, D.C. (H-index of 3); Sidebotham, M. (H-index of 3); Tuckett, A. (H-index of 3); and Wang, J. (H-index of 3).

Concerning the most critical affiliations, it was found that most are located in Australia, such as Monash University, Griffith University, Deakin University, University of Queensland, University of Melbourne, and the Queensland University of Technology. Also noteworthy are the University of Toronto in Canada, the University of Washington in the United States of America, the University of Manchester in the United Kingdom, and the University of York in the United Kingdom. This research also sought to establish the countries with the highest scientific production on the topic, whereby the United States of America with 3547 citations, Australia with 1982 citations, the United Kingdom with 1500 citations, Canada with 784 citations, and Denmark with 412 citations stand out.

The most cited documents were obtained according to the total number of citations they gathered. In this follow-up, the five most cited papers are the following: Kurtz et al. (2014) with 642 citations; Schor (2003) with 319 citations; Pedersen et al. (2012) with 299 citations; Correa-Velez et al. (2010) with 274 citations; and Duffy and Hund (2015) with 238 citations.

From a future research perspective, assessing and comparing optimal jobs and conditions for developing cross-cutting and specific activities will be equally important. In this sense, interviewing workers regardless of age (but whose age ranges should be representative) is a strategy that should be more widespread, as well as research that evaluates the ability to perform jobs throughout a career.

REFERENCES

Beers, H., & Butler, C. (2012). *Age related changes and safety critical work: Identification of tools and a review of the literature*. HSE Books Health and Safety Executive.

Bernardes, A., & Pinheiro, S. (2014). Anatomia do Envelhecimento [Anatomy of Aging]. In M. T. Veríssimo (Ed.), *Geriatria Fundamental, Saber e Praticar* [Fundamental Geriatrics, Knowledge and Practice] (pp. 41–48). LIDEL, Edições Técnicas, Lda.

Correa-Velez, I., Gifford, S. M., & Barnett, A. G. (2010). Longing to belong: Social inclusion and wellbeing among youth with refugee backgrounds in the first three years in Melbourne, Australia. *Social Science & Medicine*, *71*(8), 1399–1408. doi:10.1016/j.socscimed.2010.07.018 PMID:20822841

Crawford, J. O., Graveling, R. A., Cowie, H. A., & Dixon, K. (2010). The health safety and health promotion needs of older workers. *Occupational Medicine*, *60*(3), 184–192. doi:10.1093/occmed/kqq028 PMID:20423949

Cypel, M. C., Salomão, S. R., Dantas, P. E. C., Lottenberg, C. L., Kasahara, N., & Ramos, L. R. (2017). Status da visão, avaliação oftalmológica e qualidade de vida em idosos [Vision status, ophthalmological assessment and quality of life in the elderly]. *Arquivos Brasileiros de Oftalmologia*, *8*(3), 159–164. PMID:28832732

Damasceno, N. A., Ventura, M. P., & Damasceno, E. F. (2015). Doenças oculares em clínicas geriátricas no Rio de Janeiro: Considerações sociais e epidemiológicas em pacientes com déficit de locomoção motora [Eye diseases in geriatric clinics in Rio de Janeiro: social and epidemiological considerations in patients with motor locomotion deficit]. *Arquivos Brasileiros de Oftalmologia*, *78*(1), 40–43. doi:10.5935/0004-2749.20150011 PMID:25714537

Dharmarajan, T. S. (2021). Physiology of Aging. In C. S. Pitchumoni & T. S. Dharmarajan (Eds.), *Geriatric Gastroenterology* (pp. 101–153). Springer. doi:10.1007/978-3-030-30192-7_5

Duffy, B.E., & Hund, E. (2015). "Having it All" on Social Media: Entrepreneurial Femininity and Self-Branding Among Fashion Bloggers. *Social Media + Society, 1*(2), 1–11. dou:10.1177/2056305115604337

Ermida, J. G. (2014). Avaliação geriátrica global [Comprehensive geriatric assessment]. In M. T. Veríssimo (Ed.), *Geriatria Fundamental, Saber e Praticar* [Fundamental Geriatrics, Knowledge and Practice] (pp. 103–118). LIDEL, Edições Técnicas, Lda.

EU-OSHA, Cedefop, Eurofound, EIGE, Dubois, H., Jungblut, J-M., Wilkens, M., Vermeylen, G., & Vargas, O.L. (2017). *Towards age-friendly work in Europe: a life-course perspective on work and ageing from EU Agencies*. Retrieved from https://www.eurofound.europa.eu/publications/report/2017/towards-age-friendly-work-in-europe-a-life-course-perspective-on-work-and-ageing-from-eu-agencies

Gomes, A. M. (2011). O tempo do envelhecimento [The time of aging]. In J. Saraiva (Ed.), *Otorrinolaringologia e Envelhecimento* [Otorhinolaryngology and Aging] (pp. 1–13). LIDEL Edições Técnicas, Lda.

Hackenberger, B. K. (2020). R software: Unfriendly but probably the best. *Croatian Medical Journal, 61*(1), 66–68. doi:10.3325/cmj.2020.61.66 PMID:32118381

Hooper, C. R., & Bello-Haas, V. D. (2009). Sensory Function. In B. R. Bonder & V. D. Bello-Haas (Eds.), *Functional Performance in Older Adults* (pp. 101–129). F. A. Davis Company.

Kirkwood, T. B. L. (2005). Understanding the odd science of aging. *Cell, 120*(4), 437–447. doi:10.1016/j.cell.2005.01.027 PMID:15734677

Kurtz, S. M., Ong, K. L., Lau, E., & Bozic, K. J. (2014). Impact of the Economic Downturn on Total Joint Replacement Demand in the United States: Updated Projections to 2021. *The Journal of Bone & Joint Surgery, 96*(8), 624–630. doi:10.2106/JBJS.M.00285 PMID:24740658

Lalwani, A. K., & Snow, J. B. (2002). Distúrbios do olfato, da gustação e da audição [Disturbance of smell, taste and hearing]. In E. Braunwald, A. S. Fauci, D. L. Kasper, S. L. Hauser, D. L. Longo & J. L. Jameson (Eds.), Medicina Interna de Harrison [Harrison's Internal Medicine] (pp. 192-208). McGraw-Hill.

Lamas, M.C.R., & Paúl, C. (2013). O envelhecimento do sistema sensorial: implicações na funcionalidade e qualidade de vida [The ageing sensory system: implications on functionality and quality of life]. *Atas de Gerontologia - Congresso Português de Avaliacão Intervencão em Gerontologia Social, 1*, 1-11.

Lopes, A. A., Jayme, D. H. C., Abreu, I. L. V., Silva, I. E., Lobo, M. H. S., Oliveira, M. C., & Pinheiro, I. F. (2020). Avaliação das funções visuais e sua relação com a visão funcional e quedas em idosos ativos da comunidade [Assessment of visual functions and its relation to functional vision and falls in active community-dwelling elderly]. *Revista Brasileira de Oftalmologia, 79*(4), 236–241.

Lu, Z., Daneman, M., & Schneider, B. A. (2016). Does increasing the intelligibility of a competing sound source interfere more with speech comprehension in older adults than it does in younger adults? *Attention, Perception & Psychophysics, 78*(8), 2655–2677. doi:10.375813414-016-1193-5 PMID:27566326

Oliveira, C. R., & Pinto, A. M. (2014). Biologia e fisiopatologia do envelhecimento [Biology and pathophysiology of Ageing]. In M. T. Veríssimo (Ed.), *Geriatria Fundamental, Saber e Praticar* [Fundamental Geriatrics, Knowledge and Practice] (pp. 17–28). LIDEL, Edições Técnicas, Lda.

Paiva, A., & Paiva, S. (2014). Patologia otorrinolaringológica e envelhecimento [Otorhinolaryngological pathology and ageing]. In M. T. Veríssimo (Ed.), *Geriatria Fundamental, Saber e Praticar* [Fundamental Geriatrics, Knowledge and Practice] (pp. 245–253). LIDEL, Edições Técnicas, Lda.

Pedersen, K. M., Andersen, J. S., & Søndergaard, J. (2012). General practice and primary health care in Denmark. *Journal of the American Board of Family Medicine, 25*(Suppl 1), S34–S38. doi:10.3122/jabfm.2012.02.110216 PMID:22403249

Powell, T., & Bonito, O. (2015). *Attitudes of the over 50s to fuller working lives.* Retrieved from https://www.gov.uk/government/publications/attitudes-of-the-over-50s-to-fuller-working-lives

Santos, M., & Almeida, A. (2017). Saúde ocupacional aplicada a trabalhadores menos jovens [Occupational health applied to younger workers]. *Revista Portuguesa de Saúde Ocupacional, 3*, 39–52. doi:10.31252/RPSO.15.03.2017

Saraiva, J. (2011). Olfacto e envelhecimento [Smell and ageing]. In J. Saraiva (Ed.), *Otorrinolaringologia e Envelhecimento* [Otorhinolaryngology and Aging] (pp. 101–107). LIDEL Edições Técnicas, Lda.

Schlicht, N. (2008). Body and memory – Physical diseases and cognitive disorders. *Zeitschrift für Gerontologie und Geriatrie, 41*(3), 156–161. doi:10.100700391-008-0541-z PMID:18446304

Schor, E. L., & American Academy of Pediatrics Task Force on the Family. (2003). Family pediatrics: Report of the Task Force on the Family. *Pediatrics, 111*(6 Pt 2), 1541–1571. PMID:12777595

Silva, B. C., & Moreira, A. C. (2022). Entrepreneurship and the gig economy: A bibliometric analysis. *Management Letters. Cuadernos de Gestión*, *22*(2), 23–22. doi:10.5295/cdg.211580am

Tekles, A., & Bornmann, L. (2020). Author name disambiguation of bibliometric data: A comparison of several unsupervised approaches. *Quantitative Science Studies*, *1*(4), 1510–1528. doi:10.1162/qss_a_00081

Weyman, A., Meadows, P., & Buckingham, A. (2013). *Extending Working Life: Audit of research relating to impacts on NHS employees*. NHS Confederation.

Whillans, J., Nazroo, J., & Matthews, K. (2016). Trajectories of vision in older people: The role of age and social position. *European Journal of Ageing*, *13*(2), 171–184. doi:10.100710433-015-0360-1 PMID:27358606

Yeomans, L. (2011). *An update of the literature on age and employment*. HSE Books Health and Safety Executive.

KEY TERMS AND DEFINITIONS

Aging: A continuous, gradual, irreversible process of molecular, cellular, and functional changes that begins in adulthood.

Hearing: Sensory sense is related to hearing and processing sounds of different spectrums.

Sensory Impairment: Gradual changes in structures and functioning of organs that constitute the sensory system, compromising the performance of daily life activities and social participation.

Sensory System: It is a set of organs endowed with specialized cells with the capacity to capture internal and external stimuli. It comprises sight, hearing, smell, taste, and touch.

Smell: Sensory sense is related to the ability to sense and distinguish odors through the olfactory system.

Taste: Sensory sense consisting of chemical sensations perceived by the taste buds. It allows the recognition of tastes.

Touch: Sensory sense allows the individual to feel the world around him, perceiving and distinguishing temperatures, textures, and sensations (pain).

Vision: Sensory sense that allows, through the eyes, visualizing the external world.

Workforce: Physical, mental, and psychological capacity to perform organizational activities according to a specific function.

Chapter 3
Aging in Portugal:
The Social Development Point of View

Maria Inês Sousa
ISCTE, University Institute of Lisbon, Portugal

ABSTRACT

The chapter explores demographic aging data in Europe and the world, but more precisely in Portugal. A gradual increase in seniors and a reduction in youth characterize demographic evolution. In the chapter, the factors leading to these phenomena will be identified and duly explained, as well as the responses developed for their effect. One of the objectives is to identify solutions and answers for healthy and stimulated aging at institutions and professional areas, such as sociocultural animation. Despite several designations worldwide, its purpose is the same: to provide moments of leisure, stimulation, and learning to the entire population. In this sense, lifelong learning is a concept to be explored.

INTRODUCTION

This chapter aims to understand the concepts related to aging on a statistical, demographic, social, and individual level. It is essential to provide knowledge about the Portuguese population and the world and how it has been aging quickly.

One of the objectives is to reflect on the existing responses for this population and whether they are adequate. Another one is to perceive the transformations that have emerged over time due to this population and to reflect on the transformations that will take place in the future. It will also discuss the term mental health and how important it is for the well-being and quality of life of the elderly.

DOI: 10.4018/978-1-6684-6351-2.ch003

In addition, the term lifelong learning will be explored; what it is, what sense it makes, and what are the benefits and what is its connection to the elderly population, as much in their cognitive development as in their personal and social development.

BACKGROUND

Demographic Aging

Population aging is currently a topic of great concern and attention in European countries, as they are increasingly faced with many people at advanced ages. In the early '70s, changes began to emerge in looking at old age and the concern about caring for these populations.

The first transformations appeared at the level of social protection, namely the generalization of retirement, followed by the restructuring of social responses for the elderly, highlighting in this area the transformation of asylums into homes, as well as the emergence of new responses to support the elderly population, namely day centers, social centers, and home support services. (Fernandes, 1997; Veloso, 2008 as cited in Marinho, 2013, p. 14)

After the second half of the 20th century, European communities were faced with double aging of the age pyramid, an increase in the number of people over 65 years and a decrease in the number of people under 15 years (Ferreira et al., 2017). However, several advances in medicine, pharmacological discoveries, and technology make it possible to diagnose and/or prevent diseases, increasing the average life expectancy and reducing the mortality rate.

The United Nations (2019) asserts that:

Population ageing is poised to become one of the most significant social transformations of the twenty-first century, with implications for nearly all sectors of society, including labour and financial markets, the demand for goods and services, such as housing, transportation and social protection, as well as family structures and intergenerational ties" because "the number of older people aged 60 and over is estimated to double by the year 2050 and more than triple by 2100, from about 962 million in 2017 to 2.1 billion by 2050 and 3.1 billion by 2100. (United Nations, 2022)

However, developing and developed countries have differences in the aging process. For example, the quality and expectancy of life, economic vulnerability, educational opportunities, differences in mortality rates, birth rates, and aging, among others.

> *For example, in 2012, 6% of Africa's population was 60 years or older, compared to 10% in Latin America and the Caribbean, 11% in Asia, 15% in Oceania, 19% in North America, and 22% in Europe. By 2050, an estimated 10% of Africa's population will be 60 or older, compared to 24% in Asia, 24% in Oceania, 25% in Latin America and the Caribbean, 27% in North America, and 34% in Europe. (United Nations Population Fund, 2012, p. 4)*

In Portugal, as seen in Figure 1, from 1970 to 2014, the aging index has been rising, notably reaching 141 and still going. The same happens for the level of old-age dependency, which has been rising slowly, with an increase of only 15 between 16 and 31 recorded in 2014.

Figure 1. Aging index, old-age dependency index and working-age population renewal index, Portugal, 1970-2014
Source: Adapted from Statistics Portugal, 2015

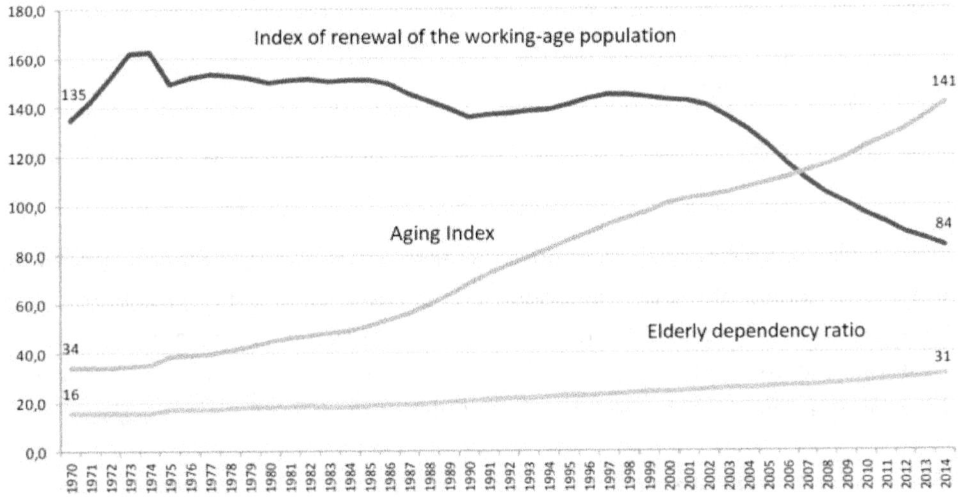

In recent years, as a result of the decrease in birth rates and the increase in longevity in Portugal, the decrease in the young population and the working-age population (0 to 64 years old) has intensified, simultaneously with an increase in the elderly population (65 and over). Figure 2 shows a considerable change in the pyramid, essentially in the ages 0-20 years old and 70-90 years old, which some authors refer to as the double aging of the age pyramid, precisely because of the decrease at the bottom of the pyramid and the increase at the top.

Figure 2. Age Pyramid, Portugal, 1991-2001
Source: Adapted from Statistics Portugal, 2002

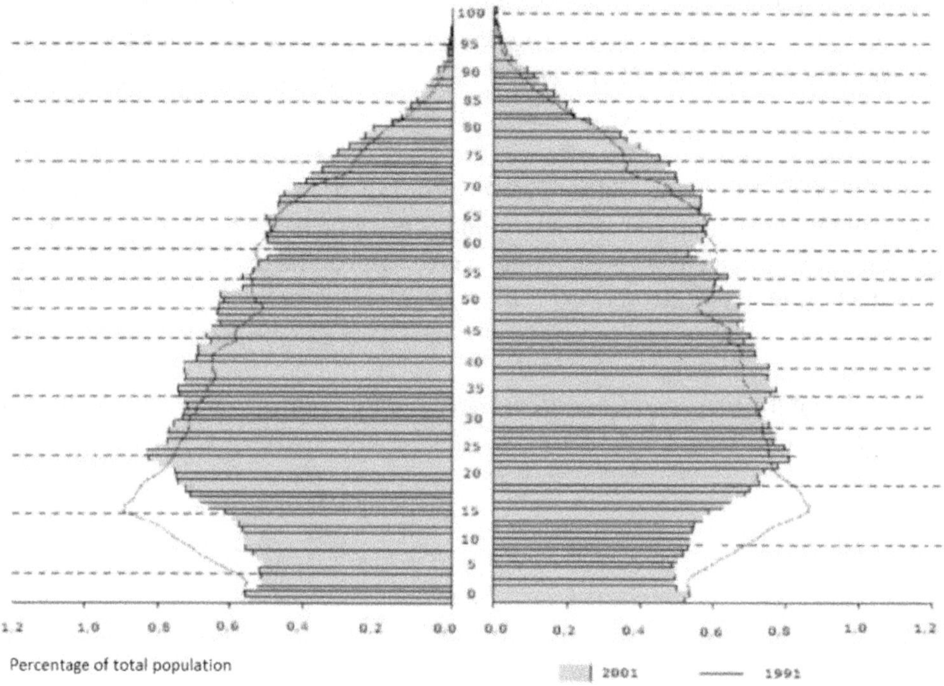

Portugal, in 2014 became the fourth country in the European Union-28 with the highest percentage of the elderly population at about 20%, although the European average is 18.5%. That said, Portugal presents changes in demographic aging to the extent that the population's age distribution reflects a more significant proportion of the aging population than the young population.

"This dynamic is a consequence of declining birth rate and increasing longevity and is understood internationally as one of the most important demographic trends of the 21st century" (Statistics Portugal, 2015, p. 2).

In 2021, 23.4% of the Portuguese national population was elderly. The aging index of the Portuguese population in 1961 was 27.5%, while in 2021 had risen to 182.7% (PORDATA, 2022). Another phenomenon relative to the elderly population in Portugal is the predominance of women, with women living longer than men.

"In 2013, worldwide, there were 85 men for every 100 women in the age group 60 and older, and 61 men for every 100 women in the age group 80 and older" (Statistics Portugal, 2015, p. 2).

Active Aging

The World Health Organization (2005, p. 13) defines active aging as:

"the process of optimizing opportunities for health, participation and security in order to enhance quality of life as people age"

According to the organization, active aging aims to provide good quality of life for the entire elderly population, without any exception, through optimizing opportunities for health, participation, and security. Meanwhile, this process depends on several factors: personal, behavioral, physical environment, social, economic, and health services.

However, two factors cut across all others: culture and gender.

"Cultural values and traditions greatly determine how a society views older people and the aging process . . . cultural diversity and complexity within countries and between regions and countries of the world" (World Health Organization, 2005, p. 20), such as ethics, human rights, etc.

"Gender is a lens through which considers the appropriateness of various policy options and their effect on the well-being of men and women" (World Health Organization, 2005, p. 20).

On the other hand, the determinants related to health and social services should favor health promotion and disease prevention. Since this age group has a higher risk of developing diseases as they age, there must be impartial and quality access to primary care to prevent serious diseases. From another perspective, the behavioral determinants concern the adoption of healthy lifestyles, which is essential for any age group. This includes eating a balanced diet, practicing sports, and not smoking or drinking alcohol to prevent diseases and increase longevity.

Personal determinants are related to biological and genetic factors.

"Genes can be involved in the etiology of disease; however, the cause of many is environmental and external rather than genetic and internal" (World Health Organization, 2005, p. 26).

Besides, psychological factors such as intelligence and cognitive ability influence how a person ages.

The determinants related to the physical environment refer to the dependence of individuals. In this sense, numerous physical barriers hinder the mobility of the elderly. For example, accessibility to transportation services; safe houses adapted to the person's health status; care with obstacles to avoid and prevent falls, among others. Regarding social determinants, social support, opportunities for education and lifelong learning, peace, and protection from violence and mistreatment are essential factors of the social environment that foster health, participation, and security as people age are essential to prevent vulnerability to crime and early death, such as loneliness, isolation, and illiteracy.

Ultimately, the economic determinants focus on three aspects: income, labor, and social protection (World Health Organization, 2005). It is of great importance that the community creates programs and actions that provide social protection, especially in situations where older people live alone as well as opportunities for decent work, and take into account the income of the elderly population to avoid situations of poverty.

All these determinants impose mutual responsibility, on the individual and the community, for the acquisition of physical, social, and mental well-being, as well as active participation in society through needs, desires, and capacity.

Individual Aging

According to the World Health Organization and in an attempt to standardize, it considers that any individual aged 65 or older is considered elderly, particularly in developing countries. However, the aging process, as a multidimensional process (biological, psychological, and social), presents itself from a differential point of view since it occurs differently from individual to individual. Depending on the individual's lifestyle, health care, and environment, among other external factors:

"the aging process does not start at the same period or develop at the same rate and does not reach the same degree of degeneration for all organ systems" (Cramês, 2012, p. 12).

Therefore, Fernandes (2016, p. 174) states that:

Aging is a natural and continuous process that, if seen under the biological cycle of life, configures the human being, in the same way as the other living beings, that is: they are born, grow, grow old and, finally, die. This process, dependent on the sociocultural context in which man is inserted, suffers internal and external influences that invariably present resonances in old age.

As far as individual aging is concerned, the researchers Ferreira et al. (2021) express that it is a gradual process of biopsychosocial change as chronological age advances, a natural aging process, usually followed by the appearance of diseases/dementias, depending on the individual. However, individual aging is conditioned by biological, social, economic, and cultural factors, and this population's heterogeneity means that opportunities for access to resources are different. All this creates social inequalities at multiple levels, including health, social mobility, income, access to goods and services, and many others. Recently, with the Covid-19 pandemic, we have faced some structural weaknesses and other problems to be solved. For example, confinement has promoted isolation situations and, consequently, the risk of social exclusion—access to essential goods for health and survival and mobility such as transport. Also, in health, there were setbacks with the delay or cancellation of consultations and exams.

For this, it is essential to take into account changes that we want to opt for shortly, such as:

- Greater consciousness and appreciation of the elderly population and their caregivers;
- Greater social inclusion of this population and new ways of living;
- Restructuring of infrastructures: foreseeing support for adapting houses and buildings to respond to the motor limitations resulting from the biological aging process.
- Adoption of new habits of life, such as the use of the Internet;
- Adherence to new techniques, such as telemedicine - contributes to a more efficient response from health services and the optimization of resources.

According to the identity of these populations, each elder has his/her own identity, so each individual must be respected. Working with the elderly, as with any other public, means being aware of their weaknesses and abilities and adjusting activities so everyone can enjoy them, but in different ways. We must consider the physical and psychological conditions (diseases and/or dementias) that sometimes make it difficult for them to move, understand, and/or communicate with others. However, old age is not homogeneous; the fragilities are not the same for everyone, so it is necessary to perform a previous evaluation of each person's needs.

In the 21st century, aging has been getting increasing visibility, with a significant advance in population aging, in the world, as in Portugal. Portugal is one of the countries where the aging rate has grown exponentially. It is necessary to reorganize services and cares for the elders and review and apply more dignified living conditions.

Fernandes (2016, p. 175) states:

that by having active older people, preserving their minds and caring for their health, it is possible to ensure a better quality of life to older people in their residence, given that, by maintaining their autonomy, they can be an important resource to their own families, delaying their institutionalization. Such purposes should not, therefore, remain invisible to the eyes of the elderly themselves, their families, and the managers and professionals in the field of care practices at home or in institutional homes.

Mental Health

"Health is a state of complete physical, mental and social well-being and not merely the absence of disease or infirmity" (World Health Organization, 2021a, p. 2).

In this way, mental health is the state in which an individual recognizes that his or her abilities are sufficient to cope with daily difficulties and to be an active member of his/her community. Governments must implement strategies to promote individuals' mental health and prevention. Access to health care for individuals with mental disorders is essential to maximize their quality of life.

The concept of mental health originated in psychiatry, where individuals were either mentally ill or mentally healthy. However, over the years, this thought has fallen into disuse. Nowadays, mental health is defined as a psychological and social balance that results from the person's interaction with the environment and allows him to develop all his human potentialities.

Aging is a stage of the life cycle that is essential for everyone. Promoting behaviors favorable to health is crucial so they can be fully lived (Oliveira et al., 2018; World Health Organization, 2021b). This phenomenon brings about multiple changes, the physical ones being the most evident, psychological, socioeconomic changes, and more. Among the physical changes, neurological changes or changes associated with the neurological system have an actual weight within the family and society.

In Nursing, the Mini-Mental State Examination (MMSE) is used to evaluate the individual's cognitive function. This neurological test assesses cognitive functions, orientation, retention, attention and calculation, evocation, language, and constructive ability. The MMSE is a system used internationally but is validated for the Portuguese population at the following cut-off points: 22 points for literacy aged 0 to 2 years, 24 points for literacy aged 3 to 6 years, and 27 points for literacy aged 7 years or more (General Direction of Health, 2011).

In a study developed by Dias et al. (2022) in a Day Care Center, it was found that the population under study had an average age of 80.92 years, which shows the aging of the population in Portugal. So, Day Centers have been a way to avoid nursing homes, and it shows by the numbers of the population attending Day Centers, which are supposed to have more independent and autonomous people.

Dementia and Pathologies

Growing old is a universal process that presents a gradual and irreversible decline in morphological capacities. However, many organs' progressive loss of function and some physical and/or psychological changes are reversed in several diseases over time. The most common diseases of the older generation are Alzheimer, Dementia, Diabetes, Parkinson, and Osteoporosis, among others.

In 2011, a study involving about 300 Residential Structures for the Elderly in Continental Portugal concluded that about 30% of residents were diagnosed with dementia. After 12 years, the perspective of decline is high, and the Alzheimer Portugal Association predicts that in 2050 there will be around 14.3 million Europeans with dementia, double the current numbers (7.8 million) (Alzheimer Portugal, n.d.).

Dementia is a chronic mental health disease diagnosed by modifying the higher nerve functions, including memory, orientation, comprehension, language, and thinking.

The term dementia refers to a series of symptoms usually seen in people with brain disease resulting from damage or loss of brain cells. The loss of brain cells is a natural process, but in the diseases that lead to dementia, this happens quickly and causes the person's brain to stop functioning in the usual way. (Alzheimer Portugal, n.d.)

Anyone can develop dementia. However, it is more common to happen after age 65. Usually, for people over the age of 85, 1 in 4 have dementia. This can also affect people between 40 and 60 (Alzheimer Portugal, n.d.). According to Kitwood (1997), the psychosocial needs of people with dementia are divided into five parts that act cooperatively without hierarchy to promote well-being in the daily lives of these people. The "Kitwood Flower" contains five petals, and they all start from the same base: love; generosity; acceptance; forgiveness; among others.

- **Comfort:** tenderness; feeling of safety; decreasing anxiety; helps dealing with feelings of loss and/or frustration;
- **Bonding:** creating close relationships, as people with dementia often feel that they are in a strange environment, surrounded by unknown people;

- **Inclusion:** valuing people's social role and allowing them to participate in society, for example, being part of a group;
- **Occupation:** allows to improve skills and feel useful, controlling feelings of apathy, social exclusion, and frustration;
- **Identity:** knowing your life story and having a sense of continuity with the past.

The need for social support in old age may increase due to changes in health, cognitive and emotional status, and, in this sense, quality of life can be combined through an individual's functional health, feelings of competence, autonomy in performing Activities of Daily Living (ADLs) and satisfaction with their social circumstances. Social support (activities, visits from family or caregivers, home visits, etc.) can mediate the effects of certain life circumstances, such as retirement, widowhood, and illness.

The age-related prevalence of neurodegenerative pathologies is higher at this age. The pathologies most affecting the nervous system are Alzheimer's disease, Parkinson's disease, and strokes (Barreto, 2020). Alzheimer's disease is a pathology that remains incurable, and it is the most common dementia that causes disability, dependence, or even death. The clinical manifestation is based on memory loss and cognitive decline. Parkinson's disease is the second most common neurodegenerative disease associated with aging. On the other hand, the diagnosis of this disease results essentially from asymmetric rest tremors. Finally, strokes in the elderly are more prevalent than in other age groups; however, they can occur in other age groups:

"about 25% of strokes occur in young people" (CUF, 2020).

These can be of two types: ischemic (by the absence of oxygen and nutrients following a blockage of blood flow) or hemorrhagic (they are flooded by blood from a ruptured artery). Several risk factors are associated with this pathology: uncontrollable diseases, such as hypertension, dyslipidemia, diabetes mellitus, and sedentarism (Barreto, 2020).

Other physical changes are quite evident in the elderly, such as in the musculoskeletal system. The imbalance, the decrease in muscle strength, and the decrease in joint range of motion may lead to falls, which are common in the elderly. In a study developed in Portugal, falls were identified as the most common domestic accident in the number of visits to the Emergency Department for Home and Leisure Accidents (Oliveira et al., 2018; Alves et al., 2021).

Considering the previously mentioned psychological changes, the most common in the aging phenomenon are social isolation, loneliness, and depression (Branson et al., 2017; Oliveira et al., 2018). Social isolation can increase the risk of the elderly developing dementia:

"due to intellectual inactivity leading to lower cognitive reserve, increased risk of depression, and precipitating vascular risk factors" (Barreto, 2020, p. 14).

This phenomenon intensified with the Covid-19 pandemic, as worldwide accepted measures for the mitigation of this Sars-Cov-2 included the confinement at the home of individuals whose work was not considered essential. As a result, the elderly population was isolated, without physical contact, as families were suggested to avoid contact with the most vulnerable groups, in which the elderly were included.

According to data from the World Health Organization (2022), the pandemic has increased pathologies such as depression and anxiety to more than 25%. This organization identified psychiatric conditions in the world mental health report. The comprehensive mental health action plan 2013-2030 was defined among the 194 member states of the World Health Organization, with the commitment to transform these mental health issues by 2030, specifically in promotion, prevention, care, and rehabilitation.

The nurse should ensure that the elderly population has an excellent active aging process. Active aging is defined as a:

"process of optimizing opportunities for health, participation, and security to improve quality of life as people age" (General Direction of Health, 2011).

For this effect, it is crucial to implement autonomous and/or interdependent interventions to promote active aging, including socio-cognitive activities, healthy eating, and physical exercise (Barreto, 2020).

A meta-analysis of 19 studies shows that the participation of individuals in cognitively stimulating activities may reduce the risk of cognitive deficit and developing dementia (Yates et al., 2016). This way, activities such as reading newspapers or books, playing music, or dancing and playing may be activities to consider with the elderly to reduce the risks mentioned above (Barreto, 2020).

Regarding diet, the Mediterranean diet has been identified as reducing the risk of neurodegenerative diseases connected with exercise, which has been reported to benefit in reducing the incidence of dementia as well as reducing the incidence of Alzheimer's (Liu-Ambrose et al., 2019).

Exercise also contributes to increased muscle strength as well as balance, preventing falls from occurring. Doing moments of physical activity enhances the autonomy of the elderly in performing activities of daily living. However, physical activity also promotes psychological health. For this reason, other social areas such as art therapy, volunteering, and occupational therapy are addressed in the topic of psychological development. Each individual's perception of health differs, and the need for self-care differs in each person's personal opinion and the need to resort to health services (Forner & Alves, 2019).

Social Responses for the Elderly

In Portugal, until the late 15th century, when the "Misericórdias" was founded, the needs of the population in need of assistance were met by the community's kindness and religious orders. "Misericórdias" are institutions that support and help sick and poor people. While some initiatives were local, associated with military orders, religious orders, brotherhoods of masters, and wealthy merchants, others were born out of charity. Beyond the "Misericórdias," "Casa Pia" of Lisbon (Portugal) was founded in the late 18th century, the first sign of the establishment of public assistance. The creation of this institution was one of the first steps to put into practice a reordering in the political way of taking on social problems.

After the implantation of the Republic, and with the arrival of the New State in 1935, a profound reform of assistance began, giving privileged status to the forms of social protection based on assistance institutions since, in the political context of the time, they shared the same religious ideology with the Clergy. The Constitution of the Republic of 1976 was a significant point of reference in the field of social protection and a reference point for both public interventions and private initiatives. As such, the creation of the Private Institutions of Social Solidarity:

"all . . . that pursue, without profit, Social Security objectives, a recognition that implies that the action of the institutions is not 'prejudiced' as long as it is framed by legal regulation and subject to the supervision of the State" (Hespanha, 2000, p.132, as cited in Pereira, 2015).

Population aging has influenced the structure of family relationships. A few decades ago, the family cared for the elderly. Nowadays, the family's limited time and capacity to occupy the time of the elderly who became dependent and/or chronically ill had to transfer the responsibility to institutions dedicated to elderly care, such as daycare centers, social centers, nursing homes, home care services, and others. Such responsibility depends on the user's needs, according to the process of institutionalization. Institutionalization means that the elderly stay in a facility for part of their time, but not necessarily for 24 hours, in which case they are referred to as institutionalized elderly residents (Jacob, 2002).

"According to INE (2001), the number of institutionalized elderly has been increasing, about 33% of patients connected to Social Security are elderly, and 12% are in nursing homes" (Belga, 2019, p. 35).

Social Security is a system that intends to ensure citizens' fundamental rights and equal opportunities:

"as well as to promote well-being and social cohesion for all Portuguese or foreign citizens who work or live in the territory" (Social Security Institute, 2021).

The principles are universality; equality, solidarity, social equity; positive differentiation; social insertion; participation; effectiveness, and many others.

The process of institutionalization has been manifesting itself as a reality that is felt by the elderly, in the sense that they no longer find within the family and the community to which they belong, a satisfactory response to their existential need. (Lourenço, 2014, p. 24)

Institutionalization requires a set of changes and adjustments in their routines, either in the space, or the integration into the environment, sharing with unknown people, as well as adapting to their new lifestyle, routines, and rules of the facilities. This way, new figures of representation emerge, such as health care providers, and caregivers, among others.

So, according to Amaro (2013), good institutionalization happens when there is stimulation and promotion of the capabilities of the elderly, an encouragement to practice physical activity, and proper cognitive stimulation that can increase the quality of life in the elderly. According to the Portuguese Social Security, there are seven types of social services:

1. Domiciliary support service.
2. Social center.
3. Day center.
4. Night center.
5. Family shelter.
6. Residential structures.
7. Holiday and leisure center.

The Domiciliary Support Service emerged in the mid-1980s, but there was a significant increase from the mid-1990s onwards. This social response consists of a proximity response, aiming to provide well-being and individual development of the elderly, especially to their autonomy and functionality. This approach happens through an individualized and personalized intervention at the patient's home, avoiding rupturing the family and/or social environment. The Domiciliary Support Service confers respect for the dignity of the elderly, pretends to combat situations of isolation and loneliness, and satisfaction of basic needs and/or activities of daily living that patients cannot perform due to illness/disability/etc.

It represents one of the alternatives available and much searched for by the elderly, in the sense of anticipating their institutionalization and not having to give up their homes and belongings due to age limitations since this service can satisfy their needs at home.

On one hand, it has a preventive character, in which the intervention focuses on preventing accidents and situations that generate dependency, creating healthy hygiene and eating habits. On the other hand, it also has a rehabilitative character since the intervention made by the specialists intends to recover or maintain functional capacities through the training of daily life activities. (Marinho, 2013, p. 68)

The Night Centers refers to a social response of night hosting:

"directed to elderly people with autonomy who during the day remain at home and by experiencing situations of loneliness, isolation, and insecurity, looked for guidance during the night" (Social Security Institute, n.d.). "The main objectives of the night center are to provide shelter and security during the night for people who still have some autonomy and promote the user's participation in his or her usual environment" (Rocha, 2018, p. 10).

Family fostering consists of temporarily or permanently integrating older adults into families that can provide them with a stable and safe environment. In this way, we welcome people in a situation of dependency and guarantee them a social and family environment. This service still has little impact in some countries because it is not so common, and it is not easy to find families willing to welcome older adults in their homes.

The Residential Structures are collective accommodations of temporary or permanent use for the elderly or people in a situation of loss of independence and/or autonomy. Also, those who live alone without a rearguard may resort to this response. Its objective is to provide permanent and adequate services to the biopsychosocial problems of the elderly by stimulating an active aging process.

Nursing Homes are an example of communal facilities for permanent or temporary accommodation, intended for patients at risk of loss of independence or autonomy.

Older adults' homes materialize an institutional model that appeared in Europe in the 16th century, designed to accommodate the mentally ill and the marginalized elders.

The Holiday and Leisure Centers or sometimes called Caregiver's Rest corresponds to a response intended:

"to all age groups of population and the family in globally to meet the leisure needs and break the routine, essential to the physical, psychological and social balance of its users" (Social Security Institute, n.d.).

Relatively to the Social Centers, these are social responses to support social, recreative, and cultural activities, organized and dynamized with the active participation of the elderly residing in a community (Social Security Institute, n.d.). The social centers have several objectives: preventing loneliness and isolation; encouraging the participation and inclusion of the elderly in local social life; promoting interpersonal and intergenerational relations; and contributing to delay or avoidance of as much as possible institutionalization.

As for Day Care Centers:

"they are (...) an open facility, halfway between home and hospitalization, and at the same time, a place of treatment and prevention (Jacob et al., 2013, p. 13)."

As a social responsibility, as an alternative to permanent institutionalization, it is designed to satisfy the basic needs of older people during the day, providing services that contribute to their permanence in their social and family environment.

For the admission of the patients, the following criteria were considered a priority:

The absence or unavailability of the family to ensure basic care, the elderly living alone or presenting socioeconomic needs, and the elderly in a situation of danger or negligence . . . situations that constitute a risk of speeding up or degrading the aging process. (Pereira, 2015, p. 22)

The Day Center works during the day, Monday to Friday:

(...) and provides a set of services ranging from the satisfaction of basic needs to psychosocial support, sociocultural animation, and other activities that intend to promote interpersonal relationships with other age groups, in order to counter isolation. (Pereira, 2015, p. 22)

This establishment provides interpersonal relationships in order to avoid isolation and loneliness of the elderly, promoting occupational activities, and also includes meal service; medication control; hygiene care; adapted transportation; and others.

There are also nursing homes (formerly known as asylums), a social responsibility for individuals with a high degree of dependence and without any family support or in which families cannot ensure their relatives' basic essential needs. They are collective equipment of temporary or permanent character, but most permanent, and are destined to offer answers to older adults at risk, with reduced or no independence and autonomy. The users search for this social response when they do not have conditions to be inserted in the others.

Lifelong Learning

Learning has no age and from this emerged the concept of lifelong learning. Education covers any age group or social category and is transversal to the several stages of life. According to Rocha (2018):

"Education is a right that belongs to everyone, and human beings, regardless of their age and circumstances, are in an educational process throughout the entire life cycle" (p. 18).

In the 1970s, the transformations to post-industrial societies emerged in which essential and transformative elements such as knowledge and information appeared. Years later, we are faced with a digital revolution in which technology changes the skills needed in the labor market and the way people work. So, in today's societies, there is an increasing complexity of tasks in the labor market and demands (Enguita, 2001).

Learning is:

"a process of human formation, creative and acquisition of knowledge and certain skills that are not limited to the training of procedures contained in instructional standards" (Enguita, 2001, p. 39), and that depends on the spaces, relationships, the educational field, values, and others."

Elderly education is more than a simple occupation of leisure time. Education in the elderly population provides moments of learning new knowledge and creating bonds of friendship that provide healthier, more active, and participatory aging.

Learning takes place in formal, non-formal, and informal education. Formal learning includes education or training provided in educational institutions, in which certification and evaluation are fundamental. A system of hierarchical succession in which successful completion of one level allows progression to higher levels. Non-formal learning occurs in training contexts, for example, professional or non-school contexts. This one does not have a system of hierarchical succession. Informal learning refers to the less structured and more diffuse processes in daily work, family, social life, or leisure activities. It is considered intentional learning.

As can be seen in Figure 3, non-formal education has earned visibility and credibility in Europe over the years, particularly in Austria, the Netherlands, the United Kingdom, and Portugal. Hungary stands out with the most significant increase, about 46 points between 2007 and 2016.

Figure 3. Participation in non-formal learning activities, countrywide, 2007, 2011, and 2016 (%)
Source: Adapted from Statistics Portugal, 2009

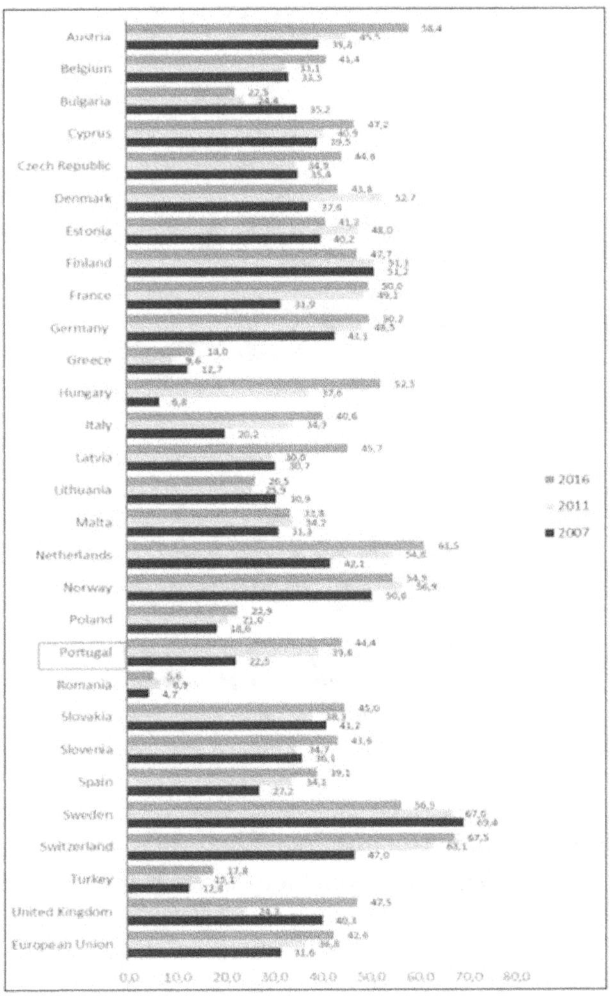

Regarding formal education (Figure 4), we see the importance and power it had about two decades ago; however, with a tendency to decrease, but still very present in Europeans' lives.

Figure 4. Participation in formal learning activities, countrywide, 2007, 2011, and 2016 (%)
Source: Adapted from Statistics Portugal, 2009

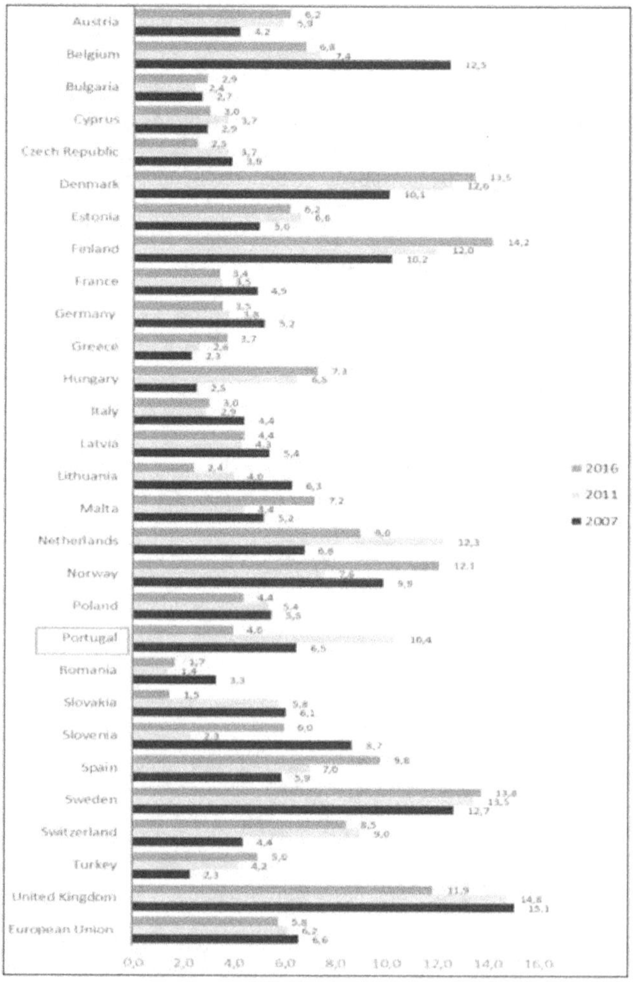

In a critique of education in the traditional, individualistic, homogeneous, authoritarian school that leaves no room for different learning rhythms, non-formal education emerges:

A set of socio-cultural practices of learning and knowledge production, which involves organizations/institutions, activities, varied means and forms, as well as a multiplicity of social programs and projects. (Gohn, 2014, p. 40)

After formal schooling, individuals are increasingly placed in situations that require new learning. However, daily life contexts require new learning, whether at work, in personal life, or in information. In this sense, non-formal and informal education includes knowledge and know-how that we acquire with intention or not. Simple things like going to a theater, a museum, and religious events are included in non-formal and informal education.

While in school, we have mandatory disciplinary knowledge that is the same for everyone, a curriculum that we have to achieve through knowledge that is neither questioned nor discussed; in non-formal education, there is more openness to questioning, practicing, and searching for other knowledge. Non-formal education has been performed in different contexts: socialization and leisure; culture; volunteering and solidarity; participation and citizenship; social movements; and sports. Having said this, the educational proposals start from:

- Mutual Help, Cooperation, and Personal Relations.
- Integrated Development of Skills.
- Self-Valorization and Quality of Life.
- Experiential Learning.
- Conflict Resolution.
- Inclusion, Integration, and Participation.
- Learner-Centered.

The first step is to define the learning and changes you want to promote for your participants by defining the action and its objectives. Next, the organization of the action with content, methodological approach, intervention modalities, and the definition of the resources you need (human, material, and financial). Finally, the evaluation in which you have to define what you want to evaluate, such as the relevance of the action, the learning achieved, and the changes generated, among others.

As a facilitator of collective learning dynamics, you will need to pay attention to the individual learning process of each participant in an open, non-judgmental register, challenging and encouraging the individual to explore new perspectives. On the other hand, you will stimulate group dynamics by promoting interactions based on equality, respect, trust, and cooperation, ensuring the participation and inclusion of all participants. In this sense, sociocultural animation is integrated into non-formal education for its essence of transformative learning. It is an area that works with many publics, including the elderly.

Sociocultural Animation

There is no certainty about the emergence of sociocultural animation. However, in Portugal, it began to have an impact after the Revolution of April 25 (1974), going through several phases. The first was the Revolutionary phase (1974 to 1976), in which sociocultural animation was seen, by the successive provisional governments and the Armed Forces movement, as a cultural development strategy with an intervening action in society based on motivation, captivation, and work. This was followed by the Constitutionalist phase (1977 to 1980), in which the State defined the guiding principles for training sociocultural animators. Then came the Heritage phase (1981 to 1985), in which the exercise of sociocultural animation was directed, essentially, to the preservation and recovery of cultural patrimony and, finally, the Globalization phase, from 1996 to the present, in which the animation works sociocultural dynamics at the level of plastic expression, musical expression, theatrical expression, physical and sportive activity, cognitive stimulation, sensorial stimulation, as well as in the realities of daily life such as cooking, hygiene, and beauty care, religion, etc., always corresponding to the needs of the population in focus (Lopes, 2006).

Over time the need for education/training and, consequently, a greater availability in the day has been noticeable.

Sociocultural animation . . . emerges historically related to several factors: the increase in free time; . . . the need for education and permanent training in a society based on the domain of knowledge and technical innovation; and the increase in the cultural divide between social classes regarding the difference in access to cultural goods. (Vilardouro, 2013)

Animation emerges to respond to problems such as rural exodus, social integration, the need to promote programs of valorization and promotion of human relations, the deficit of participation, and the lack of people's autonomy. So, it appears related to increased free time and the need for participation, education, coexistence, justice, social living, well-being, social insertion, awareness, democratization, quality of life, and transformation (Galinha, 2010).

Batista (2014, p. 41) adds that:

Sociocultural Animation is an imprecise, ambiguous activity. . . . Imprecise because it is difficult to define its boundaries. Ambiguous because of the multiple meanings attributed to the concept and that result, on the one hand, from different ideological positions and, on the other hand, from the great diversity of areas, contexts, and audiences to whom the activity is directed, as well as the great variety of instruments that it uses and activities that it develops.

Specifically, in the third idea, according to Lopes (2006), the animation is based on the principles of educational gerontology, which provides relaxed and positive moments to support individuals in dealing with their aging more naturally and finding new interests. It should also expose the importance of the role of the elderly in society in order to continue their activity in the community. In this sense, it provides new learning experiences and reinforces the existing ones; promotes group interaction and participation; promotes participation in the organization and institutional planning; involves institutionalized older people in community activities; minimizes social and cultural inequalities; and provides an environment for the exchange of experiences and personal and group experiences (Martins, 2013).

In this sense, the animator, a graduate technician, and a professional able to use various appropriate tools in order to stimulate their target must assume the critical role in transforming the free time of the elderly; preventing situations of dependence by promoting autonomy; fostering personal and intergenerational relationships; and combat demotivation (sadness, loneliness), among others (Ander-Egg, 1991). Therefore, there is a connection between professional areas and their respective elements, such as Social Work, Direct Action Auxiliary, Human Resources, Technicians, Gerontologists, and Psychologists (Giddens, 2001).

For Batista (2014), the social participation of senior citizens can be increased in various work contexts and areas where the adults in question developed their professional activity or in new contexts and areas expressing other desires impossible to implement during the so-called period of active life.

The sociocultural animator can use diversified tools to stimulate their recipients to enable them to participate and get involved in an active, autonomous, voluntary, creative, and responsible way. Is responsible for developing and implementing an intervention plan in a community, institution, or organization, using cultural, social, educational, sports, recreational, and leisure techniques (Portuguese Association for the Development of Sociocultural Animation, 2019).

The animator aims to provide the elderly with activities that improve participation, self-esteem, dynamism, and interpersonal relationships. The activities developed to cover an extensive range of actions and can be divided into seven parts, intersecting with each other, such as:

1. Physical and Motor Animation.
2. Cognitive and Mental Animation.

3. Animation through Plastic Expression.
4. Musical Animation.
5. Ludic Animation.
6. Sports Animation.
7. Among others.

CONCLUSION

Population aging is a very complex process that has been gaining visibility due to the evolution of technology and medicine in many European countries. This change has contributed significantly to the increase in life expectancy and, consequently, the reduction in the mortality rate. This being so, the development of more social responses was essential for a better quality of life for this population.

Growing old is an inevitable and progressive process, but with different characteristics due to their experiences, lifestyles, economic and environmental factors, etc. To this end, developing cognitive, physical, and social skills is fundamental so that this population does not become sedentary, isolated, or even forgotten. Areas such as occupational therapy, sociocultural animation, and gerontology are essential for this procedure.

Old age is a time of life accompanied by cognitive, physical, and social fragilities that may include the decay of all these levels or even just one. That is why the aging process differs from person to person; for example, the development of dementias and pathologies is another factor that differs from person to person.

To make this phase of life more dynamic, there are structural social responses such as day centers, home support services, and social centers so that this population can have the necessary support for their needs, whether it be in the provision of health services, moments of relaxation and interaction with other people, learning new skills, and more.

On the other hand, there are social responses at the level of professional areas such as sociocultural animation, gerontology, occupational therapy, etc. These areas allow dynamics of personal development to provide ludic and educational actions of new learning or to remember others that would already be forgotten. These are moments of relaxation connected to providing happiness, socialization, sharing, motivation, etc.

Animation, in its aspect of lifelong learning and non-formal education, provides techniques and skills for leisure and free time education, community development, social promotion, and others. The animator enhances the quality of life, dynamizes activities aimed at the population's entertainment, and stimulates and promotes learning.

In conclusion, since the population is aging, we must pay more attention to it by improving the public policies that involve them, the answers regarding health, mobility, etc., and their inclusion. In certain countries, such as Portugal, the population is getting older and older, and it seems they are the most excluded. There is a strong demand for work with children and young people, and with the older population, we notice this deficit. In this sense, we should pay more attention to the elderly and their comfort, identity, occupation, and inclusion.

REFERENCES

Alves, T., Rodrigues, E., Neto, M., Mexia, R., & Dias, C. M. (2021). Acidentes domésticos e de lazer ocorridos em pessoas com 65 e mais anos durante a pandemia da COVID-19: comparação entre 2019 e 2020 [Home and leisure accidents in people aged 65 and over during the COVID-19 pandemic: comparison between 2019 and 2020]. *Instituto Nacional de Saúde Doutor Ricardo Jorge, 10*(30), 62-66. http://hdl.handle.net/10400.18/7768

Alzheimer Portugal. (n.d.). *A Doença de Alzheimer* [Alzheimer's Disease]. Retrieved from https://alzheimerportugal.org/a-doenca-de-alzheimer-2/

Amaro, M. M. G. (2013). *A Transformação da identidade em idosos institucionalizados - Um estudo de casos múltiplos* [Identity Transformation in Institutionalized Elderly People - A Multiple Case Study] [Master's thesis, Escola Superior de Educação - Instituto Politécnico de Bragança]. Repository of Instituto Politécnico de Bragança. http://hdl.handle.net/10198/8384

Ander-Egg, E. (1991). *Introduccion à la Planificación* [Introduction to Planning]. Siglo XXI.

Barreto, T. M. C. (2020). *Fisiopatologia do envelhecimento cerebral e mecanismos anti-aging* [Pathophysiology of brain aging and anti-aging mechanisms] [Master's thesis, Universidade da Beira Interior]. Repository of Universidade da Beira Interior. http://hdl.handle.net/10400.6/10793

Batista, A. M. R. R. (2014). Animação Sociocultural: Imprecisões, ambiguidades, incertezas e controvérsias de uma ocupação professional [Sociocultural Animation: imprecisions, ambiguities, uncertainties and controversies of a professional occupation]. *Forum Sociológico, 25*(1), 23–31. doi:10.4000ociologico.898

Belga, R. I. V. (2019). *Bem-estar e qualidade de vida em idosos institucionalizados com demência - Contributos da animação sociocultural* [Well-being and quality of life in institutionalized elderly with dementia - Contributions of sociocultural animation] [Master's thesis, Escola Superior de Educação - Instituto Politécnico de Beja]. Repository of Instituto Politécnico de Beja. http://hdl.handle.net/20.500.12207/5272

Branson, S. M., Boss, L., Cron, S., & Turner, D. C. (2017). Depression, loneliness, and pet attachment in homebound older adult cat and dog owners. *Journal of Mind and Medical Sciences*, *4*(1), 38–48. doi:10.22543/7674.41.P3848

Cramês, L. (2012). *Envelhecimento activo no idoso institucionalizado* [Active aging in the institutionalized elderly] [Master's thesis, Escola Superior de Educação - Instituto Politécnico de Bragança]. Repository of Instituto Politécnico de Bragança. http://hdl.handle.net/10198/7645

CUF. (2020). *AVC - Acidente vascular cerebral* [Stroke - Cerebrovascular Accident]. Retrieved from https://www.cuf.pt/saude-a-z/avc-acidente-vascular-cerebral

Dias, S., Gonçalves, I., & Viegas, L. (2022). Risk Factors for Falls in the Elderly in a Day Care Center. *International Journal of Health Sciences (Qassim)*, *2*(62), 1–11.

Enguita, M. F. (2001). *Educar en Tiempos Inciertos* [Educating in Uncertain Times]. Editorial Morata.

Fernandes, M. H. (2016). A expressão plástica e a música erudita como recursos da animação sociocultural a idosos institucionalizados [Plastic expression and classical music as resources of sociocultural animation for institutionalized elderly people]. *Revista Kairós Gerontologia*, *19*(4), 173–203.

Ferreira, P. M., Azevedo, A. B., & Garha, N. S. (2021). Envelhecimento e COVID-19: impactos e consequências [Aging and COVID-19: impacts and consequences]. In A. Delicado & J. Ferrão (Eds.), *Portugal Social em Mudança - Impactos Sociais da Pandemia COVID-19* [Social Portugal in Change - Social Impacts of the Pandemic COVID-19] (pp. 37–47). Instituto de Ciências Sociais da Universidade de Lisboa.

Ferreira, P. M., Cabral, M. V., & Moreira, A. (2017). Introdução [Introduction]. In P. M. Ferreira, M. V. Cabral, & A. Moreira (Eds.), *Envelhecimento na Sociedade Portuguesa. Pensões, Família e Cuidados* [Aging in Portuguese Society. Pensions, Family and Care] (pp. 19–26). Imprensa de Ciências Sociais.

Forner, F. C., & Alves, C. F. (2019). Uma revisão de literatura sobre os fatores que contribuem para o envelhecimento ativo na atualidade [A literature review on the factors contributing to active aging today]. *Revista Universo Psi*, *1*(1), 150–174.

Galinha, S. A. (2010). *Sociedades Empáticas e Organizativas: Contributos Psicossociológicos em Educação* [Empathic and Organizational Societies: Psychosociological Contributions in Education]. Imprinove.

General Direction of Health. (2011). *Norma da Direção-Geral da Saúde - Acidente Vascular Cerebral: Prescrição de Medicina Física e de Reabilitação* [Norm from the General Direction of Health - Stroke: Prescription of Physical Medicine and Rehabilitation]. Retrieved from https://www.dgs.pt/directrizes-da-dgs/normas-e-circulares-normativas/norma-n-0542011-de-27122011-jpg.aspx

Giddens, A. (2001). *Sociologia* [Sociology] (6th ed.). Fundação Calouste Gulbenkian.

Gohn, M. G. (2014). Educação Não Formal, Aprendizagens e Saberes em Processos Participativos [Non-Formal Education, Learning and Knowledge in Participatory Participatory Processes]. *Investigar em Educação, 2*(1), 35–50.

Jacob, L. (2002). *O Idoso e a Comunidade-respostas Sociais* [The Elderly and the Community-Social Responses]. Academic Press.

Jacob, L., Santos, E., Pocinho, R., & Fernandes, H. (2013). *Envelhecimento e Economia Social: Perspetivas Atuais* [Aging and Social Economy: Current Perspectives]. PsicoSoma.

Kitwood, T. (1997). *Dementia Reconsidered Revisited: The Person Still Comes First* (1st ed.). Open University Press.

Liu-Ambrose, T., Barha, C., & Falck, R. S. (2019). Active body, healthy brain: Exercise for healthy cognitive aging. *International Review of Neurobiology, 147*, 95–120. doi:10.1016/bs.irn.2019.07.004 PMID:31607364

Lopes, M. S. (2006). *Animação Sociocultural em Portugal* [Sociocultural Animation in Portugal]. Editorial Intervenção.

Lourenço, P. M. R. (2014). *Institucionalização do idoso e identidade: estudo de caso de idosos institucionalizados* [Institutionalization of the elderly and identity: a case study of institutionalized elderly people] [Master's thesis, Escola Superior de Educação e Ciências Sociais - Instituto Politécnico de Portalegre]. Repository of Instituto Politécnico de Portalegre. http://hdl.handle.net/10400.26/9205

Marinho, H. I. R. (2013). *Serviço de Apoio Domiciliário: práticas e dinâmicas na ótica do utente* [Home Support Service: practices and dynamics from the user's point of view] [Master's thesis, Fundação Bissaya Barreto]. Repository of Fundação Bissaya Barreto. http://hdl.handle.net/10400.26/29499

Martins, E. C. (2013). *Gerontologia & Gerontagogia – Animação Sociocultural em Idosos* [Gerontology & Gerontagogy - Sociocultural Animation in the Elderly]. Editorial Cáritas.

Oliveira, T., Baixinho, C. L., & Henriques, M. A. (2018). Risco Multidimensional de Queda em Idosos [Multidimensional risk of falls in elderly]. *Revista Brasileira em Promoção da Saúde*, *31*(2), 1–9. doi:10.5020/18061230.2018.7058

Pereira, C. I. P. S. (2015). *A relevância do desenvolvimento humano versus desenvolvimento comunitário: uma nova perspetiva do apoio ao envelhecimento ativo no centro dia* [The relevance of human development versus community development: a new perspective on supporting active aging in the day center] [Master's thesis, Escola Superior de Educação e Ciências Sociais – Instituto Politécnico de Leiria]. Repository of Instituto Politécnico de Leiria. http://hdl.handle.net/10400.8/1683

PORDATA. (2022, June 15). *Indicadores de Envelhecimento* [Aging Indicators]. Retrieved from https://www.pordata.pt/Portugal/Indicadores+de+envelhecimento-526

Portuguese Association for the Development of Sociocultural Animation. (2019). *Estatuto da Carreira Profissional de Animador/a Sociocultural* [Statute of the Professional Career of Sociocultural Animator]. Retrieved from shorturl.at/jPUW1

Rocha, M. F. (2018). *Envelhecer ativamente em Centro de Dia* [Active aging in the Day Center] [Master's thesis, Instituto Superior de Serviço Social do Porto]. Repository of Instituto Superior de Serviço Social do Porto. http://hdl.handle.net/10400.26/26005

Social Security Institute. (2021). *Objetivos e princípios* [Objectives and principles]. Retrieved from https://www.seg-social.pt/objectivos-e-principios

Social Security Institute. (n.d). *Quem pode desenvolver respostas sociais* [Who can develop social answers]. Retrieved from https://www.seg-social.pt/como-desenvolver-respostas-sociais

Statistics Portugal. (2002). *Censos 2001 - Resultados Definitivos* [2001 Census - Definitive Results]. Statistics Portugal.

Statistics Portugal. (2009). *Aprendizagem ao Longo da Vida - Inquérito à Educação e Formação de Adultos 2007* [Lifelong Learning - Adult Education and Training Survey 2007]. Statistics Portugal.

Statistics Portugal. (2015). *Envelhecimento da população residente em Portugal e na União Europeia* [Aging of the resident population in Portugal and in the European Union]. Retrieved from https://www.ine.pt/xportal/xmain?xpid=INE&xpgid=ine_destaques&DESTAQUESdest_boui=224679354&DESTAQUESmodo=2&xlang=pt

United Nations. (2019). *Global Issues - Ageing*. Retrieved from https://www.un.org/en/global-issues/ageing

United Nations. (2022). *Envelhecimento* [Ageing]. Retrieved from https://unric.org/pt/envelhecimento/

United Nations Population Fund. (2012). *Envelhecimento no Século XXI: Celebração e Desafio - Resumo Executivo* [Aging in the 21st Century: Celebration and Challenge - Executive Summary]. Retrieved from https://www.unfpa.org/sites/default/files/pub-pdf/Portuguese-Exec-Summary_0.pdf

Vilardouro, C. F. (2013). *O contributo da animação sociocultural para o desenvolvimento pessoal e social de alunos com Necessidades Educativas Especiais no 1º ciclo do ensino básico* [The contribution of sociocultural animation to the personal and social development of students with Special Educational Needs in the 1st cycle of basic education] [Master's thesis, Universidade Católica Portuguesa]. Repository of, Universidade Católica Portuguesa. http://hdl.handle.net/10400.14/13639

World Health Organization. (2005). *Envelhecimento Ativo: Uma Política de Saúde* [Active Aging: A Health Policy]. Retrieved from https://bvsms.saude.gov.br/bvs/publicacoes/envelhecimento_ativo.pdf

World Health Organization. (2021a). *Comprehensive Mental Health Action Plan 2013–2030*. Retrieved from https://apps.who.int/iris/bitstream/handle/10665/345301/9789240031029-eng.pdf?sequence=1&isAllowed=y

World Health Organization. (2021b). *Strategies for preventing and managing falls across the life-course*. World Health Organization.

Yates, L. A., Ziser, S., Spector, A., & Orrell, M. (2016). Cognitive leisure activities and future risk of cognitive impairment and dementia: Systematic review and meta-analysis. *International Psychogeriatrics*, *28*(11), 1791–1806. doi:10.1017/S1041610216001137 PMID:27502691

KEY TERMS AND DEFINITIONS

Active Aging: Aging process with continuous participation in society's social, economic, cultural, and civil issues. It aims to increase healthy life expectancy and quality of life.

Individual Aging: Biological, psychosocial, and other changes related to old age that depends on each individual. Each human being has an aging process accompanied by differentiated experiences.

Lifelong Learning: Learning occurs outside a formal educational institute, such as a school, university, or others. Intentional learning that occurs throughout life focuses on personal development.

Mental Health: It is to feel great and healthy, personally and in relationships with others, providing the individuals with productivity, self-realization, satisfaction, and well-being.

Quality of Life (QoL): Physical, mental, and psychological well-being without the appearance of age-related diseases. This concept includes several domains: emotional state, social interaction, cultural, ethical, religious values, and satisfaction.

Social Responses: They are institutions and/or services provided to the population according to their needs. In aging, we have day centers, social centers, and nursing homes.

Sociocultural Animation: It is an area of social intervention for any age group, depending on the needs. It develops activities in several scenarios and organizations to occupy free time. It involves numerous art techniques, music, cognitive stimulation, games, etc.

Chapter 4
The Aging Workforce in Indonesia and Its Impact on Economic and Social Development

Elni Jeini Usoh
Universitas Negeri Manado, Indonesia

Linda Lambey
University of Sam Ratulangii, Indonesia

John Burgess
Torrens University, Australia

ABSTRACT

Indonesia is an emerging economy that has undergone structural change and achieved sustained growth rates that have lifted average living standards over the past three decades. Compared to advanced economies, the Indonesian population and workforce are relatively young. However, the population will age over the coming decades, and the profile will resemble that of advanced economies. Poverty and inequality are extensive, and the challenge of an aging population is that only a minority of the workforce has access to a secure post-retirement income and services that support quality aging. The challenges of an aging population and workforce are discussed in the chapter. These include the large share of workers in the informal sector and the growth of contingent work arrangements in the formal sector. Many continue to work into old age as they cannot afford to retire. Despite an increase in schooling and post-secondary education participation, the quality of education and the low investment in training has limited productivity growth.

DOI: 10.4018/978-1-6684-6351-2.ch004

INTRODUCTION

There is a global aging trend in developed and developing countries (United Nations Department of Economic and Social Affairs, 2017). The number of people aged 60 years plus will be 2 billion in 2050, up from 1 billion in 2019. However, 80 percent of older people will live in low- and middle-income countries. As age expectancy increases, the aged population, their communities, and governments will face challenges linked to healthy aging and aging with a quality of life (Basrowi et al., 2021). However, there are significant differences between countries in diverse regions and at different development stages concerning current and future population trends. While population aging is linked to economic development, with advanced economies such as Italy and Japan facing declining populations, in the coming decades, the main source for the growth in the aged population will be in developing economies like Indonesia (United Nations Department of Economic and Social Affairs, 2017). As mortality and fertility rates decline, the United Nations Department of Economic and Social Affairs (2019) predicted that one in six people globally will be over sixty-five years old by 2050 and that the proportion of aged people in Southeast Asia will double (Chomik & Piggott, 2015). The challenges associated with an aging population include impacting state finances, increasing health costs, and providing for a dignified and active retirement that supports a quality of life. For developing economies like Indonesia, the financial challenges are acute as there is a limited social safety net to support retirees, accumulated personal savings from employment are limited, and there is limited infrastructure, especially in remote regions. In terms of the workforce, aging brings challenges such as the loss of skills as workers retire and ensuring that older workers are accommodated within the workforce through, for example, the provision of flexible employment conditions and appropriate health and safety arrangements.

Population aging in developing economies generates similar challenges to those in advanced economies, such as retirement financing, the increasing dependency ratio, and the financing of adequate health services (Dhakal et al., 2022). However, in developing economies, the informal economy and informal work are significant, and there are fewer workers with sufficient savings to finance retirement. With many small businesses, high rates of self-employment, and high levels of informal employment, aging means not retirement but continued working since retirement is not a viable option (Dhakal et al., 2022).

The United Nations Department of Economic and Social Affairs (2019) identified the links between population aging and sustainable development in its global population report. The key challenges identified were that:

"Persons aged 65 or over make up the world's fastest-growing age group. Virtually all countries anticipate an increase in the percentage of older persons in their populations. Countries need to plan for population aging and ensure the well-being of older persons by protecting their human rights and economic security and by ensuring access to age-appropriate health care services, lifelong learning opportunities, and formal and informal support networks" (United Nations Department of Economic and Social Affairs, 2019, p. 37).

For Indonesia, the key challenges include providing infrastructure, income, and health support for an aging population. There is also the challenge of extensive poverty among the elderly and meeting their basic income needs, given their limited accumulated savings (Dhakal et al., 2022).

Unlike many advanced economies, the aging workforce challenges in Indonesia have quite different dimensions (Kudrna et al., 2022). These include the underlying demographic change that will contribute to the workforce's average age declining in the short term, most of the workforce being employed in the informal sector, outside the standards and protections associated with formal employment. The major policy challenge is to develop effective processes to support savings to allow the elderly to age with a quality of life.

In this chapter, we investigate the aging of the Indonesian population and workforce. We discuss the economic and social challenges associated with aging before discussing the policy responses to an aging population and workforce. The chapter concludes with a discussion of the key issues that require policy action to address the significant demographic shift that will occur in the coming decades.

BACKGROUND TO INDONESIA

Indonesia encompasses 18,108 islands, only 6,000 of which are inhabited. Despite being geographically dispersed, the Indonesian economy, politics, and population are concentrated in Java and Sumatra islands. Around 85 percent of Indonesia's Gross Domestic Product (GDP) is generated from these two locations (Burgess et al., 2020). As in nearly all emerging economies, there is a drive towards improving living standards, increasing opportunities, and developing globally competitive industries. With sustained GDP growth, increased education participation, and a shift away from agriculture and migration to urban areas, the numbers, and share of those in poverty continue to decline (Statistics Times, 2021). There has been a sustained emigration of Indonesian workers to the rest of Southeast Asia and the Middle East, working in hospitality industries, domestic work, construction, and plantations (Burgess et al., 2020; The World Bank, 2017). Indonesia has to deal with regular natural disasters – earthquakes, tsunamis, forest fires, floods, and volcanic eruptions. In addition, the economy was hard hit by the Asian financial crisis (1997–1998), the global financial crisis (2008–2009), periodic fluctuations in world oil prices, and, more recently, the COVID-19 pandemic (Afrianty et al., 2022; Burgess et al., 2020).

Indonesia has the largest population and economy in Southeast Asia. The population growth rate is estimated at 0.83 percent per year. Indonesia's economy has improved from being the world's 27th largest in 2000 to the 16th largest in the third quarter of 2018 (Statistics Times, 2021). It is the world's 10th-largest economy in terms of Purchasing Power Parity (PPP) and the fourth-largest economy in East Asia after China, Japan, and South Korea (The World Bank, 2018). There are many ethnic groups, the two largest being Javanese and Sundanese. Indonesia's main religion is Islam, which plays a key role in Indonesian culture and politics. Indonesian democracy is based on Pancasila, or five principles, as the state philosophy and a way of life. The five principles are faith in God, respect for humankind as a whole, nationalism and unity, democratic government, and social justice (Morfit, 1981).

The structure of the Indonesian economy has shifted from being heavily dependent on the agricultural sectors in the 1950s and 1960s to a gradual process of industrialization and urbanization. The process accelerated in the 1980s as falling oil prices forced the Indonesian Government to diversify away from oil exports into manufactured exports (Elias & Noone, 2011). However, the manufacturing sector is linked to the processing of agricultural products rather than elaborately transformed manufacturing, such as electronics (Elias & Noone, 2011). Indonesia's GDP composition by sector is agriculture at 13.7 percent, industry at 41 percent, and services at 45.4 percent (Central Intelligence Agency, 2022). Indonesia's economic growth has recently been driven by the non–tradable services sector (Ginting & Aji, 2015). Services contributed, on average, 3.4 percent growth per year over the past decade. The telecommunication and transport sectors have sustained double-digit growth over the past decade. Furthermore, the financial sector, trade, hotels and restaurants, and other services also expanded due to income growth in the formal sector, tourism, and ongoing urbanization (Central Intelligence Agency, 2022). However, agriculture and resources remain key sectors in the economy, with Indonesia being a major producer of rubber and palm oil, petroleum and gas, and nickel. In 2016, its major exports to Indonesia were from the agriculture and resources sector: palm oil, coal briquettes, petroleum gas, crude petroleum, and rubber (Allen, 2016).

While Indonesia has sustained a GDP growth of around 5 percent over the last decade, several structural and economic challenges remain. A feature of the economy is the large share of informal or unregulated employment at around three-quarters of the workforce and nearly all of the workforce in agriculture. There are high youth unemployment rates and underemployment throughout the economy, and the female labor force participation rate is well below that of males (Allen, 2016). Despite the ongoing structural change, per capita income growth is low, inequality is extensive, and widespread poverty (Kudrna et al., 2022; OECD, 2022). Productivity growth has been minimal, reflecting limited investment, especially in skills, and labor-intensive production, especially in agriculture, and the large share of short-term jobs in the formal sector that results in an under-investment in training (Allen, 2016). The poor infrastructure and unreliable electricity supplies contribute to low productivity growth. Despite being a significant petroleum producer and exporter, around one-third of the population cannot access reliable electricity supplies. Infrastructure such as roads, rail, ports, and airports are in poor condition and impede growth and investment (Elias & Noone, 2011). The OECD (2022) also highlighted the endemic corruption problem that contributed to the infrastructure deficit, with many major infrastructure projects being unfinished or of poor quality.

In Indonesia, social protection in old age is limited. The social security and pension system is confined to those in formal employment. For those in informal employment, old age means working for further years and being dependent on inter-generational transfers from within family groups (Kudrna et al., 2022). Less than 10 percent of the population have self-funded pension payments; the other 90 percent depend upon intra-family transfers (Basrowi et al., 2021). Population aging and workforce aging will challenge the United Nation's sustainable development agenda that includes aging with dignity (United Nations Department of Economic and Social Affairs, 2019). Implicitly the aged should be productive community members, live outside of poverty; have access to health services; and not be subject to discrimination (Dhakal et al., 2022). With aging, most of the population in Indonesia will need to continue working since they are in the informal sector, have low-paid and insecure work in the formal sector, and do not have sufficient savings to finance retirement (Kudrna et al., 2022; Kudrna et al., 2020).

From the various international development measures, Indonesia has a mixed report card. This section reports on the Human Development Index (HDI), the Human Capital Index (HCI), and the Gender Equity Index (GEI). All provide context to the issues associated with an aging population. The HDI provides an overview of a country's development trajectory based on measures of life expectancy, schooling, and Gross National Income (GNI) per capita compared with other countries. For Indonesia, the HDI value in 2017 was 0.694. It was ranked 116 out of 189 countries. The HDI for Indonesia increased from 0.528 in 1990 to 0.694 in 2017. On all measures of human development, Indonesia improved. From 1990 to 2017, Indonesia's life expectancy increased by 6.1 years, mean years of schooling increased by 4.7, and expected years of schooling increased by 2.7. Indonesia's GNI per capita increased by 152.6 percent (United Nations Development Program, 2018). The HDI for Indonesia suggests that well-being has improved as life expectancy (better health), schooling (education and opportunity), and material well-being (GNI per capita) have improved.

The HCI indicates the extent to which a child who reaches 18 years of age accesses human capital in terms of health and education (The World Bank, 2019). It indicates the extent to which children have access to potential and is an indicator of the future productivity of the workforce. In 2018, Indonesia ranked 87 out of 157 countries and lowed within Southeast Asia relative to its income. That is, there are major impediments to improvements in the HCI. The HCI score was 0.53, indicating that children who reach 18 years of age only access 53 percent of potential human capital. In other words, it has a human capital gap that it needs to address, especially around the years and quality of schooling. This is an important finding regarding its implications for productivity and skills development and addressing the challenges associated with an aging population. Survival and health rates have improved, as has the overall Human Capital Index score. However, from 2012 to 2017, the HCI score for Indonesia only increased from 0.50 to 0.53 (The World Bank, 2019).

The World Economic Forum (2015) developed the GEI, a framework for capturing the magnitude and scope of gender-based disparities. The index benchmarks national gender gaps on economic, political, education, and health criteria and provides country rankings that allow for effective comparisons across regions and income groups over time. In terms of the overall rankings of the gender gap, Indonesia was 95th out of 136 countries in 2013. Its ranking had declined from 68th in 2006 to 95th in 2013 despite its score improving. The overall disparity for women was around two-thirds of that for men in terms of participation, health, education, and empowerment. The four areas that constitute the index are economic participation and opportunity, health and survival, education attainment, and political empowerment. Throughout the Indonesian economy and governance structures, there are extensive gender differences in participation and outcomes such as employment, income, and leadership roles (Prihatiningtyastuti et al., 2020). The relevance of these measures for the discussion of population aging is as follows. First, there is a gender dimension to aging as females are disadvantaged in labor force participation (and their ability to generate savings) and excluded from business and community governance and leadership positions. Women are absent from corporate and community leadership roles (Prihatiningtyastuti et al., 2020). Second, women's quality and limited education years will limit earnings, especially lifetime earnings. This issue is important in the context of aging, as many elderly females are widows and dependent on family support (Kudrna et al., 2022). Third, while there has been material progress and improved quality of life as indicated by increased life expectancy, major challenges remain for women in terms of poverty and poor infrastructure, such as caring and community services (Prihatiningtyastuti et al., 2020).

POPULATION AGING IN INDONESIA

The population of Indonesia is 279 million (Worldometers, 2022). It is the fourth most populous country in the world, and it is currently experiencing a demographic dividend as the working-age population exceeds those at school (15 years and under) and those in retirement (65 years plus) (Basrowi et al., 2021). The median age of the Indonesian population is at least ten years below that found in advanced economies, resulting in a demographic dividend; that is, in the short term, the dependency ratio should decline as the growth in the working-age population exceeds that outside of the working age group (15 to 64 years) (Elias & Noone, 2011). However, the demographic dividend will be short-term as the school-age population will continue to decline through reduced fertility rates, and the share of the aged in the population will increase through increased life expectancy (Kudrna et al., 2020). In the longer term, this will generate a ripple effect as not only does the school-age share of the population decline, but so will the percentage of the working-age population, leading to a growing dependency ratio (Kudrna et al., 2020). However, Indonesia's population projections, and discussions of the dependency ratio, must consider the large informal sector and extensive emigration. While the official retirement age in Indonesia is 57 years, this only applies to the formal sector. For workers in the informal sector, there is no mandated retirement age. Even within the formal sector, many jobs are short-term, insecure, and insufficient to generate retirement savings (Allen, 2016). Emigration will reduce the size of the working-age population, but remittances from overseas-based workers will increase household savings and support retired family members (Burgess et al., 2020; The World Bank, 2017).

Jones (2014) indicated that there will be a significant increase of 67 million or 28 percent in the population between 2010 to 2035. The rate of population growth will gradually slow, from 1.38 percent annually (from 2010 to 2015) to 0.62 percent annually (in 2030-2035) (Jones, 2014). The projections are that the fertility and infant mortality rates will decline over this period. The projected population changes and growth rates are uneven across the country, with population aging expected to be greater in Java (the most populous province) than in other provinces. In contrast, the aging population share is projected to be low in outer provinces such as the Riau Archipelago and North Makuku (Jones, 2014). These regional differences reflect the differences in fertility rates across the provinces (Adioetomo & Mujahid, 2014). Projections from 2019 to 2050 are that the share of the population above 60 years of age will increase from 10 to 21 percent, that life expectancy for males and females will increase by around five years, and that the old age dependency ratio (+ 65 years/15-64 years) will increase from 9 to 24 percent (Help Age Global Network, n.d.). As with many other Asian economies, the longer-term projections are that falling fertility rates will eventually decrease the population (Kudrna et al., 2022).

The average life expectancy will increase and is predicted to be over 80 years by 2100 when the shares of the population over 60 will approach 30 percent across developing and developed economies (Dhakal et al., 2022).

The longer-term demographic trends suggest that the Indonesian population will age dramatically, fertility rates will decline, families will become smaller, and the average life expectancy will increase. This is in keeping with what will occur in many other Asian and emerging economies (Dhakal et al., 2022). However, unlike in advanced economies, many above retirement age do not have access to private or state-financed pensions, meaning that most of the aged population will continue to work (Kudrna et al., 2022). The concern for governments is the financing of retirement and providing services for the elderly, especially health, in the face of an increasing dependency ratio (Kudrna et al., 2022).

THE LABOR MARKET AND WORKFORCE AGING IN INDONESIA

Labor market performance improved between 1990 and 2015 in terms of employment generation, productivity, real wage growth, and increases in formal sector employment (Nomaan & Nayantara, 2018). Nomaan and Nayantara (2018) suggest that Indonesia, like many developing economies has: a high share of own-account (self-employed) workers, about one-third of total employment; a high share of contributing family workers at 12 percent of total employment; a high rate of youth unemployment, four times the average unemployment rate of 4 percent; a low rate of advanced education attainment in the workforce, at 10 percent; and nearly half of the population live in poverty with an income of less than US $5 per day. Nomaan and Nayantara (2018) indicate a trend of increased GDP per capita, improved workforce education, increased labor force participation rates for women, and a decline in the share of agricultural employment. This follows the expected trajectory of an emerging economy moving towards a service economy with an educated workforce and growing productivity. Nonetheless, there are major challenges around the large share of own account workers, the low rates of labor force participation for women, and the large share of the population in poverty and underemployment, especially in rural areas that lack industry diversity and job opportunities (Allen & Burgess, 2016).

One feature of Indonesia is a large number of community and worker cooperatives, estimated to be around 190,000. As members are self-employed, this explains the large share of own account workers who, while working for the cooperatives, are also owners of the cooperatives. Cooperatives are an important source of employment, especially for women, in rural areas (Allen & Burgess, 2016). There are also large numbers of documented and undocumented immigrant workers in Indonesia, many of whom are low-skilled, from China, Myanmar, Cambodia, Laos, and Thailand, working in the plantation sectors (Palmer & Missbach, 2019).

Another key feature of the Indonesian labor market is the large informal economy and workforce. Informal employment has remained around 80 percent of the workforce. This means that employment is insecure and irregular and that low incomes reduce the ability to save for the future. Kudrna et al. (2022) highlight that informal workers are low-skilled, have limited education, and have low incomes relative to those in the formal sector. These inequalities in earnings persist over the life course. Post-retirement age, those in informal employment are likely to continue working. Within the formal sector, many workers are on short-term contracts, resulting in insecure income flows and an inability to save for retirement and, thus, being forced to continue working post-retirement age (Allen, 2016). Overall, a large share of those aged over 60 years of age will continue working as they do not have sufficient savings to finance retirement. Kudrna et al. (2022) demonstrate that the employment rate for males is over 50 percent for the 65-74 age group. Despite the high employment rates for older cohorts, many are working on part-time arrangements (especially females) and in informal work, with the result being that average earnings for the elderly are around one-quarter of average adult earnings (Kudrna et al., 2022).

Transitions from the informal to the formal sector are related to age. Younger workers are likely to transition; older workers are not expected to transition. What emerges with an aging population is that a significant component of the post-retirement age group will continue working and with high hours of work (Kudrna et al., 2022). Unlike advanced economies, a guaranteed retirement age with pension entitlements is available to a minority of the workforce, those working in large private firms and the public sector. While labor force participation rates decline significantly in advanced economies post-retirement age, that is not the case in Indonesia (Burgess et al., 2020). Hence, a growing dependency ratio is not indicative of a growing old age cohort who are not active in the workforce. Kudrna et al. (2022) demonstrate that older adults share residences with their children, and the share of older adults co-residing with their children and grandchildren increases with age, especially for women. The most important source of income for older adults is labor income, and private (within-family) transfers become a more important source of income as people age. After 70 years of age, transfers from children become the most important income source (Kudrna et al., 2022).

Older workers and the older population in general, compared to younger cohorts, are likely to have less education, training, and qualifications and be less familiar with internet and mobile phone technology. This exclusion from new technology contributes to isolation and reduces older workers' ability to access jobs (Adioetomo & Mujahid, 2014).

The population projections indicate an aging population and workforce. Unlike advanced economies, many Indonesian workers will continue to work into old age. While the age dependency ratio will increase, older workers, especially males, will continue working. In Indonesia family, transfers and support are an essential source of income and accommodation since the elderly reside with children and grandchildren (Kudrna et al., 2020; Burgess et al., 2020). The projected demographics of falling fertility rates will result in smaller families and increased pressure on families to support the elderly (Kudrna et al., 2022). The workforce challenges associated with aging are structural, namely reducing unemployment and under-employment, increasing female labor force participation, increasing workforce training, and increasing workforce formalization while limiting the degree of contingent employment within the formal sector. Without addressing these structural problems, as the population ages, there will be increased pressure on income support and poverty reduction measures for the elderly.

THE ECONOMIC AND SOCIAL CHALLENGES OF AN AGING POPULATION AND WORKFORCE IN INDONESIA

Basrowi et al. (2021) suggest that the aged cohort in Indonesia has low literacy and educational attainment relative to younger age groups and limited access to the internet combined with limited information and communication technology literacy. As with other countries, aging is associated with health problems and poor nutritional intake. Younger generations do not have the health problems linked to aging, but they have high rates of obesity compared to older age groups. In Indonesia, the dominant religion is Islam, and alcoholism is not a problem. However, tobacco consumption is high, especially among the elderly (The Tobacco Atlas, 2019). Atmospheric pollution levels are very high, contributing to respiratory problems, especially for the elderly (OECD, 2022). Disability also increases with age, with hearing and sight problems for the elderly reducing mobility, communication, and ability to work (Adioetomo & Mujahid, 2014). Meeting the World Health Organization and United Nations agendas around healthy and productive population aging in Indonesia over the coming decades will involve meeting major policy challenges.

Ongoing structural change in Indonesia includes urbanization, growth in the services sector, and increased participation in schooling and education. However, several features of the Indonesian economy are relevant to identifying the policy challenges generated through population aging in the context of an aging population. These include the large informal sector and inadequate training and skill development levels, especially in agriculture. These, in turn, have resulted in low limited productivity growth. Other problems include widespread poverty, low levels of household savings, high rates of youth unemployment, and high rates of underemployment throughout the economy (Allen, 2016). There are gender inequities in terms of economic and political outcomes and regional disparities across the country with a west-east division in terms of average living standards. Allen (2016) suggests that the share of the formal sector is increasing, reflecting the structural changes occurring; however, many additional formal sector jobs are short-term and precarious and have more common features than the informal sector. Indonesia is both urbanizing and undergoing a slow structural adjustment process. While the transformation of the economy is ongoing with the relative growth in the manufacturing and services sector and the urbanization of the population, the share of agricultural and rural employment is around one-third. Moreover, in the rural sectors, earnings are low, and underemployment is high (Allen, 2016). A strong economic performance in GDP growth was offset by low productivity growth, extensive poverty, extensive underemployment, and growing inequality (Allen, 2016).

Kudrna et al. (2022) demonstrate that the old age dependency ratio has remained stable at around 10 percent over the past 60 years. However, they project that the ratio will be 50 percent by 2100. For every person over 65 years, there will be two working people. This reflects the working-age population's decline as fertility rates decline and the extensions in life expectancy. From this, the major societal challenges will be funding a growing share of retirees and funding those facilities that are important in contributing to healthy aging, especially health care services and age care facilities. There will be pressure on families to support elderly relatives as the average family size will decline in the future.

In developing economies, like Indonesia, social protection and pension coverage are low, and the elderly must either work or rely on family transfers to survive. Those working in the informal economy cannot save for retirement due to low and irregular incomes (Kudrna et al., 2022). The challenges of aging are partially offset by shared housing across cohorts, with the elderly sharing residences with children and grandchildren and performing and receiving caring within the family (Kudrna et al., 2022). It was estimated that less than 20 percent of the elderly in Indonesia have access to a regular pension (Kudrna et al., 2022), while 75 percent work in the informal sector and have no pension income and social security. Access to formal retirement funding is limited to formal sector workers and includes government officials, army officers, large firms, and government-owned companies (SMERU Research Report, 2020; Noveria, 2006).

There is a strong gender element to vulnerability in old age. Women are disadvantaged as they have low savings and earnings and lower participation in the formal sector and the labor market (Help Age Global Network, n.d.; Prihatiningtyastuti et al., 2021). Post-retirement age, the participation rates of men in the labor market are much higher than those for women (Prihatiningtyastuti et al., 2021). With aging, there is an increase in single-women households, and through time as family size declines, there will be a decline in support for the old aged from families (Kudrna et al., 2022). This problem is exacerbated in rural areas by outmigration to urban areas, leaving the elderly without family support and networks (Adioetomo & Mujahid, 2014). Around 42 percent of the elderly in Indonesia are living either in poverty or just above the poverty line (Priebe & Howell, 2014). Since the size of families will decline in the future, traditional family support mechanisms for the elderly have diminished and will decrease with the ongoing aging population (Kudrna et al., 2022). With smaller families, reduced family support, and the migration of the young from rural to urban areas, Indonesia could face the social problems experienced by the aged in advanced economies; these include isolation, loneliness, exclusion, and marginalization (Dhakal et al., 2022).

Despite having a young population, aging in Indonesia will result in workforce and skill shortages, especially developing skill gaps as the structure of the Indonesian economy moves more into services and IT-based activities (Burgess et al., 2020). The skills shortages result from what is perceived as a low-quality education system, and the inability of the education system to support skill development results in graduate unemployment and underemployment (Priyono & Nankervis, 2020). Skills shortages will be exacerbated by the ongoing migration of unskilled, semi-skilled, and skilled workers to higher-paying jobs in Asia and the Middle East (Burgess et al., 2020).

Nomaan and Nayantara (2018) identified decent work challenges facing Indonesia. These included the absence of basic social protection through social safety nets, the growing disparity between Java and Sumatra and other regions, and the vulnerable position of overseas migrant workers. Despite the Government's efforts to advance social protection in Indonesia, which includes both contributory and non-contributory schemes for workers and their families in the formal and informal sectors, a signiðcant proportion of the population still does not have access to basic social protection provisions. Socio-economic exclusion of the marginalized and vulnerable is still a continuing concern and remains a critical challenge for policymakers. Regarding regional development, the disparity in economic growth rate among the provinces is signiðcant. Java and Sumatra account for more than 82 percent of the total national GDP, while Eastern provinces lag far behind (Nomaan & Nayantara, 2018).

Allen (2016) identifies low productivity growth as a major impediment to future development. Moreover, informal and short-term formal employment impedes skill and training (Allen, 2016). Further challenges to sustainable development are poor infrastructure, the quality of education, and poor graduate work skills (Pryono & Nankervis, 2020; Allen, 2016; Jones, 2014). Despite a shift towards services and manufacturing and increasing educational attainment, there are barriers to skill development and transitioning to secure and well-paid jobs in the formal sector (Burgess et al., 2020). These barriers impede the ability of the working-age population to save for retirement and provide inter-family transfers to support retired family members.

A further consequence of population aging and increased life expectancy is the pressure placed on the health system, especially as with age, the incidence of medical conditions such as diabetes, cataracts, high blood pressure, Alzheimer's disease, and viral infections increases. With underdeveloped health systems and an absence of access to reliable health services in rural areas, there is doubt over the ability of Indonesia to cope with the health-related demands of aging, including meeting the nutritional needs of the elderly with their limited income (Basrowi et al., 2021).

POLICY RESPONSES TO AN AGING POPULATION AND WORKFORCE

In Indonesia, the cultural and religious context elevates family and community support for the elderly. It bestows recognition to the elderly for their contribution to family and community development (Lestari et al., 2022). There is a tradition of family and local community support for elderly parents and neighbors and resistance to placing the elderly in care facilities. Despite this tradition, the economic challenges of aging are considerable in the context of limited national, local, and family financial capabilities. The Indonesia Government is aware of the policy problems and challenges associated with an aging population and workforce. Sanusi (2014) classifies the challenges as physical, economic, social, and legal. Physical covers reduced mobility and degenerative disability linked to aging. In turn, this places pressure on financing the health care system and its suitability to reach the needs of the elderly with suitable health and care services. Throughout Indonesia, the infrastructure to support a healthy aging agenda is underdeveloped and inadequate (Arifianto, 2006). Economic covers extensive poverty in old age, dependence on family transfers, and the overall increase in the dependency ratio. Underlying poverty is associated with low and insecure earnings, the lack of personal savings, and the need to continue working past the legal retirement age, especially for those in the economy's informal sector. Social challenges include exclusion, neglect, and loneliness. These challenges especially apply to single females and those living in remote regions. Legal challenges include managing violence, fraud, and asset theft perpetrated against the elderly.

Laws and decrees have been enacted since 1998 that directly address the welfare of the elderly or incorporate the elderly into a broader agenda, such as poverty reduction and income support. Arifianto (2006) provided an overview of the legislative developments and challenges linked to an aging population in Indonesia. The legislation identified by Arifianto (2006) included the Social Welfare Law of

1974, the Old Age Welfare Law of 1998, and the National Social Security System Law of 2004. These laws incorporated aging into the national welfare agenda and attempted to develop a national retirement income program. Arifianto (2006) observed that while the challenges were acknowledged, policy, especially around pension systems and income support, remained underdeveloped or underfunded. He also suggested that there would be ongoing pressure as the size of families declined and through the ongoing migration to cities placing burdens on the elderly who remain behind in regional areas.

Sanusi (2014) identified relevant laws and decrees that included: Government Regulation No. 43/2004 on Older Person Welfare Improvement Efforts; Presidential Decree 93/M/2005 on Appointment and Membership of National Commission for Older Persons; Law No. 40/2004 on the National Social Security System (NSSS); Law No. 11/2009 on Social Welfare; and Law No. 13/2011 on Poverty Eradication. Institutional support for developing, applying, and evaluating programs to support aging is progressed through the National Plan on Aging (NPA) and the National Commission for Older Persons (NCOP). The NPA encompasses the following objectives (Sanusi, 2014):

- Political support of policymakers, non-governmental organizations (NGOs), community, and religious leaders, as well as experts in aging in efforts to improve older person welfare;
- Informal support for older persons by maintaining family and community support for the older population;
- Formal support for older persons by increasing improvement in health services and development of the system in protection and social security for older persons;
- Establish older person institutions through improving inter-sector cooperation at national and international levels.

Beyond the above objectives, the suite of supporting policy programs included expanded home care programs and support for training home care providers; fare concessions for the elderly on public transport; the incorporation of age-friendly support programs into community health centers; income assistance for those elderly in poverty; and support for NGOs that provide elderly services (Sanusi, 2014). However, local governments are responsible for enacting and implementing programs to support the elderly. The national government provides the policy direction and finance, while local governments are responsible for delivery. This brings flexibility into policy and recognizes differences across the regions. However, to date, many of the listed programs have been partially applied or limited by restrictions of coverage and eligibility. This is especially the case for access to state pensions, residential and home-based aged care, and contribution-based pension programs (Lestari et al., 2022).

Basrowi et al. (2021) provide a health profile of the aging population in Indonesia. They highlight the health improvements in the aging cohort over time. While the government has an active aging program, there remain challenges to realizing a healthy aging agenda because of widespread cigarette consumption, inappropriate diets, and an inactive lifestyle across the population. They suggest that there is a need for a more active preventative health program across the population that takes in government, NGOs, and communities. Elevated levels of atmospheric pollution compound the health challenges from burning fossil fuels, deforestation programs, burn-offs to develop the palm oil sector, and growing urbanization and motor vehicle pollution supported by fossil fuel subsidies.

Taking preventive health measures reinforces the point that developing an effective aging policy agenda must accommodate the challenges faced by the aged now and the aged in the future. The immediate need of the aged is to support healthy aging, and aging with dignity requires an integrated health and income support program, community infrastructure development, and community social program development.

Addressing future challenges linked to aging requires that policies be developed to address – full employment, education, and training; equity and inclusion; social security and savings programs to finance retirement; increased formal economy participation; and effective preventive health programs are required. In the labor market, the Indonesian government must consider the transition to larger formal employment, limiting short-term employment in the formal sector, improving access to and the quality of education, supporting the improvement in skills and training programs, and reducing graduate and youth unemployment. Other challenges include removing barriers to female participation in the workforce, reducing regional inequalities, and supporting the financing of pension and health insurance for retirement (Burgess et al., 2020; Prihatiningtyastuti et al., 2020; Allen, 2016).

CONCLUSION

Indonesia has achieved considerable improvements in living standards across the population regarding standard economic performance indicators. Behind this economic success, there have been improvements in literacy, education, and health. Despite this success, challenges remain, such as widespread poverty, inequality, and gender and regional disparity. There remains a large informal sector and high rates of underemployment and youth unemployment. The population profile of Indonesia, relative to advanced economies, has a large youth component that will generate a population dividend in the coming decades as the population dependency ratio declines. However, in the longer-term fertility rates, the average family size will decrease, life expectancy will increase, and the population dependency ratio will increase.

The challenges of financing retirement and providing the services that support a productive retirement and retirement with dignity are present in Indonesia, as they are in advanced and developing countries. The features that make Indonesia different from advanced economies are the extensive poverty and large share of the workforce in the informal sector. Funded state and employer pensions apply to a small component of the population. Many of the population, especially males, continue working beyond 60 years of age as they do not have sufficient savings to finance retirement. The elderly live with extended families and are dependent on intra-family transfers. However, the longer-term demographic projections indicate that the average family size will decline with falling fertility rates. Those elderly at risk of isolation, poverty, and exclusion are likely to be single females and those living in rural areas.

Major workforce issues must be addressed to support the capacity of individuals and the community to address the challenges of an aging population. These include underemployment, high rates of youth unemployment, and the large informal sector. In turn, these issues contribute to poverty and an inability to finance retirement. Low productivity growth reflects the quality of education and the under-investment in training because of the large share of the informal workforce and the large numbers of short-term jobs in the formal sector. Major equity issues to be addressed include the large inequalities in pay and conditions across the workforce and the large numbers living in poverty. Addressing gender and regional inequalities and exclusion remains a major policy priority. These barriers reduce the ability of the current workforce to plan for and support retirement and, in the longer term, make it difficult for the government to finance programs that support aging with dignity. The quality of aging and retirement requires extensive investment in supporting infrastructure, especially health, the development of preventive health programs, and addressing the ongoing health problems associated with urbanization, pollution, and deforestation.

No one policy can address the challenges associated with population aging. As the above indicates, there is a need for a suite of programs that encompasses macroeconomic policy to promote growth and employment; microeconomic policies to support structural change; social policies to extend support and safety nets to retirees; education policy to improve access and quality; health policy to improve services, access, and quality; and regional development policies to support infrastructure access.

REFERENCES

Adioetomo, S. M., & Mujahid, G. (2014). *Indonesia on the Threshold of Population Ageing*. United Nations Population Fund.

Afrianty, T. W., Artatanaya, I. G., & Burgess, J. (2022). Working from home effectiveness during Covid-19: Evidence from university staff in Indonesia. *Asia Pacific Management Review*, *27*(1), 50–57. doi:10.1016/j.apmrv.2021.05.002

Allen, E. R. (2016). *Analysis of Trends and Challenges in the Indonesian Labor Market - ADB Papers on Indonesia No. 16*. Asian Development Bank.

Allen, E. R., & Burgess, J. (2016). Using Targeted Jobs Programs to Support Local Communities: The Case of Indonesia. In M. F. Rola-Rubzen & J. Burgess (Eds.), *Human Development and Capacity Building: Asia Pacific Trends, Challenges, and Prospects* (pp. 117–139). Routledge.

Arifianto, A. (2006). *Public Policy Towards the Elderly in Indonesia: Current Policy and Future Directions*. SMERU Research Institute.

Basrowi, R. W., Rahayu, E. M., Khoe, L. C., Wasito, E., & Sundjaya, T. (2021). The Road to Healthy Ageing: What Has Indonesia Achieved So Far? *Nutrients*, *13*(10), 3441. doi:10.3390/nu13103441 PMID:34684441

Burgess, J., Dayaram, K., Lambey, L., & Afrianty, T. W. (2020). The Challenges of Human Resource Development in Indonesia. In K. Dayaram, L. Lambey, J. Burgess, & T. Wulida Afrianty (Eds.), *Developing the Workforce in an Emerging Economy: The Case of Indonesia* (pp. 1–17). Routledge. doi:10.4324/9780429273353-1

Central Intelligence Agency. (2022). *The World Fact Book - Indonesia*. Retrieved from https://www.cia.gov/the-world-factbook/countries/indonesia/

Chomik, R., & Piggott, J. (2015). Population Ageing and Social Security in Asia. *Asian Economic Policy Review*, *10*(2), 199–222. doi:10.1111/aepr.12098

Dhakal, S. P., Burgess, J., & Nankervis, A. (2022). Population Ageing: Challenges in the Asia Pacific and Beyond. In S. Dhakal, A. Nankervis, & J. Burgess (Eds.), *Ageing Asia and the Pacific in Changing Times* (pp. 3–17). Springer. doi:10.1007/978-981-16-6663-6_1

Elias, S., & Noone, C. (2011). *The Growth and Development of the Indonesian Economy*. Retrieved from https://www.rba.gov.au/publications/bulletin/2011/dec/4.html

Ginting, E., & Aji, P. (2015). *Summary of Indonesia's Economic Analysis - ADB Papers on Indonesia No. 2*. Asian Development Bank.

Help Age Global Network. (n.d.). *Ageing population in Indonesia*. Retrieved from https://ageingasia.org/ageing-population-indonesia/

Jones, G.W. (2014). *The 2010-2035 Indonesian Population Projection - Understanding the Causes, Consequences and Policy Options for Population and Development*. United Nations Population Fund (UNFPA).

Kudrna, G., Le, T., & Piggott, J. (2020). *Review report on demographics, labor force and older people in Indonesia*. Retrieved from https://www.cepar.edu.au/publications/working-papers/review-report-demographics-labour-force-and-older-people-indonesia

Kudrna, G., Le, T., & Piggott, J. (2022). Macro-Demographics and Ageing in Emerging Asia: The Case of Indonesia. *Journal of Population Ageing*, *15*(1), 7–38. doi:10.100712062-022-09358-6 PMID:35399208

Lestari, M., Stephens, C., & Morison, T. (2022). Constructions of older people's identities in Indonesian regional ageing policies: The impacts on micro and macro experiences of ageing. *Ageing and Society*, *42*(9), 2046–2066. doi:10.1017/S0144686X20001907

Morfit, M. (1981). Pancasila: The Indonesian State Ideology According to the New Order Government. *Asian Survey*, *21*(8), 838–851. doi:10.2307/2643886

Nomaan, M., & Nayantara, S. (2018). *Employment and Growth in Indonesia (1990-2015)*. International Labour Organization.

Noveria, M. (2006, June 7-9). *Challenges of Population aging in Indonesia* [Paper Presentation]. Conference on Impact of Ageing: A Common Challenge for Europe and Asia, Vienna, Austria.

OECD. (2022). *Indonesia Economic Snapshot*. Retrieved from https://www.oecd.org/economy/indonesia-economic-snapshot/

Palmer, W., & Missbach, A. (2019). Enforcing Labour Rights of Irregular Migrants in Indonesia. *Third World Quarterly*, *40*(5), 908–925. doi:10.1080/01436597.2018.1522586

Priebe, J., & Howell, F. (2014). *Old-age Poverty in Indonesia: Empirical evidence and policy options - A role for social pensions*. TNP2K Working Paper.

Prihatiningtyastuti, E., Dayaram, K., & Burgess, J. (2020). Skills development and challenges for regional women. In K. Dayaram, L. Lambey, J. Burgess, & T. W. Afrianty (Eds.), *Developing the Workforce in an Emerging Economy: The Case of Indonesia* (pp. 53–67). Routledge. doi:10.4324/9780429273353-5

Priyono, S., & Nankervis, A. (2020). Graduate work readiness in Indonesia: challenges and opportunities. In K. Dayaram, L. Lambey, J. Burgess, & T. W. Afrianty (Eds.), *Developing the Workforce in an Emerging Economy: The Case of Indonesia* (pp. 110–124). Routledge. doi:10.4324/9780429273353-9

Sanusi, M. (2014, October 21-23). *Inter-generational family and community support: implication to social participation and contribution of older persons* [Paper Presentation]. *12th ASEAN and Japan Meeting on Caring Societies*, Tokyo, Japan.

SMERU Research Report. (2020). *The Situation of the Elderly in Indonesia and Access to Social Protection Programs: Secondary Data Analysis.* The National Team for The Acceleration of Poverty Reduction.

Statistics Times. (2021). *Projected GDP Ranking.* Retrieved from http://statisticstimes.com/economy/projected-world-gdp-ranking.php

The Tobacco Atlas. (2019). *State of global tobacco.* Retrieved from https://tobaccoatlas.org/

The World Bank. (2017). *Indonesia's Global Workers: Juggling Opportunities and Risks.* The World Bank.

The World Bank. (2018). *The World Bank In Indonesia.* Retrieved from https://www.worldbank.org/en/country/indonesia/overview

The World Bank. (2019). *Human Capital Index.* Retrieved from https://databank.worldbank.org/reports.aspx?source=3698&series=HD.HCI.EYRS

United Nations Department of Economic and Social Affairs. (2017). *Population Aging and Sustainable Development.* United Nations.

United Nations Department of Economic and Social Affairs. (2019). *World Population Prospects 2019: Highlights.* United Nations.

United Nations Development Program. (2018). *Human Development Index (HDI).* Retrieved from https://hdr.undp.org/data-center/human-development-index#/indicies/HDI

World Economic Forum. (2015). *The Global Gender Gap Report 2015.* Retrieved from https://www.weforum.org/reports/global-gender-gap-report-2015/

Worldometers. (2022). *Indonesia Population.* Retrieved from https://www.worldometers.info/world-population/indonesia-population/

KEY TERMS AND DEFINITIONS

Dependency Ratio: The ratio of those in employment to those outside of employment, usually represented by the ratio of the 15-64 years age group (those of working age) to those outside of working age.

Gender Equity Index (GEN): The index measures gender equity and estimates national gender gaps on economic, political, education, and health criteria.

Human Capital Index (HCI): Measures the extent to which a child who reaches 18 years of age has access to health and education.

Human Development Index (HDI): A measurement of a country's development trajectory based on measures of life expectancy, schooling, and Gross National Income per capita.

Informal Employment: Unregulated and unrecorded employment associated with family businesses, the self-employed, seasonal, and daily work.

Informal Sector: That component of the economy that is outside regulations and difficult to track.

Pancasli: Indonesian state philosophy is based on five principles: faith in God, respect for humankind, nationalism, and unity, democratic government, and social justice.

Chapter 5
The Importance of Aging in the Innovation Process of Organizations

Bruno de Sousa Lopes
University of Aveiro, Portugal

Vanessa Amorim
https://orcid.org/0000-0001-9738-5485
Porto Accounting and Business School, Polytechnic of Porto, Portugal

Orlando Lima Rua
Porto Accounting and Business School, Polytechnic of Porto, Portugal

Maria Céu Lamas
School of Health, Polytechnic of Porto, Portugal

ABSTRACT

The authors of this chapter aim to present the links between an aging workforce, innovation, and creativity. They address each of these themes individually, and then analyze the interconnection between the central theme (i.e., the aging workforce with creativity and innovation), and in the last point, analyze the innovative work behavior as a conclusive way of using the knowledge and skills of the aging workforce as a competitive advantage for an organization. Thus, this chapter demonstrates that the aging workforce, contrary to popular belief, is one of the age segments of organizations that contributes most to the innovation process since there is a symbiotic process between older and younger workers, and this is also evident in the creative process since innovation and creativity are intrinsic processes.

DOI: 10.4018/978-1-6684-6351-2.ch005

INTRODUCTION

Many myths have been created regarding the creative capacity of senior employees, stating that they contribute little to the creative process and, consequently, to the innovation process within organizations. However, despite this being the portrait passed on in society, the truth is that the literature states that senior employees are crucial elements in the creative process and, consequently, in the innovation process, mainly by combining the technical and digital capabilities of younger employees with the knowledge and experience of older employees, thus creating a preferential environment for the creation of innovation within organizations. Furthermore, it is essential to talk about creativity and innovation in the aging workforce; since aging is a growing and rampant phenomenon that mainly affects organizations, it will be increasingly necessary to retain older employees since worldwide forecasts point to an increase in the retirement age and consequently a longer time of permanence in organizations. Thus, it becomes essential to combine the permanence of the aging workforce and therefore take and make the most of their greatest assets which consist of their professional and life experience, combined with practical knowledge of the function, the organization, and the market, thus adding their skills, with the reinforcement of new blood in organizations with more excellent dexterity and digital skills and greater freshness. Both are endowed with great sense and critical thinking but have different perspectives. Thus, this chapter intends to fight the myths about the aging workforce and highlight the critical role of the aging workforce in the process of creativity and innovation in organizations.

BACKGROUND

Aging

Aging is characterized by the natural biological process innate to any human being that occurs throughout their lifetime. At the same time, the phenomenon of demographic aging directly impacts the amount of labor available in each organization and country (Cepellos, 2018).

Derived from reduced fertility and mortality rates and increased life expectancy, and improved health and hygiene systems, concerns about economic expansion, growth, and workforce shortages have arisen as a result of population aging, as it is projected that unless there is a change in work patterns and retirement age the vast majority of individuals will be of retirement age (Settels, 2022). Thus, the Organisation for Economic Cooperation and Development projections indicated that between 2000 and 2020, there would be an increase of 63% of the labor force aged 50 to 64 (The Organization for Economic Cooperation and Development, 2020).

This is already verified in developed countries such as those belonging to the European Union, Sweden, Canada, Australia, Israel, China, and Mexico, among others, thus showing that this is a worldwide phenomenon (Rinsky-Halivni et al., 2022; Rodriguez & Saenz, 2022; Stengård et al., 2022; Stone & Harkiolakis, 2022; Zhang & Wood, 2022). To combat labor shortages in developed countries due to an aging population and a low birth rate, most countries have adopted policies such as postponing the retirement age to extend working life in order to mitigate a possible shortage of workers in the current labor market, and as aging has become a global phenomenon, this practice has also become prevalent worldwide (Rinsky-Halivni et al., 2022; Rodriguez & Saenz, 2022; Stengård et al., 2022; Stone & Harkiolakis, 2022; Zhang & Wood, 2022). On the other hand, this issue is only being discovered in underdeveloped countries such as Bangladesh. However, experts are already saying that the retirement age will have to be raised for retirees to be economically self-sufficient and independent (Islam et al., 2022).

Times have changed, and currently, many individuals intend to work beyond retirement age, either because they wish to remain active, either physically or intellectually, or to make up for some insufficiencies in the pension they will receive, or even due to the difficulties of social security systems. Simultaneously, new knowledge about physiology and human anatomy and cumulatively about human aging was developed and acquired (Pinto et al., 2015). Individuals must realize that aging does not translate into something negative but may very well be the opposite to be something positive for the individual, such as improved health, financial security, and social and family participation (Pinto et al., 2015). Due to an increasingly aging population, but also more active, it was considered necessary to define the concept of Active Aging based on three pillars: health, participation, and security, with the perspective that people can maintain productive lives in society (World Health Organization, 2012).

Innovation

Innovation can be defined as the goal of creating something new; there is innovation when a concrete action is performed and results in something completely new, not necessarily having to be an innovation made from scratch (Viswanathan & Sridharan, 2011).

Innovation is also defined as a process that results in a new concept or a new way of seeing and solving a problem, resulting in the transformation of the same in a new product, technology, or service or through the redesign and restructuring of a product, technology, service or even form of production. The impact of innovation in organizations and societies translates into increased economic growth of a country in economic development, more jobs, and perhaps an improvement in living conditions (Urabe et al., 2018; Corodescu-Roşca et al., 2023).

Globalization has accelerated the process of innovation in organizations increasing technological complexity allied to the globalization process, the fierce competition currently felt in the markets, and the scarcity of resources forced organizations to change their way of acting (Corodescu-Roşca et al., 2023; Zhang et al., 2023). This pressure results in a goal of always being ahead of the competition, thus forcing organizations to attract and retain the most qualified employees to promote and foster an environment of innovation for the development of new strategic sectors, promote digitalization and innovation in the existing sectors of the organization (Corodescu-Roşca et al., 2023). This way, innovation has been widely explored in academia, business, and governments.

The literature shows that more than entrepreneurial organizations and entrepreneurs alone are needed to guarantee economic growth. However, in these organizations and economic agents, the highest rates of innovation are found, leading to more significant economic development and growth and a more remarkable change in society (Pindado et al., 2023). Entrepreneurs need always to pay attention to and interact with all existing stakeholders in their action process; thanks to this interaction, entrepreneurial organizations can drive innovation within their organization and consequently enable the organization's development (Pindado et al., 2023).

There are two types of innovation, open innovation and closed innovation. Open innovation is based on the assumption that organizations do not use only their resources going to seek information and references outside the organization, seeking such information within universities, public opinion, an innovation center for creative and technological companies, or even among other organizations because the sum of all information allows to expand the market and apply this innovation externally when it is fully developed (Chesbrough, 2006; Zhang et al., 2023). Compared to closed innovation, it is assumed that organizations only explore knowledge uniquely and exclusively within them. The entire creative and innovative process takes place within the organization; as such, organizations that invest in this type of innovation seek to gather and retain the best and most qualified professionals in the area to seek solutions and innovative answers. Everything is treated with strict confidentiality, and only after the completion of the product is there an external disclosure (Zhang et al., 2023). Contrary to the internal innovation process that may have to disclose and share patents and copyrights, this only sometimes happens; in closed innovation, the rights and intellectual property are uniquely and exclusively of the organization. A wide variety of ecological and social problems can be solved now and in the future through innovation, the applicability of new technologies, and new approaches to thinking, approaching, and developing problems (Gaspar & Mabic, 2015).

Innovation emerges in this way as a critical factor for social development since many of the innovations that have occurred recently have resulted in a benefit for society and, in many cases for humanity, not only thanks to innovative thinking but also innovative environments, a correct and effective implementation allows to face obstacles in a world in constant evolution and change (Gaspar & Mabic, 2015; Makridis & McGuire, 2023; Zhang et al., 2023).

Creativity

Creativity is an innate characteristic of human beings, either by curiosity for a novelty or by approaching a specific subject (Das et al., 2023). Creativity originated in psychology, focusing mainly on identifying creative traits and, consequently, the creative process (Curnin et al., 2022). Only when solutions as tangible and intangible forms, such as strategies, ideas, and solutions to current problems, were equally analyzed and studied were addressed in studies in management, for example (Curnin et al., 2022).

Globalization and rampant technological advances have created complex challenges and fierce competition for organizations (Destiana & Handayani, 2022). Thus, creativity emerges as a critical factor for the success of organizations because creativity is the embryonic phase of innovation, through the production of innovative and effective ideas in the market, being often confused creativity with innovation, which translates into the practical application of the innovative idea that was obtained through the creative process (Destiana & Handayani, 2022; Pedota & Piscitello, 2022).

The fierce competition existing in the markets translates thanks to the digitalization and emergence of new technologies and technological innovation and, as such, requires organizations to have a rapid capacity for change in order to meet the needs and, therefore, the demands of their customers to remain competitive in the market, as such organizations need to constantly find themselves ahead concerning presenting innovations in order to meet the demands, tastes, and preferences of their customers (Destiana & Handayani, 2022).

Nowadays, creativity is one of the main skills sought in the labor market, regardless of the industry or business area, provided that the function at home imperatively requires the ability to create new ideas, new technologies, and new products, among others (Katz et al., 2022). According to Cerne et al. (2022), creativity also presupposes the creation of innovative and valuable ideas for society. Das et al. (2023) also refer to the importance of creativity in creating original and valuable ideas as a critical factor for organizations to meet the challenges of an increasingly competitive market, meeting the needs and demands of customers in a complex and unpredictable environment.

Thus, an organization's human capital is the main asset when it comes to the creative capacity of the organization. However, for this to be possible, it is necessary that the organization can motivate and encourage employees (Destiana & Handayani, 2022).

Aging and Innovation

As a result, there is a relationship between the exchange of knowledge and experience between older employees and the other employees in an organization, in the sense that this exchange of information and knowledge allows for the creation of a space for the exchange of ideas, which results in the development of organizational innovation processes. According to Hargadon and Bechky (2006) and Cirillo et al. (2013), this mixes the expertise and knowledge of older employees, which has been strengthened by years of experience, with the innovation and freshness of younger employees (Guillén & Kunze, 2019). Although older employees traditionally have fewer academic skills, they have more work and social experience, whereas younger employees have the inverse of these characteristics. Combining each age group's strengths provides more leverage for developing creative and inventive thinking (Chand & Markova, 2019).

According to the authors Anzola-Román et al. (2018) and Bouncken et al. (2021), innovation emerges from the interaction of various players from different professional areas and hierarchical levels within an organization, necessitating a set of characteristics that must be combined and owned by the various participants, such as creative expertise, knowledge, and learning processes.

Regarding the notion that aging influences the innovation process, Guillén and Kunze (2019) point to a lack of consistency in the current literature, as well as in the existing literature that supports and refutes the perception of aging as a hindrance to innovation, however, according to the authors of their study, there is a loss in the potential for creativity because of the passage of time. On the other hand, organizational interaction can readily bridge this gap, allowing for diverse knowledge and new ideas. Chand and Markova (2019) support this notion by stating that, even though older employees remain in the organization for a more extended period, work for a longer period, and are more loyal to the organization, they have slightly lower levels of creativity and innovation than younger employees.

While Johnson et al. (2018) argue that aging may be the new driver for innovation, business development, and economic growth in the long run, they also point to several opportunities that should be exploited to enable innovative development while encouraging active aging.

Aging and Creativity

Since creativity and innovation are inextricably linked, it is only possible to discuss innovation by addressing the issue of creativity. The literature also states that creativity is a critical differentiator compared to the competition (Vasconcelos, 2018).

Thus, as with innovation, senior employees play an essential role in organizations regarding creativity, as they have greater confidence to develop and suggest more creative ideas. However, some authors caution that the most effective way to produce creative ideas that inherently lead to innovation within organizations is through the interaction between older and younger employees (Binnewies et al., 2008; Verworn & Hipp, 2009; Vasconcelos, 2018).

In contrast to the invention, there is no evidence that aging causes a decline in creativity because this quality is related to a person's personality (Vasconcelos, 2018). Even though innovation and creativity are two notions that are frequently associated with one another, they do not signify the same thing. Although the differences appear evident, the definitions of the ideas need to be more frequently understood and even conflated. To put it another way, we can say that creativity is a stage in the process of thinking and structuring ideas and that it is a situation from which innovation develops with the materialization and implementation of the idea obtained by an individual through his or her creativity, which is derived from his or her creative thinking. In other words, innovation occurs due to creativity (Bousinakis & Halkos, 2021).

Innovative Work Behavior

The aging of the workforce, as well as the increasing cognitive demands placed on the duties performed by the employees of companies, have been demonstrated to have resulted in characteristics that will have an impact on the labor market and organizations throughout time (Hernaus et al., 2019). Job roles that require higher levels of cognitive capacity, such as those requiring creative thinking, problem-solving abilities, and decision-making processes, highlight the necessity of developing the notion of Individual Innovative Work Behavior (IWB) in the workplace (Hernaus et al., 2019).

IWB is essential for guaranteeing the long-term viability of an enterprise because it gives reciprocal benefits to the firm and its personnel. In this view, there are many definitions of IWB in the literature. However, it is also feasible to assume that it is fundamentally translated into individual behaviors that aim to produce, promote, and implement new ideas (Jankelová et al., 2021).

These workers' cognitive capacities can be impaired by age, as indicated by their slower information processing speed and shorter attention span. This is especially true in a labor market where the workforce is becoming increasingly elderly. In this sense, the concept of IWB may be diminished in specific age groups, particularly in the younger generation (Hernaus et al., 2019).

Furthermore, it is important to remember that the more complicated a specific working function is, the more significant mental effort is necessary to complete the task. Complicated situations can be considered a technique for enhancing employees' IWB by presenting them with obstacles. Once a situation has been identified, employees must respond by generating innovative solutions (Hernaus et al., 2019).

Growing importance has been placed on recognizing and identifying factors that impact the IWB, particularly in the context of small and medium-sized enterprises, which are regarded as essential structural parts of economic growth and influential employment providers. Knezovic and Drkic (2020) did a study in which they discovered that IWB is positively associated with psychological empowerment, participation in decision-making, and organizational justice. Transformational leadership also functions as a mediator between organizational justice and IWB in the linkage between the two concepts.

CONTRIBUTIONS, LIMITATIONS, AND FUTURE RESEARCH DIRECTION

This study aims to provide an opportunity for reflection, increasing the understanding of the importance of studies related to senior workers, notorious the scarcity of studies on the vast majority of themes that address the aging workforce, deserving a more holistic approach by academics. It is also expected that this chapter will allow us to demystify some myths and preconceived ideas about the role of older employees in the process of creativity and innovation in organizations, as they are identified as critical elements in the innovation and economic growth of countries.

Therefore, it is hoped that this chapter will provide the necessary resources for decision-makers in the five-way helix to adopt solutions for a new social and economic reality with a direct impact on the workforce by promoting the transfer of knowledge and experience in organizations and society in order to promote economic growth and development.

A limitation of this chapter is that it only analyzed a theoretical perspective on the issues addressed in the chapter. There is no practical application of it either from a quantitative data collection perspective or a qualitative case study, among others, so that this study can be more robust in the future. It should be analyzed how organizations use their older employees to drive and provide an environment of creativity and innovation.

CONCLUSION

It is concluded that aging is an unstoppable process and innate to any human being; combined with the fact that there is a significant increase in average life expectancy, an improvement in health and hygiene systems, and a reduction in birth and mortality rates makes this same aging will have a direct impact on the available workforce, so it becomes essential for governments and organizations to think about the best way to ensure the permanence of older employees in organizations.

This phenomenon of demographic aging and aging of the workforce translates not only at the European level, where this phenomenon was first recorded, but there is a globalization of the same since it already affects the European, American, Asian, and Oceanic continent, even in the African continent the most developed countries of that continent are already projecting changes in their age pyramid in the medium-long term. As such, the state has used as measures to maintain the aging workforce the increase in the retirement age and penalties for those who want to retire before the age set by law to retire.

Innovation is the creation of something new, be it a concept, a new way of approaching a problem, a new product, technology, service, or restructuring. The impact of innovation on organizations, individuals, and society is undeniable since it translates into economic growth, more jobs, and improved quality of life.

Creativity is an innate characteristic of many individuals, and organizations do everything they can to attract and retain the best and most qualified employees who possess this skill, much due to the fierce competition existing in today's market due to globalization and digitalization so that they are ahead of their competitors. Creativity is the phase after innovation. Creativity is the idea behind the practical execution of a new product, being this product is what we call innovation.

This chapter allows us to verify a positive direct correlation regarding the exchange of knowledge and experiences between older and younger employees. This exchange creates an innovative environment within the organization. As both have their strengths, in the case of older employees, they have significant strengths in terms of having more years of experience and more practical knowledge allied to the better technological and innovative capacity of younger employees; the potent combination of these strengths enables the development of critical and inventive thinking. Although traditionally, in society, it is thought that older employees have a lower capacity for innovation, this chapter allows us to demonstrate that this is not true.

As creativity and innovation are two intrinsically linked themes, it is also mentioned in this chapter that the best way to enhance creativity in an organization is through interaction and exchange of knowledge and experiences between older and younger employees.

REFERENCES

Anzola-Román, P., Bayona-Saez, C., & García-Marco, T. (2018). Organizational innovation, internal R&D and externally sourced innovation practices: Effects on technological innovation outcomes. *Journal of Business Research, 91*, 233–247. doi:10.1016/j.jbusres.2018.06.014

Binnewies, C., Ohly, S., & Niessen, C. (2008). Age and creativity at work: The interplay between job resources, age and idea creativity. *Journal of Managerial Psychology, 23*(4), 438–457. doi:10.1108/02683940810869042

Bouncken, R. B., Ratzmann, M., & Kraus, S. (2021). Anti-aging: How innovation is shaped by firm age and mutual knowledge creation in an alliance. *Journal of Business Research, 137*, 422–429. doi:10.1016/j.jbusres.2021.08.056

Bousinakis, D., & Halkos, G. (2021). Creativity as the hidden development factor for organizations and employees. *Economic Analysis and Policy, 71*, 645–659. doi:10.1016/j.eap.2021.07.003

Cepellos, V. (2018). Envelhecimento nas Organizações: Os Grandes Debates sobre o Tema nos Estudos de Administração de Empresas [Aging in Organizations: The Major Debates on the Topic in Business Administration Studies]. *Teoria e Prática em Administração, 8*(1), 138–159. doi:10.21714/2238-104X2018v8i1-37614

Cerne, M., Bunjak, A., Wong, S.-I., & Moh'd, S. S. (2022). I'm creative and deserving! From self-rated creativity to creative recognition. *Creativity and Innovation Management, 31*(4), 664–679. doi:10.1111/caim.12518

Chand, M., & Markova, G. (2019). The European Union's aging population: Challenges for human resource management. *Thunderbird International Business Review, 61*(3), 519–529. doi:10.1002/tie.22023

Chesbrough, H. W. (2006). *Open innovation: The new imperative for creating and profiting from technology*. Harvard Business Press.

Cirillo, B., Brusoni, S., & Valentini, G. (2013). The rejuvenation of inventors through corporate spinouts. *Organization Science, 25*(6), 1764–1784. doi:10.1287/orsc.2013.0868

Corodescu-Roşca, E., Hamdouch, A., & Iatu, C. (2023). Innovation in urban governance and economic resilience. The case of two Romanian regional metropolises: Timişoara and Cluj Napoca. *Cities (London, England), 132*, 104090. Advance online publication. doi:10.1016/j.cities.2022.104090

Curnin, S., Brooks, B., & Brooks, O. (2022). Assessing the influence of individual creativity, perceptions of group decision-making and structured techniques on the quality of scenario planning. *Futures, 144*, 103057. doi:10.1016/j.futures.2022.103057

Das, K., Patel, J. D., Sharma, A., & Shukla, Y. (2023). Creativity in marketing: Examining the intellectual structure using scientometric analysis and topic modeling. *Journal of Business Research, 154*, 113384. doi:10.1016/j.jbusres.2022.113384

Destiana, R., & Handayani, W. (2022). Exploring the Role of Levers of Control in a Work Environment That Supports Innovative Behavior (An Empirical Study at PT. SEMB). *Quality - Access to Success, 23*(199), 253–265. doi:10.47750/QAS/23.191.30

Gaspar, D., & Mabic, M. (2015). Creativity in Higher Education. *Universal Journal of Educational Research, 3*(9), 598–605. doi:10.13189/ujer.2015.030903

Guillén, L., & Kunze, F. (2019). When age does not harm innovative behavior and perceptions of competence: Testing interdepartmental collaboration as a social buffer. *Human Resource Management, 58*(3), 301–316. doi:10.1002/hrm.21953

Hargadon, A. B., & Bechky, B. A. (2006). When collections of creatives become creative collectives: A field study of problem solving at work. *Organization Science, 17*(4), 484–500. doi:10.1287/orsc.1060.0200

Hernaus, T., Maric, M., & Černe, M. (2019). Age-sensitive job design antecedents of innovative work behavior: The role of cognitive job demands. *Journal of Managerial Psychology, 34*(5), 368–382. doi:10.1108/JMP-10-2018-0478

Islam, M. S., Ng, T. K. S., Manierre, M., Hamiduzzaman, M., & Tareque, M. I. (2022). Modifications of Traditional Formulas to Estimate and Project Dependency Ratios and Their Implications in a Developing Country, Bangladesh. *Population Research and Policy Review, 41*(5), 1931–1949. doi:10.100711113-022-09720-8 PMID:35572094

Jankelová, N., Joniaková, Z., & Mišún, J. (2021). Innovative Work Behavior—A Key Factor in Business Performance? The Role of Team Cognitive Diversity and Teamwork Climate in This Relationship. *Journal of Risk and Financial Management, 14*(4), 1–16. doi:10.3390/jrfm14040185

Johnson, J. H. Jr, Parnell, A. M., & Lian, H. (2018). Aging as an Engine of Innovation, Business Development, and Employment Growth. *Economic Development Journal, 17*(3), 32–42.

Katz, J. H., Mann, T. C., Shen, X., Goncalo, J. A., & Ferguson, M. J. (2022). Implicit impressions of creative people: Creativity evaluation in a stigmatized domain. *Organizational Behavior and Human Decision Processes, 169*, 104116. doi:10.1016/j.obhdp.2021.104116

Knezovic, E., & Drkic, A. (2020). Innovative work behavior in SMEs: The role of transformational leadership. *Employee Relations: The International Journal, 43*(2), 398–415. doi:10.1108/ER-03-2020-0124

Makridis, C. A., & McGuire, E. (2023). The quality of innovation "Booms" during "Busts.". *Research Policy, 52*(1), 104657. doi:10.1016/j.respol.2022.104657

Pedota, M., & Piscitello, L. (2022). A new perspective on technology-driven creativity enhancement in the Fourth Industrial Revolution. *Creativity and Innovation Management, 31*(1), 109–122. doi:10.1111/caim.12468

Pindado, E., Sánchez, M., & Martínez, M. G. (2023). Entrepreneurial innovativeness: When too little or too much agglomeration hurts. *Research Policy, 52*(1), 104625. doi:10.1016/j.respol.2022.104625

Pinto, A. M. G. L. R. S., da Silva Ramos, S. C. M., & Nunes, S. M. M. D. (2015). Managing an Aging Workforce: What is the Value of Human Resource Management Practices for Different Age Groups of Workers? *Tékhne (Instituto Politécnico do Cávado e do Ave), 12*, 58–68. doi:10.1016/j.tekhne.2015.01.007

Rinsky-Halivni, L., Hovav, B., Christiani, D. C., & Brammli-Grinberg, S. (2022). Aging workforce with reduced work capacity: From organizational challenges to successful accommodations sustaining productivity and well-being. *Social Science & Medicine, 312*, 115369. doi:10.1016/j.socscimed.2022.115369 PMID:36162364

Rodriguez, F. S., & Saenz, J. (2022). Working in old age in Mexico: Implications for cognitive functioning. *Ageing and Society, 42*(11), 1–21. doi:10.1017/S0144686X2100012X

Settels, J. (2022). The Health Effects of Workforce Involvement and Transitions for Europeans 50–75 Years of Age: Heterogeneity by Financial Difficulties and Gender. *Canadian Journal on Aging, 41*(3), 304–319. doi:10.1017/S0714980821000556 PMID:35859357

Stengård, J., Leineweber, C., Virtanen, M., Westerlund, H., & Wang, H.-X. (2022). Do good psychosocial working conditions prolong working lives? Findings from a prospective study in Sweden. *European Journal of Ageing, 19*(3), 1–12. doi:10.100710433-021-00672-0 PMID:36052189

Stone, A., & Harkiolakis, N. (2022). Technology Boom(ers): How US Multinational Technology Companies Are Preparing for an Ageing Workforce. *Administrative Sciences, 12*(3), 1–14. doi:10.3390/admsci12030091

The Organization for Economic Cooperation and Development. (2020). *OECD Data: Labour Force Participation Rate.* Retrieved from https://data.oecd.org/searchresults/?q=labour+force+participation+rate

Urabe, K., Child, J., & Kagono, T. (2018). *Innovation and Management: International Comparisons* (13th ed.). De Gruyter.

Vasconcelos, A. F. (2018). Older workers as a source of wisdom capital: Broadening perspectives. *Revista de Gestão, 25*(1), 102–118. doi:10.1108/REGE-11-2017-002

Verworn, B., & Hipp, C. (2009). Does the ageing workforce hamper the innovativeness of firms? (No) evidence from Germany. *International Journal of Human Resources Development and Management, 9*(2/3), 180–197. doi:10.1504/IJHRDM.2009.023452

Viswanathan, M., & Sridharan, S. (2011). Product Development for the BoP: Insights on Concept and Prototype Development from University-Based Student Projects in India. *Journal of Product Innovation Management, 29*(1), 52–69. doi:10.1111/j.1540-5885.2011.00878.x

World Health Organization. (2012). *World Health Day 2012: ageing and health: toolkit for event organizers.* Retrieved from https://apps.who.int/iris/handle/10665/70840

Zhang, W., & Wood, S. (2022). Awareness of age-related change, chronological age, subjective age and proactivity: An empirical study in China. *Frontiers in Psychiatry, 13*, 915673. doi:10.3389/fpsyt.2022.915673 PMID:36245881

Zhang, Z., Jin, J., Li, S., & Zhang, Y. (2023). Digital transformation of incumbent firms from the perspective of portfolios of innovation. *Technology in Society, 72*, 102149. doi:10.1016/j.techsoc.2022.102149

KEY TERMS AND DEFINITIONS

Aging: Is based on the demographic aging of the population inherent to the increase in average life expectancy and improvements in health and hygiene conditions, together with the decrease in birth and mortality rates.

Creativity: This is a competency described as the ability to imagine, produce, create, or invent new ideas or concepts; such thinking is the predecessor of the innovation process through the creation of a new idea or way of looking at a problem or a new process.

Economic Growth: It consists of the increase in the production of one or several economic units over one or several periods. Such an increase presupposes the nation's enrichment and improving the standard of living.

Innovation: Its goal is to create something new or introduce novelties through the renewal or re-creation of a given product or way of producing. Such a process necessarily means changing or improving a given product or way of producing and is one of the engines of economic growth.

Innovative Work Behavior: This translates as the innovative behavior of an individual, applying his or her creativity, skills, and knowledge in a process capable of generating innovative ideas and elaborate projects that allow putting those ideas into practice regarding new products, new ways of producing, or reinventing a product.

Knowledge Transfer: Refers to the exchange of life experiences, technical knowledge, and practical knowledge among the various employees of the organization, either between age segments or within the same age segment.

Skills: Consists of the knowledge, skills, and attitudes inherent to an individual user in performing an individual's function.

Chapter 6
Restructuring the Workforce Through Non-Ageist Hiring and Retention Practices That Value Aging Workers' Expertise:
Recognizing the Need for Workplace Age Diversity

Nadine E. Franz
https://orcid.org/0000-0002-2713-3108
Baylor University, USA

ABSTRACT

The aging workforce faces obstacles in a youth-obsessed society. Ageist assumptions dominate the airwaves, where society celebrates youth while undervaluing older people. These stereotypes permeate as companies marginalize older people while sending veiled messages that diminish their worth. Older people endure barriers, whether seeking new opportunities or promotions. Ageism is widespread, and hiring and retention practices often neglect older workers. The disregard for more senior talent results from ageist stereotypes. These biases ignore older employees' worth. Employer mistreatment of older employees signals their lack of commitment to diversity. Employers must implement non-ageist HR initiatives while continuously holding themselves accountable for executing fair employment policies. This chapter explores ageist issues, controversies, problems, and steps employers must take to create and implement non-ageist hiring and retention policies to safeguard a diverse workforce.

DOI: 10.4018/978-1-6684-6351-2.ch006

INTRODUCTION

Older employees often face barriers, whether seeking new employment opportunities or promotions and career progression within their existing places of employment (Hirsch et al., 2000). These career blockades result from ageism, also called *age discrimination*. Workplace ageism is prevalent, and hiring and retention practices often neglect older workers and further undervalue their talents and expertise (Osborne & McCann, 2004). Older workers offer tremendous value to the workplace, yet some employers perpetuate ageist practices (Capowski, 1994) that snub older people's talents (Hujsak, 2015). As a result, many older job seekers feel overlooked and frustrated while seeking new employment (Franz et al., 2022). For example, in a 2020 study of 30 job seekers aged 50–83 across the United States (U.S.), the participants unanimously expressed feeling unappreciated and disrespected in a labor market that made them feel worthless (Franz, 2021). In addition, 93% of the participants voiced disgust because they knew they were the victims of ageism but had no way to prove it because of age discrimination's obscureness (Franz, 2021). This obscureness makes ageism difficult to prove objectively because of carefully hidden ageist practices within seemingly legitimate human resources (HR) and hiring policies (Franz, 2021). Moreover, this obscureness perpetuates ageism's omnipresence within many companies (Franz et al., 2022). For this reason, ageism's veil is difficult, if not impossible, to detect, enabling employers to sidestep employment laws (Lesonsky, 2017). Moreover, there is evidence that some job descriptions target a younger audience (North & Fiske, 2013) through ageist language that dissuades older employees from applying for positions they are qualified to perform (Petery & Grosch, 2022).

The unfair workplace exclusion of aging employees is wrong and causes career damage for older employees (Hujsak, 2015). Age discrimination is an atrocity, and change requires corporate prioritization through targeted recruitment and retention initiatives that hold company leaders accountable. In addition, the aging workforce wants to work and rely on employment for financial security, their sense of well-being, and to feel like they are still a part of society (Schulte et al., 2018).

This chapter discusses the problem of ageism and explores transformational steps for employers to create and implement non-ageist hiring and retention policies and procedures to safeguard a diverse workforce. The aging population potentially augments and fosters diverse and inclusive workplaces that engender organizational growth (Kulik et al., 2014). As the population ages rapidly, employers must adapt their mindsets to capitalize on the older workforce's vast expertise. According to Kulik et al. (2014), some countries are adopting numerous national policies to respond to an aging population. Consequently, companies must develop, implement, and sustain innovative, comprehensive talent acquisition practices to attract, train, and retain their aging employees (Kulik et al., 2014).

This chapter aims to help organizations get honest about their ageist hiring practices, so they can engender non-ageist inclusive recruiting, hiring, and retention policies that appreciate older employees' knowledge, skills, and abilities (KSA). This author accomplishes this mission in five steps. First, the author highlights the issues of ageism. Second, the author explains the depth and breadth of controversies about ageism with evidence from the empirical literature. Third, the author discusses the problem that impedes progress toward eradicating ageism. Fourth, the author offers solutions and recommendations for companies to develop and implement non-ageist hiring and retention policies. Finally, the author suggests future research directions.

BACKGROUND AND KEY TERMS

Butler (1989) coined the term *ageism* and described it as the premeditated classification and discriminatory treatment of older people. This form of discrimination is problematic, especially in a rapidly aging society that results from lower birth rates and an increase in the average lifespan that has caused upsurges in the elderly population (Kulik et al., 2014). For this chapter, older and aging employees interchangeably refer to any employee or job seeker aged 50 and older. Aging workers are great resources for employers because they offer skills and knowledge that potentially help their younger counterparts gain new insights. Therefore, a corporate focus on implementing fair, equitable, and non-ageist employment practices has significant implications for companies and their younger employees, who reap the benefits of the expertise and wisdom of a qualified, aging workforce.

The number of people aged 60 and older will rise to an estimated two billion by 2050 (Viviani et al., 2021). These data are alarming, considering that companies' ageist practices limit the aging workforce's ability to obtain new employment or achieve promotions, thus limiting their career progression (Stypinska & Turek, 2017). The aging population's growth highlights a need for companies to hire and retain older employees to fill job openings while fostering cross-generational collaborations to drive company growth, productivity, and development. Unfortunately, the aging population takes their knowledge, skills, and abilities with them when they exit the labor market (Franz et al., 2022). This knowledge and skills gap presents a brain drain. This talent drain has dire consequences, one that employers cannot easily replace by hiring younger, less experienced employees (Cortijo et al., 2019). In addition, employers' failure to recognize the need to hire and retain an older workforce conveys a disregard for cross-generational workplaces that benefit from the expertise shared between younger and more senior employees. This indifference signals a biased perception of the value of age. Moreover, the problem of ageism is proof of top leadership's indifference to the value that older employees offer the workforce (Lyons et al., 2014).

Employers' failure to prioritize the recruitment, hiring, and retention of older talent stems from employers' stereotypical biases towards more senior employees (Gringart et al., 2005; Taylor & Walker, 1998). This unfair ageist typecast sidelines the aging workforce (Lyons et al., 2014) and sends covert messages that lessen their worth compared to younger people (Malinen & Johnston, 2013). Additionally, these disguised ageist hiring policies suggest that the aging workforce is incapable of competing in the labor market (Hujsak, 2015). Conversely, there is no proof of older workers' incompetence and zero indication of productivity differences between younger and more senior employees (Viviani et al., 2021). Furthermore, little empirical evidence proves that older employees are less productive than younger people (Schulte et al., 2018).

Age discrimination results from ageist values dominating the airwaves, where society celebrates youth while underestimating older people as feeble and less capable. This disregard for older people is troubling and further compounded by the fact that approximately 10.9% of the aging workforce became unemployed at the onset of the COVID-19 pandemic (Davis et al., 2020). The obsession with youth is worrisome, considering unemployed people aged 55 to 70 in developed countries represent a viable, overlooked, and under-utilized talent pool (Kulik et al., 2014). Yet, despite the availability of this untapped aging candidate pool, ageism persists.

An understanding of the key terms in this chapter is essential for readers. Therefore, key terms plainly and unswervingly entwine throughout this section and other chapter areas to elucidate terms that ensure comprehensive understanding (Creswell, 2014). In addition, the author also uses human resource industry jargon for which there are no citations. Ageism results from prejudice or discrimination solely based on a person's age and embody biased attitudes and discriminatory practices toward older people (Oliveira, 2017). These ageist attitudes prevail and manifest in the unfavorable treatment of individuals solely based on age (Berger, 2009).

In the U.S., the aging workforce receives protection under federal employment laws (U.S. Department of Labor, Bureau of Labor Statistics, 2018). These laws fall within the Bureau of Labor Statistics (BLS), the federal agency within the U.S. Department of Labor (DOL) that evaluates workplace events, the treatment of employees, and economic factors and fluctuations that impact society (U.S. Department of Labor, Bureau of Labor Statistics, 2018). The laws aim to prevent discrimination, the practice of inflicting prejudicial treatment individually and categorically against members of a protected group (U.S. Equal Employment Opportunity Commission, 2019). The Equal Employment Opportunity Commission (EEOC) oversees and enforces civil rights laws involving workplace discrimination at the federal level (U.S. Equal

Employment Opportunity Commission, 2019). Incidentally, the *macroculture*, the shared White-dominated core culture of the U.S. (Banks, 2016), inflicts ageist biases against older employees and job seekers (U.S. Department of Labor, Bureau of Labor Statistics, 2018).

Additionally, the Older Workers Benefit Protection Act (OWBPA) defends older workers and job seekers from discrimination by companies due to age throughout the recruitment, hiring, performance of job duties, and separation of the employment process. U.S. employment laws categorize these employees as a protected class or a group of employees or job seekers entitled to special protection under U.S. laws concerning age, race, color, national origin, sex, physical or mental disability, religion or creed, and veteran status (U.S. Equal Employment Opportunity Commission, 2019). Employment laws should protect the aging workforce from unfair recruiting practices or companies' questionable hiring practices that disenfranchise protected class members (U.S. Equal Employment Opportunity Commission, 2019) in a youth-obsessed society that promotes youthfulness as the standard of beauty and relevance (Roscigno, 2010).

Despite the societal obsession with youth, many organizations support the hiring, retention, training, and development of an older workforce. For example, the following three organizations promote initiatives addressing staffing gaps with an older, experienced workforce. First, The Older Worker Initiative drives strategies to improve older Americans' ability to maintain employment, pursue alternative work, or pursue entrepreneurship (Taskforce on the Aging of the American Workforce, n.d.). Second, the Age-Friendly Institute spearheads lucrative approaches to enhancing excellent results for the aging population in workplaces, communities, and other locations (Age-Friendly Institute, n.d.). Finally, Back To Work 50+, an AARP Foundation program, offers employment training and resources to older Americans through partnerships with local employers (AARP Foundation, n.d.). These organizations, among others, understand the value that older employees offer the labor market and are unwavering in their commitment to exterminating workplace ageism.

Before offering solutions to the problem of workplace ageism, it is crucial to demonstrate the corporate embeddedness of workplace ageism, which Veldon (2013) described as unfair treatment of applicants or employees because of age. Therefore, this chapter discusses the problem of ageism and ageism's prevalence by engaging the scholarship to support the position that workplace ageism is a problem. Ageism impacts older workers' employment and job searches (Franz et al., 2022; Rippon et al., 2014; Veldon, 2013). This prevalence is troubling because of its implications for older job seekers who miss employment opportunities and promotions because employers fail to recognize and validate their worth in the labor market (Hujsak, 2015; Capowski, 1994). The problem of age discrimination negatively impacts employees, resulting in decreased morale and an ethical quandary (Kulik et al., 2014). Ageism is rooted in society's obsession with youth (Nolan, 2011), an obsession celebrated daily in the media.

Age discrimination spills over from society into the workplace, where the aging workforce is falsely stereotyped and denied employment opportunities based on falsehoods (Malinen & Johnston, 2013). Ageism is the damaging treatment of people due to their age (Roscigno, 2010). Research shows that some employers evaluate older prospective hires and employees through ageist recruiting, hiring, and retention practices and policies (Franz et al., 2022). Additionally, in a study of 20 countries around the globe, including the U.S., the United Kingdom, and Sri Lanka, the researchers described ageism as a phenomenon less focused on the demographics of aging and instead on society's cultural values (Ng & Lim-Soh, 2021) focused on youthfulness and ageist stereotypes.

Not only are these stereotypes untrue, but they are challenging to detect, making them harder to fight. In addition, these roundabout practices (Stypinska & Turek, 2017) manifests in unsubstantiated stereotypes about older people, further isolating the aging population from employment opportunities (Barrington, 2015). Furthermore, these prejudices and groundless labels about the aging population are often obscure (Lesonsky, 2017) and problematic to distinguish (Franz et al., 2022). For example, according to Wanberg et al. (2016), there is an indication of a parallel between age and reemployment status, particularly for people over age 50. Accordingly, this alarming correlation circumvents employment opportunities and promotions for older employees.

Some employers disregard legislation protecting the older workforce (Franz et al., 2022). The EEOC levies the Age Discrimination in Employment Act of 1967 (U.S. Equal Employment Opportunity Commission, 2019). Additionally, the OWBPA shelters employees over the age of 40 from age-related discrimination by employers based on age during the hiring, working, and termination of employment (U.S. Department of Labor, Bureau of Labor Statistics, 2018); yet, some employers disregard these laws (Grossman, 2013). Many employers establish and perpetuate abstruse hiring and retention practices to defy employment laws, thus evading penalties. Research highlights ageism's rise as companies discover and leverage loopholes and lawful tactics that safeguard their unfair hiring practices (Lesonsky, 2017). This perpetual evasion of the law leads to harsh consequences for older job seekers and employees, such as depression and long-term unemployment (Franz et al., 2022; Mandal et al., 2011).

Long-term unemployment and a lack of employment growth opportunities damage older job seekers and employees (Gibson et al., 2010). These aging employees lose their resolve when companies reject their skills and knowledge (Franz et al., 2022). The ageist exclusion of qualified older people oppresses them and causes despair and anxiety. Furthermore, the financial strain resulting from long periods of unemployment further victimizes older people (Clark, 2012) and causes depression (Mandal et al., 2011).

Employers obtain cumulative benefits from the older workers' knowledge and skills (Powell, 2010). Older workers are more experienced and educated, offering inestimable value to the workforce (Clark, 2012). Aging employees are vital resources, and employers who hire them benefit significantly from their vast contributions to the workplace (Clark, 2012). Older employees and job seekers deserve the same opportunities bestowed upon younger employees. For this reason, employers benefit when they recognize the need for equitable hiring practices (Friedman et al., 2016).

Employment discrimination based on age is wrong, as people do not control the aging process and should not suffer penalties for growing older. The literature established workplace ageism's deep-rooted manifestation within employers' practices. Age discrimination entrenchment in the labor market is undeniable. Its perpetuation of youth-obsessed decision-making based on false stereotypes about older employees has negative implications for an aging workforce. Moreover, ageism's ugly veil makes it easy for employers to circumvent labor laws. Unfortunately, this skirting of the rules creates forced long-term unemployment for older people, cheating their talents and expertise in the labor market. The following sections discuss the issues, controversies, and problems of workplace ageism and the failure of many companies to implement non-ageist hiring and retention policies and procedures to safeguard a diverse workforce.

AGEIST HIRING AND RETENTION PRACTICES NEGLECT OLDER WORKERS

This section discusses the issues, controversies, and problems of ageism and the associated impacts on older employees. These impacts result from ageist recruitment, hiring, retention, and promotion policies devaluing older talent in the labor market. As a result, some employers alienate an aging workforce, forcing these older talents into involuntary unemployment or early retirement (Franz et al., 2022; Stypinska & Turek, 2017; Wanberg et al., 2016; Powell, 2010). In addition, ageism's unprovable nature nests within unscrupulous HR policies and procedures, sending the message to an aging workforce that they are powerless (Wanberg et al., 2016; Powell, 2010).

Ageism practices prevail with no signs of ageist employers desiring to implement fair and equitable hiring policies and procedures (Capowski, 1994). For example, some companies use ageist job descriptions to support their discriminatory hiring practices that deny older job seekers employment opportunities throughout the candidate evaluation process (Richardson et al., 2013). In addition, many employers use untruthful stereotypes to prolong workplace ageism (Taylor & Walker, 1998; Capowski, 1994).

Some ageist stereotypes ignore the pros and focus on the fabricated cons of hiring older workers. Some pros include the skills and expertise older employees offer, their unwillingness to job-hop, their immense work ethic, and their track record of taking fewer days off from work (Columbia Public Health, 2022). The cons include employers' biases that older workers may be reluctant or incapable of following instructions, lack technical understanding to perform their duties, and display insubordination when reporting to younger managers (Capowski, 1994). Much of the cons result from ageist, unfair biases toward older employees (Franz, 2021), and the following sections expound on the depth of the issue of ageism, the associated arguments, and the difficulties resulting from ageism.

The Issues of Ageism Prevails, From Recruitment to Termination

Workplace ageism is an issue that begins for many older job seekers throughout the job search process and prevails until they willingly or reluctantly depart the labor market (Franz et al., 2022). The number of older employees will upsurge in the upcoming decades as the workforce ages (Truxillo et al., 2015). A 2013 AARP study of employees aged 45–74 revealed that roughly 60% of the employees claimed that their motivation for working derived from a financial necessity (Perron, 2013). This high percentage is astounding and demonstrates the need for employers to hire and retain older employees to maintain financial independence and support their lifestyles.

The aging population finds that, despite their willingness to work and vast skills and expertise, employers choose to overlook them in favor of younger talent. This oversight is challenging for older employers and leaves them feeling unwanted, inadequate, and discriminated against (Veldon, 2013). Additionally, employers often overlook aging employees for promotions because they think they are a flight risk and will soon depart the workforce because of their age (Roscigno, 2010; Lippmann, 2008). As a result, many older employees feel stuck because they are either denied new employment opportunities or overlooked for promotions. For many aging employees, this experience with ageism forces them prematurely out of the workplace because they lose faith in a labor market that denies them opportunities and a sense of belonging (Franz et al., 2022).

Age discrimination is concerning because it is often unprovable and masked behind seemingly ethical HR policies, practices, and procedures. Unfortunately, some companies develop and implement these veiled policies to alienate the older workforce while protecting themselves from discrimination lawsuits (Franz et al.,

2022; Stypinska & Turek, 2017; Wanberg et al., 2016; Powell, 2010). The Age Discrimination in Employment Act of 1967 (ADEA) is an American labor law prohibiting workplace discrimination against employees and job seekers 40 years of age or older (Nolan, 2011). Yet, employers carefully conceal these policies to defy longstanding employment laws, including the ADEA and OWBPA, which protect older employees from workplace discrimination. Although labor laws protect older employees aged 40 and older from workplace age-related bias that results in the unfair and unjust treatment of employees or job candidates 40 years of age or older (U.S. Equal Employment Opportunity Commission, 2019), some employers continue to implement ageist employment practices (U.S. Equal Employment Opportunity Commission, 2019). Moreover, some companies continually snub laws established by the BLS, the federal agency within the DOL that assesses companies' conduct towards older employees. Although older employees are members of a protected class because of their age (U.S. Department of Labor, Bureau of Labor Statistics, 2018), some companies still ignore EEOC guidelines to prolong ageism.

Ageism penetrates the workforce, and it does not appear that some employers are doing enough to create age-inclusive hiring practices (Capowski, 1994). Additionally, employers' defiance of the laws persists through the embeddedness of HR policies and procedures and bars opportunities for older employees. Some of these entrenched behaviors include policies about job description language, candidate sourcing, recruiting, interviewing, training, promotion, and retention (Barrington, 2015). These ageist HR policies intentionally ignore the aging workforce and convey that youth trumps experience (Roscigno, 2010). The following section discusses ageist hiring practices that impact the aging workforce.

There is evidence that some employers use ageist job descriptions as part of their hiring practices aimed at denying older job seekers opportunities during these employers' evaluation of the aging workforce's resumes and job applications (Richardson et al., 2013). In addition, some employers often write descriptions that target a younger talent pool through masked, ageist language (Franz et al., 2022). Some of this veiled language includes terms like *energetic*, *tech-savvy*, *innovative*, and *fast-paced*, even for positions where these requirements make very little sense (Franz et al., 2022).

Companies use ageist job descriptions to deter older candidates from applying for job openings (Roscigno, 2010). A recent review of over 50 job postings on Career Builder, LinkedIn, Glassdoor, Indeed, SimplyHired, company websites, and other job boards revealed signs of ageism, even though equal employment opportunity (EEO) statements accompanying the job announcements (Franz et al., 2022). For example, some descriptions signal a desire to hire tech-savvy and energetic employees, motioning a desire to hire a younger workforce (Lahey, 2005). When the ageist language fails to prevent older job seekers from applying, companies find creative ways to exclude their resumes, which are typically easy to detect because of their long work history, which sometimes reveals signs of age (Franz et al., 2022).

In a study of over 40,000 job applications, Neumark (2021) discovered ageism, with more evidence of age discrimination for older women than men. Additionally, in Carlsson and Eriksson's (2019) field study of 6,000 fictitious resumes submitted for fictitious candidates aged 35–70 in Sweden, the data revealed that the call-back rate for interviews gradually decreased as the ages of the fictitious candidates increased, much more so for women than men. There was an indication of employer typecasts about older employees' capacity to learn new skills, take on new tasks, demonstrate flexibility, and maintain motivation (Carlsson & Eriksson, 2019). Some of these stereotypes include notions that older employees lack technical aptitude, making them unsuitable for filling employment openings.

Additionally, many companies use social media recruitment strategies (Hosain et al., 2020), frequently alienating the aging workforce (Thompson & Mayhorn, 2012). Many employers utilize social media and technology-based hiring strategies and platforms to source, recruit, and interview a younger audience. These platforms include LinkedIn and Facebook (Rafique et al., 2021). Moreover, some employers use social media platforms geared toward younger audiences, including Twitter, Instagram, Tik Tok, Snapshot, and WhatsApp, to hire employees. Using social media platforms to recruit in an environment where many employees falsely claim that older people are not social media savvy sends the message that older candidates need not apply. Some employers' use of social media platforms relays a message that their workplaces are not interested in hiring and retaining older workers (Midtsundstad, 2011). Furthermore, this recruitment strategy enables some employers to find ways to discriminate without breaking the law (Lesonsky, 2017; Roscigno, 2010).

Some employers deny older workers career advancements based solely on unfair, ageist stereotyping despite the many benefits of hiring older employees. Many employers deny older employees career advancement opportunities when they block aging employees from training and promotion opportunities. In addition, some employers perpetuate false stereotypes of older employees' capacity to learn new tasks as they age (Davies et al., 2017; Findsen, 2015). The changing workplace demographic shift signals a need for employers to offer training and advancement opportunities for their aging workforce (Williams van Rooij, 2012). Although older workers make up a large portion of the labor market and offer valuable skills, many companies fail to provide the aging workforce with the same training opportunities as their younger coworkers (Davies et al., 2017).

Contrary to some employers' biased beliefs, older employees can learn and apply new skills, despite their age (Davies et al., 2017). There are numerous advantages to hiring older workers who have continually grown their knowledge and skills while enhancing their abilities to remain employable and competitive in the workplace.

Education and training improve the aging workforce's capacity to contribute to the workplace (Karmel & Woods, 2004). Karmel and Woods (2004) also posited that, at times, older employees who acquire new credentials, knowledge, and skills offer more significant benefits to employers. Unfortunately, some employers are hesitant to hire, train, retain, and promote older employees. This reluctance is due to employers' ageist attitudes and perceptions around the aging workforce's ability to learn, handle physical tasks, avoid workplace accidents, innovate, and collaborate with their younger counterparts (Taylor & Walker, 1998). These biases are unfounded and impede older employees' ability to thrive in the workplace.

Older employees face many obstacles throughout the job search process (Franz et al., 2022; Wanberg et al., 2016; Roscigno, 2010), and these problems persist after they obtain employment as many face challenges in gaining valuable training and promotion opportunities (Davies et al., 2017; Findsen, 2015). These challenges are disheartening for many older employees who feel devalued (Stypinska & Turek, 2017). Ageist hiring and retention practices also prematurely force older out of the workforce. Ageist job descriptions discourage older job-seekers from applying, making them feel they would not be hired simply because of their age (Roscigno, 2010). Furthermore, once hired, employers fail to recognize the demographic shift in the workplace, imposing the need for employers to train and develop their aging employees (Williams van Rooij, 2012). To create inclusive workplaces, employers must work to eradicate ageism in the workplace. Companies must cease using stereotypical arrogance and ageist blockades to target and alienate older employees (Taylor & Walker, 1998).

Ageism's Controversies Based on False Stereotypes

As stated in the previous section, employers use false stereotypes to perpetuate workplace ageism (Taylor & Walker, 1998; Capowski, 1994). For example, many employers stereotype older employees as less flexible, unwilling to learn and train, less healthy, more likely to have family issues, and less motivated and trusting (Ng & Feldman, 2012). As a result, some ageist stereotypes appear in job descriptions, hiring policies, and procedures (Burn et al., 2021). However, studies show that, for older job seekers, age plays a role in whether companies hire them, not a lack of skills, proving that some companies base their hiring decisions solely on age (Richardson et al., 2013).

Older people are underrepresented in the media, and when represented, the youth-obsessed media portrays them as frail and irritable. Ageist biases persist as some employers view older employees as less knowledgeable and less likely to perform their duties (Harris et al., 2018). Workplace ageism causes a lack of employee confidence and impartiality predicament (Kulik et al., 2014). The media undoubtedly spreads ageist stereotypes, which spill over into the workplace (Kulik et al., 2014).

The Problems of Ageism's Impact on the Aging Workforce

Many problems persist when employers use ageist employment practices to alienate the aging workforce. Furthermore, society suggests that older adults serve no value in the workplace (Hujsak, 2015). As a result, companies miss out on older talent that can fill critical job openings (Capowski, 1994). Employers also prevent the collaboration and benefits of a multigenerational workforce (Hujsak, 2015). The literature reveals the gross underutilization of older people in the workplace, whose talent subsequently goes to waste (Cortijo et al., 2019). Unemployed older people cannot stimulate the economy without gainful employment. Employers prevent older people's ability to stimulate the economy (Altmann, 2014) when they fail to hire older talent. Many companies talk about corporate social responsibility yet fail to do so to overcome the economic and emotional impact caused by workplace ageism.

Workplace ageism impacts millions of older Americans, and some employers continually refuse to hire and value older employers based on ageist stereotypes (Capowski, 1994). Older workers offer tremendous talents to the workplace (Hujsak, 2015). Employers should consider their organizational system and values concerning how they treat older job seekers in an aging society. Ageism overlooks older employees' vital knowledge and expertise honed over several years (Grossman, 2013). The problem of age discrimination and the undervaluing of older talent in the workplace is judiciously obscure and almost impossible for older employees to verify (Stypinska & Turek, 2017). Ageism further permeates the workplace through ageist job descriptions, unfair hiring practices, and employment policies that spew negative preconceptions of older workers to keep them out of the workplace (Roscigno, 2010).

In conclusion, ageism's prevalence is disturbing, and ageist practices preserve the underutilization of qualified older employees' skills and knowledge (Cortijo et al., 2019). Ageist employment practices immeasurably distress older employees throughout the employment lifecycle, from recruitment to termination (Franz et al., 2022; Powell, 2010). Discriminatory employment practices often result from inaccurate stereotypes about older people (Capowski, 1994), ultimately alienating aging talent emotionally and causing financial anguish. Unhappy and unemployed older people cannot stimulate the economy without gainful employment (Franz, 2021). Companies can advance an agenda for contesting an aging society's financial and social consequences by considering and hiring older people based on their merits (Cortijo et al., 2019). To do so, companies must leverage the diversity of thoughts, experiences, and skills of an age-diverse workforce to develop and maintain a workplace that demonstrates social responsibility (Cortijo et al., 2019). This shift will only materialize when employers advertise age-inclusive job descriptions and implement social media recruitment practices that target and attract older workers. Additionally, employers must train and promote older employers in the absence of stereotypes that marginalize older workers.

SOLUTIONS AND RECOMMENDATIONS

Training and ongoing professional development are critical to addressing the issue of ageism (Wang & Fang, 2020). Older workers bring value to the workforce, and their talent is needed. In a study of 30 American job seekers engaged in active job searches, the participants overwhelmingly felt qualified to perform their jobs successfully (Franz, 2021). Yet, despite their confidence in their professional abilities, companies failed to recognize their value in the workplace (Franz, 2021). The study's results implied the need for employers to offer training and development for their recruiters and leadership teams to meet the needs of older employees, so older Americans gain opportunities to contribute their skills and knowledge to the workplace (Franz, 2021). Therefore, training is necessary for HR professionals, recruiters, and hiring decision-makers to drive change (Wegge & Meyer, 2020). In-depth training must include self-reflection of hiring teams' and leadership's biases to acknowledge their internal biases and role throughout and after the hiring process. Additionally, this proposed professional development training includes learning and understanding the impact of ageism on older job seekers, the benefits of hiring older workers, and the importance of hiring older workers similar to other marginalized groups (Franz, 2021).

The training intervention program provides hiring decision-makers and stakeholders (recruiters, managers, peers, and others who may participate in selecting, interviewing, and hiring candidates) tools to recruit and retain older workers without prejudice (Franz et al., 2022; Franz, 2021). These tools help recruiters, and their hiring counterparts recognize and change discriminatory hiring practices towards older job seekers to attract and retain qualified older job seekers and employees (Franz, 2021; North & Hershfield, 2014). This understanding creates a gateway for understanding the issues contributing to the problem of ageism while identifying solutions to the problem of ageist hiring practices. The following steps guide the processes necessary to create age-inclusive hiring and retention policies and procedures.

1. Perform an internal recruiting and retention SWOT analysis (strengths, weaknesses, opportunities, and threats) to identify and capitalize on what they are doing right, address areas needing improvement, identify and seize new opportunities, and minimize risks.

2. Review HR policies for signs of ageism and other forms of marginalization.
3. Evaluate each employee to determine their biases and provide HR training to address gaps in employee skills and core competencies.
4. Overhaul the HR, hiring, and retention policies to ensure age-inclusive hiring practices.
5. Continually assess the new policies and procedures to ensure adherence to age-inclusive hiring practices.
6. Make changes as needed to ensure the policies and procedures keep up with societal changes and workplace demands.

Hiring and retaining older employees is essential because they offer tremendous knowledge and wisdom to the workplace (Clark, 2012; Hujsak, 2015). Therefore, not only is it necessary to implement non-ageist hiring practices to attract and retain older employees, but it is also important to continually assess these hiring and retention policies to ensure compliance by all hiring decision-makers (Franz et al., 2022; Franz, 2021). Furthermore, this assessment identifies signs of the recruiters' and hiring stakeholders' compliance with preventing internal biases from impacting how they treat older candidates and employees to endure age-inclusive hiring and retention policies.

There are zero risks to retaining older Americans in the workforce (Hujsak, 2015). On the contrary, older workers' contributions are necessary for the U.S. labor market, as younger employees are more likely to face unemployment and psychological issues because of the COVID-19 pandemic recession (Achdut & Refaeli, 2020). Moreover, this rising unemployment rate of younger Americans embeds in their newfound focus on life purpose and their idealistic view of life after the pandemic (Troger, 2021). This increased unemployment for younger workers leaves vacant positions for the older workforce to fill. Employers who seize the opportunity to fill job vacancies with qualified, available older workers positively impact the aging society and their ability to work and stimulate the American and global economies (Franz, 2021).

The inclusive employment practices suggested in this chapter enable employers to identify and evaluate ageism practices within their organizations. In addition, this chapter proposes techniques to develop and implement non-ageist hiring and retention policies that foster productivity and success. Consequently, the chapter includes the benefits of continuous policy assessments to sustain age-inclusive hiring and retention policies to prevent repeat violations of ageist practices (Franz et al., 2022; Franz, 2021). Comprehensive, unbiased, non-ageist hiring, retention, mentoring, promotion, and retention policies bridge generational workplace gaps while leveraging older employees' vast knowledge and skills.

FUTURE RESEARCH DIRECTIONS

The author hopes to conduct further research in this area focused on understanding hiring managers' and decision-makers planning and execution strategies for hiring, mentoring, training, and promoting an aging workforce. In doing so, the author hopes to identify the strategic planning or the lack thereof, that drives their decisions to develop hiring practices that alienate the aging workforce from the labor market.

This future research will result in a step-by-step instruction manual for employers to internally assess and implement or improve their hiring practices while driving change to implement and sustain non-ageist hiring practices. The researcher also plans to conduct future research on the intersection of ageism with gender and race. Additionally, the author intends to write a comprehensive diversity, equity, and inclusion (DEI) handbook that fosters a hands-on approach and ownership of their DEI policies and procedures, so they become more invested in the DEI policies. Companies often rely on consultants to tell them what to do regarding their DEI policies. Unfortunately, this approach handicaps employers, causing the implementation of DEI, hiring, and retention policies that are cookie-cutter and not tailored to their company's unique needs. This impending DEI handbook will disclose the importance of leadership buy-in to the policies they create and broadcast, so they live their diversity policies by practicing what they preach.

Additionally, corporate leaders fail to completely buy into consultant-focused DEI plans because they typically play a passive role in developing their policies and procedures. This researcher hopes to end the practice by introducing common sense DEI, HR, hiring, and retention procedures that are inclusive and meet the needs of diverse employees. This future book's theme is compelling as it highlights a closer look at the aging workforce and steps companies must take to be age-inclusive.

Moreover, companies must enforce an affirmative action policy that requires hiring a specific percentage of older qualified employees. HR laws already exist to include older workers but are often ignored. As a result, older workers are marginalized, and their employment must now be prioritized and protected in a more welcoming and accepting workplace that values them.

CONCLUSION

Older employees face many challenges in the labor market based solely on age. Workplace ageism robs older people of job opportunities and career advancement. Ageist stereotypes are prevalent in the workplace (Lyons et al., 2014). As a result, employers send aging employees veiled messages that make them feel worthless (Malinen & Johnston, 2013). Unfortunately, older people deal with employment barriers throughout the employment lifecycle. Ageism is widespread, and hiring and retention practices often neglect and devalue older workers (Lahey, 2005). Ageist biases discount older employees' worth.

This chapter discussed issues, controversies, and problems surrounding ageism and the harmful impacts of age discrimination on older employees. Some unfair hiring practices toward older employees include ageist job descriptions, social media job search strategies that alienate older employees, and discriminatory hiring practices and decisions based on false stereotypes. Furthermore, the author suggests steps employers must take to identify and mitigate their hiring practices to ensure age inclusiveness.

Employer mistreatment of older employees signals their lack of commitment to age diversity. Employers must implement non-ageist human resource initiatives while continuously holding themselves accountable for executing fair and equitable employment policies. Change is necessary at the policy and legal levels. Society must tackle ageism as a policy and legal importance to protect older employees and crush workplace ageism if employers refuse to observe legal decrees (Veldon, 2013). Employer non-compliance with employment laws creates inequities that cheat older employees of deserved opportunities (Veldon, 2013). The legal system must enforce existing laws to protect aging employees from ageist employers.

REFERENCES

AARP Foundation. (n.d.). *Compete with confidence for full-time jobs*. Retrieved from https://www.aarp.org/aarp-foundation/our-work/income/back-to-work-50-plus/?cmp=RDRCT-BCK2WK50PL_APR22_015

Achdut, N., & Refaeli, T. (2020). Unemployment and psychological distress among young people during the covid-19 pandemic: Psychological resources and risk factors. *International Journal of Environmental Research and Public Health*, *17*(19), 1–21. doi:10.3390/ijerph17197163 PMID:33007892

Age-Friendly Institute. (n.d.). *About the Age-Friendly Institute*. Retrieved from https://institute.agefriendly.org/about/age-friendly-institute/

Altmann, R. (2014). *Older workers benefit businesses and the economy*. Retrieved from http://search.proquest.com/docview/1747605274/citation/72F1F155507442E3PQ/1

Banks, J. A. (2016). Issues and concepts. In J. Banks & C. Banks (Eds.), *Multicultural education: Issues and perspectives* (9th ed., pp. 2–23). John Wiley & Sons.

Barrington, L. (2015). Ageism and bias in the American workplace. *Generations, 39*(3), 34–38.

Berger, E. D. (2009). Managing age discrimination: An examination of the techniques used when seeking employment. *The Gerontologist, 49*(3), 317–332. doi:10.1093/geront/gnp031 PMID:19377045

Burn, I., Button, P., Corella, L. M., & Neumark, D. (2021). Does ageist language in job ads predict age discrimination in hiring? *Journal of Labor Economics, 40*(3), 613–667. doi:10.1086/717730 PMID:35845105

Butler, R. N. (1989). Dispelling ageism: The cross-cutting intervention. *The Annals of the American Academy of Political and Social Science, 503*(1), 138–147. doi:10.1177/0002716289503001011

Capowski, G. (1994). Ageism: The new diversity issue. *Management Review, 83*(10), 10–15.

Carlsson, M., & Eriksson, S. (2019). Age discrimination in hiring decisions: Evidence from a field experiment in the labor market. *Labour Economics, 59*, 173–183. doi:10.1016/j.labeco.2019.03.002

Clark, K. A. (2012). *Long-term unemployment among the baby boom generation: An exploration of coping strategies and subjective well-being* [Ph.D. dissertation, Fielding Graduate University]. ProQuest Dissertations Publishing.

Columbia Public Health. (2022). *The advantages of older workers.* Retrieved from https://www.publichealth.columbia.edu/research/age-smart-employer/advantages-older-workers

Cortijo, V., McGinnis, L. P., & Şişli-Ciamarra, E. (2019). The AGE model: Addressing ageism in the workplace through corporate social responsibility. *Journal of Labor and Society, 22*(1), 197–213. doi:10.1111/wusa.12387

Creswell, J. W. (2014). *Research design: Qualitative, quantitative, and mixed methods approaches* (4th ed.). Sage.

Davies, E. M. M., Hanley, K., Jenkins, A. K., & Chan, C. (2017). Learning and training for older workers. In M. Flynn, Y. Li, & A. Chiva (Eds.), *Managing the ageing workforce in the east and the west* (pp. 185–206). Emerald Publishing., doi:10.1108/978-1-78714-638-920171009

Davis, O., Fisher, B., & Radpour, G. (2020, October 20). *A first in nearly 50 years, older workers face higher unemployment than mid-career workers*. Retrieved from https://www.economicpolicyresearch.org/jobs-report/a-first-in-nearly-50-years-older-workers-face-higher-unemployment-than-mid-career-workers

Findsen, B. (2015). Older workers' learning within organizations: Issues and challenges. *Educational Gerontology*, *41*(8), 582–589. doi:10.1080/03601277.2015.1011582

Franz, N. E. (2021). *A phenomenological case study to describe the ageism-induced anxiety of job seekers aged 50–83* [Ed.D. Problem of Practice Dissertation]. Baylor University.

Franz, N. E., Werse, N. R., & Talbert, T. L. (2022). Ageism-induced anxiety of job seekers aged 50–83: Preliminary findings from a phenomenological case study problem of practice dissertation. *Impacting Education: Journal on Transforming Professional Practice*, *7*(2), 11–18. dou:10.5195/ie.2022.199

Friedman, H., & Friedman, L., & Leverton. (2016). Increase diversity to boost creativity and enhance problem solving. *Psychological Issues in Human Resource Management*, *4*(2), 7–33.

Gibson, J. W., Jones, J. P., Cella, J., Clark, C., Epstein, A., & Haselberger, J. (2010). Ageism and the baby boomers: Issues, challenges and the team approach. *Contemporary Issues in Education Research*, *3*(1), 53–60. doi:10.19030/cier.v3i1.161

Gringart, E., Helmes, E., & Speelman, C. P. (2005). Exploring attitudes toward older workers among Australian employers. *Journal of Aging & Social Policy*, *17*(3), 85–103. doi:10.1300/J031v17n03_05 PMID:16219595

Grossman, R. J. (2013). Invest in older workers. *HRMagazine*, *58*(8), 20–25.

Harris, K., Krygsman, S., Waschenko, J., & Laliberte Rudman, D. (2018). Ageism and the older worker: A scoping review. *The Gerontologist*, *58*(2), e1–e14. doi:10.1093/geront/gnw194 PMID:28082278

Hirsch, B. T., Macpherson, D. A., & Hardy, M. A. (2000). Occupational age structure and access for older workers. *Industrial & Labor Relations Review*, *53*(3), 401–418. doi:10.1177/001979390005300303

Hosain, S., Manzurul Arefin, A. H. M., & Hossin, M. A. (2020). E-recruitment: A social media perspective. Asian Journal of Economics. *Business and Accounting*, *16*(4), 51–62.

Hujsak, J. (2015). Older workers: The value proposition-A sustainable enterprise imperative. *Cost and Management*, *29*(6), 6–15.

Karmel, T., & Woods, D. (2004). *Lifelong learning and older workers*. Retrieved from https://eric.ed.gov/?id=ED494053

Kulik, C. T., Ryan, S., Harper, S., & George, G. (2014). Aging populations and management. *Academy of Management Journal*, *57*(4), 929–935. doi:10.5465/amj.2014.4004

Lahey, J. N. (2005). *Do older workers face discrimination? (Issue Brief No. 33)*. Retrieved from https://crr.bc.edu/briefs/do-older-workers-face-discrimination/

Lesonsky, R. (2017). *Small business trends: 8 signs of ageism in the workplace and what to do about them*. Retrieved from http://search.proquest.com/docview/1939712583/citation/D3A138FA00F54167PQ/1

Lippmann, S. (2008). Rethinking risk in the new economy: Age and cohort effects on unemployment and re-employment. *Human Relations*, *61*(9), 1259–1292. doi:10.1177/0018726708094912

Lyons, B. J., Wessel, J. L., Tai, Y. C., & Ryan, A. M. (2014). Strategies of job seekers related to age-related stereotypes. *Journal of Managerial Psychology*, *29*(8), 1009–1027. doi:10.1108/JMP-03-2013-0078

Malinen, S., & Johnston, L. (2013). Workplace ageism: Discovering hidden bias. *Experimental Aging Research*, *39*(4), 445–465. doi:10.1080/0361073X.2013.808111 PMID:23875840

Mandal, B., Ayyagari, P., & Gallo, W. T. (2011). Job loss and depression: The role of subjective expectations. *Social Science & Medicine*, *72*(4), 576–583. doi:10.1016/j.socscimed.2010.11.014 PMID:21183267

Midtsundstad, T. I. (2011). Inclusive workplaces and older employees: An analysis of companies' investment in retaining senior workers. *International Journal of Human Resource Management*, *22*(6), 1277–1293. doi:10.1080/09585192.2011.559099

Neumark, D. (2021). Age discrimination in hiring: Evidence from age-blind vs. non-age-blind hiring procedures. *The Journal of Human Resources*, 0420-10831R1. Advance online publication. doi:10.3368/jhr.0420-10831R1

Ng, R., & Lim-Soh, J. W. (2021). Ageism linked to culture, not demographics: Evidence from an 8-billion-word corpus across 20 countries. *The Journals of Gerontology: Series B*, *76*(9), 1791–1798. doi:10.1093/geronb/gbaa181 PMID:33099600

Ng, T. W. H., & Feldman, D. C. (2012). Evaluating six common stereotypes about older workers with meta-analytical data. *Personnel Psychology, 65*(4), 821–858. doi:10.1111/peps.12003

Nolan, L. C. (2011). Dimensions of aging and belonging for the older person and the effects of ageism. *BYU Journal of Public Law, 25*(2), 317–339.

North, M., & Hershfield, H. (2014). *Four ways to adapt to an aging workforce.* Retrieved from https://hbr.org/2014/04/four-ways-to-adapt-to-an-aging-workforce

North, M. S., & Fiske, S. T. (2013). Subtyping ageism: Policy issues in succession and consumption. *Social Issues and Policy Review, 7*(1), 36–57. doi:10.1111/j.1751-2409.2012.01042.x PMID:24523829

Oliveira, E. A. da S. (2017). *Ageism in the workplace: Stereotype threat, work disengagement and organizational disidentification among older workers* [Doctoral dissertation, Universidade do Porto]. ProQuest Dissertations Publishing.

Osborne, T., & McCann, L. A. (2004). Forced ranking and age-related employment discrimination. *Human Rights (Chicago, Ill.), 31*(2), 6.

Perron, R. (2013). *Staying ahead of the curve 2013: AARP multicultural work and career study.* Retrieved from https://www.aarp.org/research/topics/economics/info-2014/staying-ahead-curve-work.html

Petery, G. A., & Grosch, J. W. (2022). Broadening the view of workplace ageism. *Work, Aging and Retirement, 8*(4), 379–382. doi:10.1093/workar/waac015 PMID:35923432

Powell, M. (2010). Ageism and abuse in the workplace: A new frontier. *Journal of Gerontological Social Work, 53*(7), 654–658. doi:10.1080/01634372.2010.508510 PMID:20865626

Rafique, T., Asif, F., Afridi, J., & Mahmood, K. (2021). Credibility of social networking sites: Impact on organizational attraction in recruitment field. *Sarhad Journal of Management Sciences, 6*(2), 2414–2336.

Richardson, B., Webb, J., Webber, L., & Smith, K. (2013). Age discrimination in the evaluation of job applicants. *Journal of Applied Social Psychology, 43*(1), 35–44. doi:10.1111/j.1559-1816.2012.00979.x

Rippon, I., Kneale, D., de Oliveira, C., Demakakos, P., & Steptoe, A. (2014). Perceived age discrimination in older adults. *Age and Ageing, 43*(3), 379–386. doi:10.1093/ageing/aft146 PMID:24077751

Roscigno, V. J. (2010). Ageism in the American workplace. *American Sociological Association, 9*(1), 16–21. doi:10.1525/ctx.2010.9.1.16

Schulte, P. A., Grosch, J., Scholl, J. C., & Tamers, S. L. (2018). Framework for considering productive aging and work. *Journal of Occupational and Environmental Medicine, 60*(5), 440–448. doi:10.1097/JOM.0000000000001295 PMID:29420331

Stypinska, J., & Turek, K. (2017). Hard and soft age discrimination: The dual nature of workplace discrimination. *European Journal of Ageing, 14*(1), 49–61. doi:10.100710433-016-0407-y PMID:28804394

Taskforce on the Aging of the American Workforce. (n.d.). *Older worker initiative*. Retrieved from https://www.dol.gov/agencies/eta/reports/older-worker-initiative

Taylor, P., & Walker, A. (1998). Employers and older workers: Attitudes and employment practices. *Ageing and Society, 18*(6), 641–658. doi:10.1017/S0144686X98007119

Thompson, L. F., & Mayhorn, C. B. (2012). Aging workers and technology. In W. Borman & T. Hedge (Eds.), *The Oxford handbook of work and aging* (pp. 341–361). Oxford University Press. doi:10.1093/oxfordhb/9780195385052.013.0113

Troger, H. (2021). *Human resource management in a post Covid-19 world: New distribution of power, individualization, digitalization and demographic developments*. Springer. https://link.springer.com/book/10.1007/978-3-030-67470-0

Truxillo, D., Cadiz, D., & Hammer, L. (2015). Supporting the aging workforce: A research review and recommendations for workplace intervention research. *Annual Review of Organizational Psychology and Organizational Behavior, 2*(1), 351–381. doi:10.1146/annurev-orgpsych-032414-111435

U.S. Department of Labor, Bureau of Labor Statistics. (2018). *Age discrimination*. Retrieved from https://www.dol.gov/general/topic/discrimination/agedisc

U.S. Equal Employment Opportunity Commission. (2019). *Home*. Retrieved from https://www.eeoc.gov/

Veldon, B. (2013). Ageism and age discrimination in the workplace. *CRIS-Bulletin of the Centre for Research and Interdisciplinary Study, 2013*(2), 33–41. doi:10.2478/cris-2013-0008

Viviani, C. A., Bravo, G., Lavallière, M., Arezes, P. M., Martínez, M., Dianat, I., Bragança, S., & Castellucci, H. I. (2021). Productivity in older versus younger workers: A systematic literature review. *Work (Reading, Mass.), 68*(3), 577–618. doi:10.3233/WOR-203396 PMID:33612506

Wanberg, C. R., Kanfer, R., Hamann, D. J., & Zhang, Z. (2016). Age and reemployment success after job loss: An integrative model and meta-analysis. *Psychological Bulletin*, *142*(4), 400–426. doi:10.1037/bul0000019 PMID:26011790

Wang, M., & Fang, Y. (2020). Age diversity in the workplace: Facilitating opportunities with organizational practices. *The Public Policy and Aging Report*, *30*(3), 119–123. doi:10.1093/ppar/praa015

Wegge, J., & Meyer, B. (2020). Age diversity and age-based faultlines in teams: Understanding a Brezel phenomenon requires a Brezel theory. *Work, Aging and Retirement*, *6*(1), 8–14. doi:10.1093/workar/waz017

Williams van Rooij, S. (2012). Training older workers: Lessons learned, unlearned, and relearned from the field of instructional design. *Human Resource Management*, *51*(2), 281–298. doi:10.1002/hrm.21466

KEY TERMS AND DEFINITIONS

Age Bias or Age Prejudice: The prejudicial treatment of employees 40 years of age or older.

Ageism: The prejudgment or discrimination based on a person's age.

Aging Workforce: Individuals within the workforce who are aged 50 or older.

Discrimination: The practice of discriminating against marginalized groups.

Hiring Practices: Companies hiring policies that govern their recruiting strategies.

Human Resource (HR) Policies and Procedures: The policies and procedures employers use to handle affairs concerning employees.

Protected Classes: A group of employees or job seekers who received legal protection from employers based on age, race, color, national origin, sex, physical or mental disability, religion or creed, and veteran status.

Chapter 7 The Journey Between the Final Stage of Career and the Adaptation to Retirement

Bruno de Sousa Lopes
University of Aveiro, Portugal

ABSTRACT

This chapter aims to understand the organizational practices of disengagement of senior employees, focusing primarily on the final phase of the careers of this class of employees and their entry into retirement. It analyzed the challenges of adaptation to retirement, as well as the disengagement practices used by organizations, and characterized the individual career management of seniors. The methodology used was qualitative, using a semi-structured interview complemented by a socio-demographic survey for data collection. The results of the study point to the fact that the whole process of end-of-career and retirement has a significant impact on both individuals and organizations. The evidence shows that factors such as aging and the importance of health and family are some of the main concerns of individuals. At the same time, organizations focus mainly on career management, succession processes, and employee satisfaction at the end of their careers and, consequently, on acceptable entry into retirement.

INTRODUCTION

Aging is a natural and unstoppable biological process in any individual's life; this phenomenon directly impacts each country's available labor force (Cepellos, 2018; de Oliveira & Anderson, 2020). Of the various factors that have contributed

DOI: 10.4018/978-1-6684-6351-2.ch007

to the increase in demographic aging, we can mention that the most important and impactful have been the low birth rate associated with a better quality of life and public health systems leading to an increase in average life expectancy (Cepellos, 2018; de Oliveira & Anderson, 2020).

We are currently experiencing a phenomenon of demographic aging as never been seen before. This phenomenon is no longer European, where it initially occurred, but is now a global reality. Such an event forces the countries to adjust, by increasing the retirement age, to guarantee not only the general maintenance of the labor force but, in many cases, the very subsistence of the Social State or the States' Welfare systems. Organizations are currently facing an exodus regarding the departure of senior employees, and consequently, much of the knowledge was neither written down nor passed on to future generations. Adjacent to this phenomenon, it is easy to see that in the coming decades, population aging is expected to continue to be one of the main problems of current and developed societies due to the globalization of demographic aging (Cepellos, 2018; de Oliveira & Anderson, 2020).

As mentioned by Tavares (2020), aging will have a direct and marked impact on the available workforce within each country and, consequently, within each organization, which implies that societies and organizations need to start looking with special care to this segment of the population (older or senior people), since global trends simultaneously project an increase in average life expectancy and an increase in this age segment. On the other hand, a decrease in the young population is launched, which necessarily implies that a large part of this aging workforce that until then was seen as expendable and without a place in current organizations will remain active, thus demonstrating the critical role that senior employees will play in organizations and society.

Tavares (2020) reiterates that organizations must start preparations for the challenges inherent in this paradigm shift regarding the aging workforce available to organizations. Therefore, investing in the quality of work life is essential to mitigate the effects of an aging workforce on organizational performance. Since human capital is the differentiating factor in organizations, this capital inevitably includes the added value of senior employees with the skills and knowledge inherent in their years of experience. Thus, it is essential to create specific career management for this particular stage of individuals' working lives to, on the one hand, optimize their potential and, on the other hand, allow this knowledge and skills to flow naturally to employees of younger generations, thus improving a better succession when the senior employee leaves (Rupp et al., 2006; Ramos, 2010).

The central theme of this study is the career management of senior employees, more specifically, the whole process inherent to the final phase of the career until the succession process and consequently the entry into retirement since there is little literature on the interaction and relationship of the transition phase to retirement and the adaptation of retirement.

Thus, the present study will use a qualitative research methodology of an inductive nature since it is a subject on which there is little literature. It also aims to understand the phenomenon under study more deeply. Thus, the research question "How are senior employees' disengagement practices defined in organizations?" was identified. The general objective of this study is to understand the organizational practices of disengagement of senior employees, and more specifically: to identify the challenges in adaptation to retirement (of senior employees), to define the disengagement practices used by organizations, and to characterize the individual career management (of senior employees) in preparation for retirement.

BACKGROUND

Aging

Aging is an innate, natural, and uncontrollable process in the life of human beings. This term has always existed; however, it was attached to the characterization of individual aging. More recently, it has been used to characterize collective, societal, and global aging (Saad, 2016; Cepellos, 2018). In this prism, aging directly impacts the available labor force in each country, derived from the fact that population aging has moved from a merely continental (European) phenomenon to a reality and a worldwide phenomenon (Saad, 2016; Cepellos, 2018).

The forecast for the coming decades points to rapid and constant population growth, leading to demographic transformations because directly linked to the increase in average life expectancy, improved health care, and reduced birth rates, among other factors, foster population aging (Saad, 2016; Cepellos, 2018).

According to data from Euromonitor International (2019), Japan, Italy, Greece, Finland, and Portugal are considered the five most aged countries worldwide, demonstrating how demographic aging is a universal reality that has been gaining weight and prominence globally. However, this problem is not new and has been gradually addressed since industrialization (Nazareth, 2009).

In a broad sense, the phenomenon of aging results from the transition from a demographic model in which birth and mortality rates were exceptionally high to a new model in which both demographic factors are increasingly lower. This phenomenon has led to a progressive and rapid deformation of the age pyramid, with a reduction in the young population and a considerable increase in the elderly population (Daniel et al., 2016). It is estimated that in 2080 we will have a graph that cannot be considered a pyramid. The base, comprised of the younger population, will be narrower than the levels corresponding to the middle-highest ages. This will represent a trend toward the inversion of the old and traditional demographic pyramid, where the base was higher than the top (Statistics Portugal, 2014).

This change can be explained by several factors, such as the numerous advances in medicine and improvements in basic sanitation and other general living conditions of the population, thus enabling a significant increase in the average life expectancy of human beings (Daniel et al., 2016).

This phenomenon first appeared in the Old Continent of Europe but soon spread to all developed countries. It is seen more intensely in developing countries, which still have favorable growth rates of the young population (Pestana, 2003). However, global trends forecast that this continent will reach zero youth growth from 2030 onwards (Eurostat, 2015). The United Nations projects that by 2050 the youth population will be around 21%, while the elderly population will reach 15.6% (Statistics Portugal, 2014). Likewise, it should be noted that the growth rate of the senior population is four times higher than that of the young population (Statistics Portugal, 2014). Therefore, it is estimated that, in 2080, one in eight European Union citizens will be over 80 years old (Eurostat, 2015).

In Portugal, this change occurred more precisely between 1960 and 2001, with demographic aging being associated with a decrease of about 36% in the young population and an increase of 140% in the elderly population. In 2001 there was, for the first time, a predominance of the older population over the younger population, and it is estimated that in 2060 more than half of the Portuguese population will be over 65 years old (Statistics Portugal, 2014).

By analyzing global perspectives and trends, it is predicted that societies will increasingly grow and age in absolute and percentage terms. This leads to a phenomenon that has led to a change in the outlook of today's society, i.e., we have gone from a "1,2,4" society (one grandparent, two parents, and four children) to today's "4-2-1" society (four grandparents, two parents, and one child). This demonstrates the worldwide trend of a shrinking population considered young to the detriment of an increasingly aging population (Rosa, 2012).

The accentuation of aging in the demographic pyramid shows an emerging and growing problem, which will become one of the biggest challenges in the reformulation of the workforce, bringing immediate and long-term repercussions in the international organizational context, forcing a rethinking of the role of senior workers in society, together with the fact that for several countries it is necessary to rethink the welfare state (Pestana, 2003).

Senior Employee Concept

The literature (e.g., Johnson & Lopes, 2008; Schalk et al., 2010; Ramos, 2010) highlights the need to clarify the concept of a senior employee, drawing attention to the definition of an age beyond which an employee can be considered as "older." At the same time, organizations need to take care and plan the management and retention of senior employees to maintain knowledge and talent since, increasingly, the reality in which organizations are inserted seems not to be aligned with the aging population recorded all over the world.

Despite repeated calls from several authors (e.g., Schalk et al., 2010; Finkelstein et al., 2013) for the creation of a construct and a definition of what a senior worker is, this is not possible due to the lack of consensus on this topic, and the perception of aging, which creates a problem for several researchers and policymakers (Gonyea, 2009; Painter et al., 2012).

In an attempt to determine the current and prospective future number of older people and senior workers, it is first essential to safeguard the homologation of a definition, as it is challenging to study a topic when we do not know what we are defining when the word "old" is used. For Pitt-Catsouphes and Smyer (2006), the age range for older workers may vary - depending on circumstances - from 40 to the legal retirement age in each country.

Drawing on several perspectives on aging, Hedge et al. (2006) refer to five approaches to defining the concept of an older worker: (I) chronological, that is, the definition of a senior worker is based on his or her age; (II) performance-based, that is, as performance declines underlying the deterioration of capabilities directly related to the individual's aging; (III) psychosocial, i.e., the age perceived by oneself and society; (IV) organizational, i.e., the perception held by one's employer; (V) life course, i.e., the approach related to the change in behaviors resulting from age, along with environmental or biological factors. From this perspective, older people tend to be considered a heterogeneous group.

The World Health Organization (2012), in order to delimit the "third" and "fourth" ages, agreed that "elderly" is an individual aged sixty-five years or more. Similarly, according to the European Commission's Green Paper (EUR-Lex, 2006), the aging population is divided into "older workers" (55 to 64 years old), "seniors" (65 to 79 years old), and "very old" (80 or older). This distinction was necessary due to a lack of consensus in the literature and across cultures about what a senior worker is (EUR-Lex, 2006). According to Riach (2009), the population group of "older" people is becoming the dominant population group in terms of the labor force. However, it is unrealistic to assume that a 40-year-old worker has similar work values, attributes, and expectations as a 65-year-old worker. Therefore, it is essential to look at the generational concept, that is, to see what is most important to each generation.

In summary, workers considered senior are people who come from two main generations: (1) the silent and great generations (from 1945 or earlier, who are currently 75 or older) and (2) the baby boom generation (from 1946 to 1964, currently aged 56 to 74), according to Pew Research Center (2019).

Career Management

The 2nd Industrial Revolution and the post-war period brought an era of economic growth that led institutions and companies to rethink their structural organization. Thus, during the 20th century, the concept of career emerged as a synonym for an individual's career path (Moore et al., 2007; Alis et al., 2012).

There are several definitions of a career, depending on how it is approached and the area of study (Cunha et al., 2015). For Nicholson and West (1989), the concept of career can be seen and analyzed from three perspectives: the first consists of the psychological constructs that give meaning to careers, the second in the analysis of the concept of career, according to the perspectives of a particular culture and subculture, and the third in the chronological sequence of functions performed by an individual.

According to Arthur et al. (2005), we can define a career as a succession of functions performed by a person throughout his or her active life within a single organization. For Alis et al. (2012), on the other hand, a career is understood as the set of salaried functions that an individual performs throughout his or her life. From Ivancevich's (2010) perspective, the concept of a career does not need to be related to a paid position or an organization.

Since the concept of career has several definitions (Baruch, 2006), the concept of career management also adopts several explanations according to how the concept of career is observed, that is, whether it is analyzed from an individual or organizational perspective (Arthur et al., 2005; Alis et al., 2012; da Silva et al., 2016; Greenhaus et al., 2018).

da Silva et al. (2016) aggregate these two concepts, referring that the definition of career consists of the sequence of functions that an individual performs, being able to earn retribution or not, and experiencing a feeling of belonging to a professional or non-professional group. This concept, linked to the concept of organizational career, brings together several types of performance, such as, for example, a volunteer mission, liberal professionalism, and service provision, among others, introducing the perspective not only of organizational career but also of individual career.

Gunz and Peiperl (2007) define career management as an organizational activity that applies Human Resources practices, such as selection, training and development, coaching, promotions, evaluation, and compensation. These practices make it possible to stimulate and control careers within the organization. Authors such as Palade (2010) or Veloso et al. (2012) go further, saying that these Human Resources practices should consist of structuring a development strategy for each function existing in the organization. This argument reinforces the idea that all employees have the perception and awareness of what is needed for that function to guide their actions and efforts to achieve the desired place, fulfilling their goals. In turn, Alis et al. (2012) refer that the concept of career management represents the set of actions, attitudes, and activities performed by an individual to define and command the course of his or her career path, thus developing the necessary skills to progress professionally. Career management emerges with the purpose of organizations achieving a balance between the career needs/objectives of individuals and the needs/objectives of the organization (Veloso et al., 2012).

Succession Plan

Succession planning is currently an essential strategy for organizational sustainability, creating measures and activities to ensure the satisfaction of the needs resulting from an employee's departure and, consequently, the occupation of the position left open (Charbonneau & Freeman, 2016).

The existing literature on this topic is not very exhaustive and addresses it predominantly in terms of succession in family businesses (e.g., Tondo, 2008; Garg & van Weele, 2012; Pimentel, 2019) since 70% to 80% of companies in Europe are family-owned (Duh, 2015), and represent between 65% and 80% of companies worldwide (Sharma et al., 2000). However, several authors (e.g., Ip & Jacobs, 2006; Garg & van Weele, 2012; Godinho, 2016) have defined the issue of succession planning. According to Ip and Jacobs (2006, p. 327), succession planning *"entails a longer term and more extensive approach towards the training and replacement of key individuals."* For Garg and van Weele (2012, p. 97), succession planning is *"a process which ensures the continued effective performance of an organization by establishing a process to develop and replace key staff over time."* Succession planning is transversal to all organizations, regardless of their size, social nature, geographical area, and area of operation (Godinho, 2016).

For Sharma et al. (2000), the actions that constitute succession management consist of selecting the successor, which includes identifying potential successors, developing the criteria for selecting them, communicating the decision, training the successor, developing a business strategy after succession, and defining the role of the outgoing leader /employee after succession.

Although it is possible to define a strategic succession plan for all functions in an organization, this is usually not done due to the complexity of the process and its cost. Therefore, a succession plan is usually only defined for those roles considered to be senior, critical, and key (Government of Newfoundland and Labrador, 2008).

Succession Plan for Employees at the End of their Career

Succession plan management involves mapping out future vacancies in critical functions and preparing candidates to fill those vacancies. Succession management encompasses activities and measures to ensure that, regardless of the timing and the critical and senior role, there are people with the necessary knowledge, skills, and experience to take on that vacancy and its role (Murty et al., 2016).

Succession management can take either informal or formal modes. Informal succession management appears when the person who will be replaced identifies and prepares his or her successor, thus not considering the possible changes that the organization may go through, either in strategic or structural terms and often not based on the talents as a requirement. When this type of succession is carried out, other employees face greater difficulty accepting it because it is a process done without the knowledge of the remaining organization (Garg & van Weele, 2012). When succession management happens formally, it follows a series of steps previously defined and disclosed to the organization (Garg & van Weele, 2012). This process considers the needs of the company and employees and thus receives greater credibility and acceptance from colleagues. In the case of employees at the end of their career, the successor is often identified and has a period of adaptation and acquisition of knowledge, skills, and experience. In this way, when the time comes for the surrendered element to leave the organization, the successor is already fully capable of taking over the position (Leibowitz et al., 1991; Garg & van Weele, 2012).

By 2020, about 50% of the existing workforce was occupied by Millennials (born between 1982 and 2004), making them the predominant workforce in the labor market (Kosterlitz & Lewis, 2017). This circumstance leads to the need to prepare for the succession of Generation X (born between 1961 and 1981), the Baby Boomers (born between 1943 and 1960), and also some cases of people from the Great and Silent Generation (born between 1901 and 1942), as they will enter the retirement process (Kosterlitz & Lewis, 2017).

There is no consensus in the literature regarding how long it takes to prepare for succession. Kosterlitz and Lewis (2017) argue that it should start between three to ten years before the exit, while others (e.g., Ip & Jacobs, 2006) argue that only twenty weeks will be needed, i.e., five months. For Lee et al. (2003), time is an essential factor for succession to be successful since a margin must be provided in case changes need to be made in the event of problems or unforeseen events. Thus, the ideal time to start the plan is five years before the departing employee leaves (Garg & van Weele, 2012).

It is also recommended that the succession plan be reviewed annually to ensure that candidates are prepared to assume the role at any time. In this perspective, performance and training evaluations are critical to determining if the candidate for succession is appropriately prepared, showing us that, since there is no exact period to start a succession plan, it is up to the organizations to identify the most appropriate way to carry it out successfully (Garg & van Weele, 2012).

Professional Detachment

The concept of work has recently acquired a meaning of individual identity, a sign of status and social interaction, as it consists of a continuous process in the active life of an individual (Fonseca, 2012). This meaning has complemented the idea that work only consisted of a person's primary source of income (Fonseca, 2012). Xavier (2004) adds that, in addition to the traditional concept of work as a source of income, it allows individuals to create a social status, influencing their personality, since it allows for personal fulfillment, while the loss or change of work causes damage in the lives of individuals. This last point is increasingly relevant since many of the problems concerning labor relations lead to the rupture/dissociation from the organization, which can often transpose labor problems to personal problems (Xavier, 2004).

Turnover and Retirement

As mentioned in the aging section and advocated by Schmidt and Lee (2008), personal characteristics (health, family, and income) are the main factors an individual considers when considering retirement. Among several socio-demographic factors, a range of reasons makes these factors predictors of a possible turnover intention and effective turnover.

Domingues (2011) and Pereira (2011) argue that the variables age and seniority have the same behavioral pattern, i.e., the older the individual or, the more significant his seniority in an organization, the lower his intention to leave. In the first case, this happens because the older the worker is, the less attractive he/she is in the labor market and, consequently, the less likely he/she is to find a new lay opportunity (Domingues, 2011; Pereira, 2011). In the second case, the same happens to the extent that employees with more seniority tend to be more committed to their organization, "wearing the company's jersey," especially since, for many, it was either the only organization where they worked, or the one where they worked the longest and, consequently, created their relationships there (Domingues, 2011; Pereira, 2011).

However, in these cases, it is only when the time for retirement approaches that the employees encompassed by these variables (higher age and seniority) tend to show a behavior of intention to leave the organization, that is, when people get close to meeting the requirements to request retirement, they tend to show a behavior of unwillingness to stay in the organization, wishing to leave it (Domingues, 2011; Pereira, 2011).

There is no consensus in the literature relating turnover intentions and retirement. Hanisch and Hulin (1990) argue that both intentions have the same characteristics. However, Schmidt and Lee (2008) argue that both intentions correspond to different transitions an individual faces during his or her time in the labor market.

Although there is plenty of literature on turnover and retirement (e.g., Smith et al., 2011; Corbin, 2020), there is little correlation between the two topics. This is justified by the fact that, generally, older workers have a lower intention to change jobs since they are closer to retirement. On the other hand, younger workers, since they are further away from retirement, see the option of leaving an organization as a form of change (Schreurs et al., 2011).

The traditional literature on retirement refers to health, education, income, and family life as the main factors to consider when an individual begins to consider this intention (Schmidt & Lee, 2008). Traditionally, retirement intention is based on more work-related characteristics, unlike retirement intention, which has more personal characteristics. Thus, characteristics such as self-domination, the possibility of career evolution, and the possibility of personal development are the predominant elements for a possible intention to consider change (Domingues, 2011; Pereira, 2011) and, for this reason, turn turnover intention into a turnover. However, the probability of turnover decreases with age, proportionally increasing the intention to retire (Schmidt & Lee, 2008).

Both the intention to disengage and the intention to retire have a similar outcome, i.e., leaving the organization where the individual is working (Smith et al., 2011). Nevertheless, while the intention to disengage only consists of the willingness to leave a company, the decision to retire involves the decision to end a career and, implicitly, to extinguish several personal relationships and to separate oneself from the labor market. Thus, voluntary job turnover is a distinct role transition from an individual's retirement (Smith et al., 2011).

Transition to Reform

A retirement is an event of high social and psychological relevance in an individual's life. It has gained increasing interest from governments, researchers, and society in general, as there has been a substantial increase in the number of retirees due to demographical aging (Fonseca, 2012; Wang & Shi, 2015).

Retirement is the state that follows the definitive process of detachment from the labor market (Wang & Shi, 2015). Thus, to define whether a person is retired or not, he or she must meet criteria such as (a) having left the labor market, (b) earning a public or private pension, and (c) recognizing himself or herself as a retired person (Ekerdt, 2000).

Several authors (e.g., Matour & Prout, 2007; Osborne, 2012) refer that transitions to retirement have a set of psychological implications, which can be positive or negative. Therefore, the individual who retires must perform a restructuring of his purposes and goals in life in order to reduce identity and anxiety problems, to identify and restructure his role in society, his interpersonal relationships, and all his time because one of the most significant losses for people is the deconstruction of the life/work concept into the retirement/work concept (Osborne, 2012).

Thus, a set of reasons and motives lead to the origin of this event - retirement. First, we must consider whether it was voluntary or forced. Then, if it took place early, for various reasons, or if it was an early retirement, a retirement at the age eligible for retirement, or if it took place beyond the age limit (Fonseca, 2012). The next point to analyze is the reason that led to this reality, i.e., if it was for negative reasons, such as health problems, or if, on the contrary, it resulted from positive motivations, such as wanting to spend more time at home, travel, devote more time to a hobby, or redefine their social and family role, for example as a grandfather or grandmother (Fonseca, 2012).

METHODOLOGY

The starting question was formulated to prepare this chapter and the respective study: "How are the disengagement practices of senior employees defined in organizations?". Thus, the general objective of this study is to understand the organizational practices of disengagement of senior employees and, more specifically, to:

- Identify the challenges in retirement adaptation (of senior employees);
- Define the separation practices used by organizations;
- To characterize the individual career management (of senior employees) in preparation for retirement.

Considering that the practices of disengagement of senior employees are a theme that there is not much literature about it and consequently much information allied to the defined objectives, it was decided to conduct a study with a qualitative research methodology of inductive nature. This is considered the most appropriate to be applied in these cases because there is not much-standardized information; thus, the researcher has the chance to create and develop constructs, theories, and hypotheses, which might not be evident until initially, based on the empirical evidence observed and obtained (Sparkes & Smith, 2013).

Flick (2007) states that the qualitative methodology requires a more significant effort from the researcher, a process in which the researcher's power of description is essential for the accomplishment of the research, as it requires a description as detailed and accurate as possible. Given that there is a direct relationship between the researcher and the participant, and also between the study and the life context in which the person is inserted, the use of an inductive method - as is the case of the qualitative study - allows for the constant collection of data, which will later be processed in order to obtain a general theory through the various realities experienced and felt by the participants.

One of the main objectives of qualitative studies is to analyze small samples with great depth, thus allowing for a deep understanding of reality or phenomenon in concrete situations and cases, since this methodology allows obtaining great detail and knowledge about the studied phenomenon through the interpretation of all verbal and non-verbal language used by the study participants, as this is the only way to assess and analyze emotions and feelings about a particular phase of the participant's life, in this case, the process of disengagement and retirement (Charmaz, 2006; Fàbregues & Paré, 2007).

Collecting Technique

Regarding data collected in this study, the techniques used consisted of a sociodemographic questionnaire and a semi-structured interview to obtain qualitative data that, when put together, lead to understanding and interpreting the perception of seniors about their career management and the process of disengagement from the organization, and consequent adaptation to retirement.

Procedure for Gathering and Processing Information

To choose the research methodology for this study, it was necessary to carry out a bibliographic search on the chosen theme, thus allowing the development of an analysis of state of the art on this theme and enabling the establishment of a working basis for the creation of data collection instruments (sociodemographic survey and interview script). After creating the instruments and analyzing the state of the art, it was necessary to identify the target population for the study, and some parameters were defined for scrutinizing the possible participants in the study. Thus, the individuals to be elected as ideal targets should be:

- People aged 65 and over (as that is the definition used for senior citizens in the European Union);
- People who had retired up to 5 years (to avoid information bias).

After creating the instruments and defining the target population, it was necessary to identify a possible participant who met the target population's criteria. It was decided to use a non-probability sampling technique, convenience sampling. After this identification, and after the participant accepted the invitation to participate, the date, place, and time were set for the test interview, during which the sociodemographic questionnaire and the interview script were applied to make sure that the questions asked were understood and that the questions proposed were pertinent and precise. Before each interview, the participants were asked to fill out a sociodemographic questionnaire with twelve closed questions to characterize the study sample. An informed consent signed by both interviewee and interviewer was also given and collected.

The mission of this pilot interview was to test the script and verify whether its structure allowed obtaining viable and relevant data that could be coded and analyzed, taking into account the study's objectives. Thus, the pilot interview did not reveal the need to modify any questions because it was found that the interview script allowed obtaining of the necessary data and that it was easy to understand for the participants. To begin with, the objective was to contact known companies to find out if any former employees could be considered as possible participants in this study. However, there was some reticence from some companies due to General Data Protection Regulation. After exhausting the existing contacts in the companies, the author proceeded to communicate and disclose the study on several professional social networks such as LinkedIn and Facebook, in this case, more specifically in existing groups where its members are students or professionals in the area of human resources.

Nevertheless, after an unexpected difficulty was verified, it was decided to use as a preferential method the capture of participants in senior universities, which turned out to be a very lengthy and bureaucratic process, because it was often necessary to wait for authorizations from Parish Councils, and then even from the Directions of the universities. Subsequently, and as in the case of the participants selected through the network, it was still necessary to contact the participants to check their availability for the interview and sociodemographic survey. Thus, of the ten participants needed, only two were indicated by the senior universities, and the remaining eight resulted from selection through the network.

Another factor that made it challenging to obtain participants for this study was the fact that some people, due to their age, no longer fit the parameter of being retired for a maximum of 5 years, together with the fact that many, given the initial contact by an unfamiliar person, did not trust openly enough to show availability for the collaboration that was requested.

Additionally, the pandemic caused by the SARS-Cov-2 coronavirus, and the declaration of a state of emergency that occurred in Portugal during the data collection period, was an additional obstacle in that the target population of this study belongs precisely to the highest-risk group in COVID-19 disease.

Contacts were initiated at the beginning of January 2020, and the first interviews took place at the end of that same month, and this process lasted until the end of May 2020. Seven face-to-face and three telephone interviews were held, with the participant's availability always being confirmed and the dates for the interviews being set according to the interviewees' preference and availability at their chosen locations. All interviews were recorded after the participant gave his/her authorization. The interviews lasted an average of fifteen minutes, and all of them were transcribed using the verbatim method, with the exact words and the description of non-verbal reactions.

After transcribing the interviews, it is necessary to analyze the data obtained; thus, the Grounded Theory was used (Strauss & Corbin, 1998). Grounded Theory essentially has three phases of data coding: open coding, axial coding, and selective coding (Strauss & Corbin, 1998). Once the process of transcribing the interviews 'verbatim' was completed, they were placed in a previously structured Excel file, thus allowing for content analysis, in which the units of analysis/coding of the data collected in the interviews were initially identified, thus allowing for the development of theories and constructs adjacent to the collection and analysis of data and the creation of new knowledge. This whole set of systematic and rigorous processes used in data coding and analysis allows the researcher to develop his or her theories and explanation for a phenomenon being studied (Strauss & Corbin, 1998; da Silva, 2019).

Characterization of the Study Participants

The cooperating population in this study was composed of ten individuals aged 65 years or older who were in the situation of retirement up to a maximum of 5 years, some of whom may be taking advantage of retirement but continuing to perform professional activities. All of whom were located in the Northern area of Portugal (Table 1).

In this way, we can refer that this is a theoretical sample since the participants of this study dominate and know and have experienced the phenomena that they wish to be studied in this study (Fernandes & Maia, 2001). The interviews ended when theoretical saturation was reached, i.e., when the data started to become repetitive, and the appearance of new information became rare or did not bring anything new to the study.

At the time of data collection, participants were assured that anonymity and data confidentiality would be maintained throughout the research. To identify participants, the designations Participant 1 and Participant 2 were used, maintaining this sequence until Participant 10, and each time they referred to the organizations where they worked, codes would also be used to ensure maximum anonymity and confidentiality, making it as difficult as possible to track participants.

RESULTS

The author will present the main results through the data collected from the semi-structured interviews and analyze the information according to the principles of Grounded Theory. The main categories obtained in this study were: 1) Characterization of Retirement, 2) Career and 3) Characterization of Disengagement.

Category Retirement Characterization

Retirement is an event of enormous social and psychological relevance in an individual's life, making it necessary for the retiree to restructure his personal goals to reduce any chances of this event causing adverse reactions in the individual's life. In the same way, it is necessary to investigate the reasons that led to the request for retirement because situations of illness or personal/family problems can negatively impact the individual's life.

The category Characterization of Retirement (Figure 1) emerged from the following subcategories, Physical Activity, Family Life Characteristics, Personal Development, Aging, Importance of Health in Retirement, Financial Independence, Transition to Retirement, Satisfaction with Retirement, Household Responsibilities, Maintenance of Mental Activity, and Interaction with the Community.

The subcategory Physical Activity consists of body movement associated with an energy expenditure above the usual resting level that can influence an individual's physical and psychological health, with participants mentioning Sports Practice as the main practice of Physical Activity. Participant 4 refers precisely to this practice.

"I go to the gym all morning in the afternoon and just walk with my wife."

Table 1. Participants' Sociodemographic Characteristics

Participant	Gender	Age	Civil Status	Level of Education	Training Area	Function in the Company	Antiquity	Age at which you started the Active Life	Years in Active Life	Age at which you Retired	Years in Retirement
1	F	70	Married	High School	Accounting	Accounting Officer	27	22	44	66,3	3,7
2	M	71	Married	Middle School	Nursing	Nurse	28	20	49	69	2
3	M	70	Married	High School	High School General Course Sciences	Client Banking Manager	35	18	47	65	5
4	M	65	Married	High School	Industry	Production Supervisor	47	14	50	63	2
5	F	67	Widow	High School	Sales	Sales to Foreign Markets	46	18	46	65	2
6	M	65	Married	High School	Purchase	Inventory Management and Purchasing	49,6	12	53	65	0,4
7	F	66	Widow	High School	Female Formation	Technical Administrative Assistant	30	17	49	66,5	0,5
8	M	71	Married	High School	Welder	Managing Partner	26	14	57	66	5
9	M	66	Married	Bachelor	Mechanical Engineering	Human Resources Director	42	22	44	65	1
10	M	68	Divorced	MBA	Economics	Commercial Director	15	20	48	64	4
Average years	-	**67,9**	-	-	-	-	**34,6**	**17,7**	**48,7**	**65,48**	**2,42**

Source: Own elaboration, 2022

Figure 1. Categories and Subcategories of the Characterization of the Reform
Source: Own elaboration, 2022

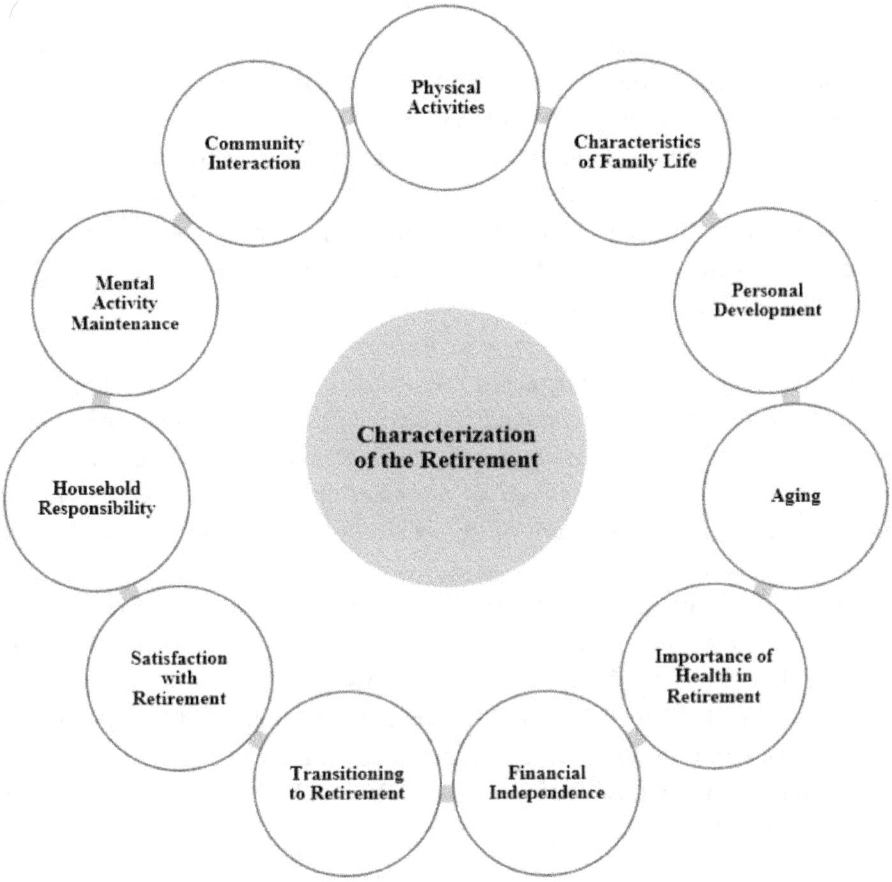

The Family Life Character consists of the set of responsibilities, rights, and duties that an individual has towards a primary social group, consisting of two or more people, existing a relationship of descent or ancestry; biological, ancestral, legal or affective, here is also referred by the participants the importance of Family and Friends Pressure. An illustrative example of this sentiment is demonstrated by Participant 1, who states:

"And having my son to guide me because he was finishing college to support him at the beginning of his professional career and also ready at the family level. I had also to give my support because I have people already of a certain age, and they needed me (...) Moreover, all that and also ready at the family level, I had to give my support because I had people already of a certain age, and they needed me so

in that aspect, as I had already fulfilled what my organization says, I felt it was time to leave."

The importance of health in retirement from the perspective of individuals is based on the fact that often the stress and problems that are frequently usual in the work process and that directly affect the health of a person when one retires, it is essential to have a break of these factors that cause disease by trying to take more care of oneself and one's health, precisely this topic of health was addressed by the interviewees. Participant 10 also adds to this information the fact that often even having several benefits in monetary terms, they do not always compensate for the damage caused to their health.

"Professional life is very stressful, the other day, my dentist said to me you cannot imagine how your teeth have changed since you left X, even the teeth, ahhh even the teeth, they pay well, but you wear out the constant pressure, the goals, if you meet the goals no one bothers you if you do not meet them it is a permanent massacre daily, they pay well, but that is how things work, there was nothing else besides this."

Similarly, Retirement Satisfaction is one of the main factors of the Characterization of Retirement; this process allows one to ascertain the degree of satisfaction of the person in his perspective as a retiree and also what is his predisposition for a possible re-entry into the labor market, this is referred by respondents as feelings for total satisfaction of retirement too, Unwillingness to re-enter the labor market, Achievement with Personal Retirement and Personal Achievement in Retirement, as mentioned by Participant 9.

"(Laughs) four point nine, (...) hence my fulfillment as a retiree is almost great because I am swamped intellectually not only physically, and above all, I am the helmsman of my boat. I do what I want when and how I think is right."

It also addressed the importance and the obligation of Domestic Responsibilities; at the time of retirement, they get a greater relevance, especially in the passage of part of the day of retirees, such as cleaning and tidying the house, among other activities, so it is referred at this point the Domestic Tasks as one of the central factors in these obligations, as is visible by what was transmitted by the Participant 7.

"I take care of the house, I clean the house, I iron, I am on the internet a little bit, and anything that I may have to do, I go to mass; now things are a little different, isn't it."

Category Career

The Career category differs from how individuals and organizations interpret it; here, some factors are highlighted, such as the meaning given to the career, the feeling/emotions that individuals have during their career, and the existence or not of a career management or reward for performance or merit. This is the constant succession of professional roles/categories that an individual holds throughout his or her career. These roles may or may not be paid and may or may not be linked to organizations.

The selective category Career (Figure 2) emerged subcategories, particularly: Challenges of Adaptation to Function, Demotivation, Satisfaction with Career, Permanence at Work, Institutional Integration, Soft Skill, Management Tools, No Career Management, and Career Management.

Figure 2. Categories and Subcategories of the Career
Source: Own elaboration, 2022

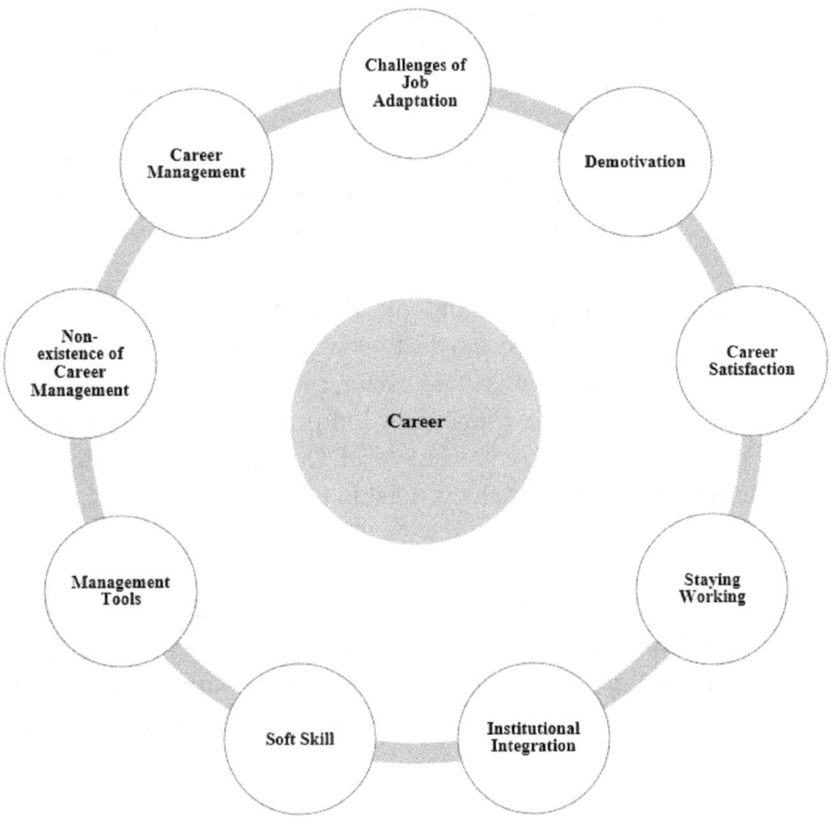

It is possible to verify that the individuals refer that the Challenges of Adaptation to Function are a concern taken along the career from when it begins until when it ends, mainly according to the Particularities of the Function, because a bad adaptation to the function that is going to be played or a bad passing of baton or teachings is the beginning for the failure in playing the function. Participant 5 is an enlightening example of the Challenges of Adaptation to Function, mainly of passing the baton of functions to avoid this problem.

"The way they were transmitted was ahhh see in practice see how things worked or how I worked with things ahhh I was giving indications, and I was showing what I thought was correct in terms of functioning, and I still think it was correct, and I think it transmits more or less well also depends on people how they receive or not what is transmitted to them, but I think I transmitted in a more or less correct way what was to have been taken into account."

In the subcategory, Demotivation analyzed the factors that this feeling can have on participants throughout their careers and the disadvantages adjacent to it, so the participants also refer that feeling Demotivation in their career is interconnected with the feeling of devaluation that leads to a feeling often of giving up. Participant 7 is an illustrative example of the demotivation factor and its adverse effects.

"Ahhh, sometimes yes, once or twice I felt like leaving (...), so it often led me to give up and say I have not been training. I have not been, ahhh, training others to come now and impose on me what I know I am doing wrong."

One of the positive advantages/feelings mentioned by the participants as opposed to the feeling of Demotivation is Satisfaction with the Career; when making an extrospective of the past and their whole career, the participants mainly refer to a feeling of satisfaction with their whole path and professional evolution, they also refer that there is a feeling of Achievement of Goals, Personal Achievement in professional terms and Personal Achievement in Career Management, as stated by Participant 10.

"On a scale of one to one hundred, ahhh, one hundred and twenty, I always felt fulfilled. I always liked what I did, I always got results I always fought for things I do not have, so I do not have hurts from the past; I think I had an enriching professional career ahhh umm where I learned a lot ahhh where I got results this is like everywhere."

Career Management is a common practice in most organizations and is also considered fundamental by the participants in the Career Process. Thus, Career Management involves two areas, the organizational and individual parts. First, careers are defined according to the needs and objectives of the organization. In contrast, individual career management allows careers to be managed according to the objectives and aspirations of individuals.

Participants refer that the application of this process is essential because it allows for the creation and definition of careers, the ability to analyze their career path and to envisage a post-retirement career definition. As an illustration, it is possible to check Participant 5.

"And I had some effective progression throughout all the years I worked there. I started by being in the center, what was it called to let me see if I remember, the cost center where the production data of the factory was noted; it was a textile company; after three years in that job, I ended up moving to the secretariat, a much more interesting area than the previous one, I was in the secretarial department from about seventy-four years before the revolution, about seventy-three at the end of seventy-three until eighty-five, maybe I do not know exactly, and at that time I moved to the foreign sales department."

In parallel to the process described above, some participants mention the lack of Career Management as a demotivating and dissatisfying factor during the career because understanding that it is impossible to develop more within the organization becomes a demotivating factor and consequently translates into a reduction of quality and productivity because the future perspective is the same as the current one. There are no more goals to achieve. This situation led Participant 3 to request retirement.

"the main reason was that I did not find more motivation to continue; that is, I was not upset with anyone, and no one was upset with me, but I thought that if there was no perspective of career development."

Disengagement Category

The dimension of Disengagement Characterization consists of the processes that organizations opt for at the moment of termination of employment with an employee or the understanding and emotions that the individual went through during this period, such as the process of replacement and passing on of the baton when there is a succession plan or, conversely, how to operate when there is no such process. This dimension emerged from the subcategories: Characterization of the Succession Plan and Feeling about the Disengagement (Figure 3).

Figure 3. Categories and Subcategories of the Characterization of Disengagement
Source: Own elaboration, 2022

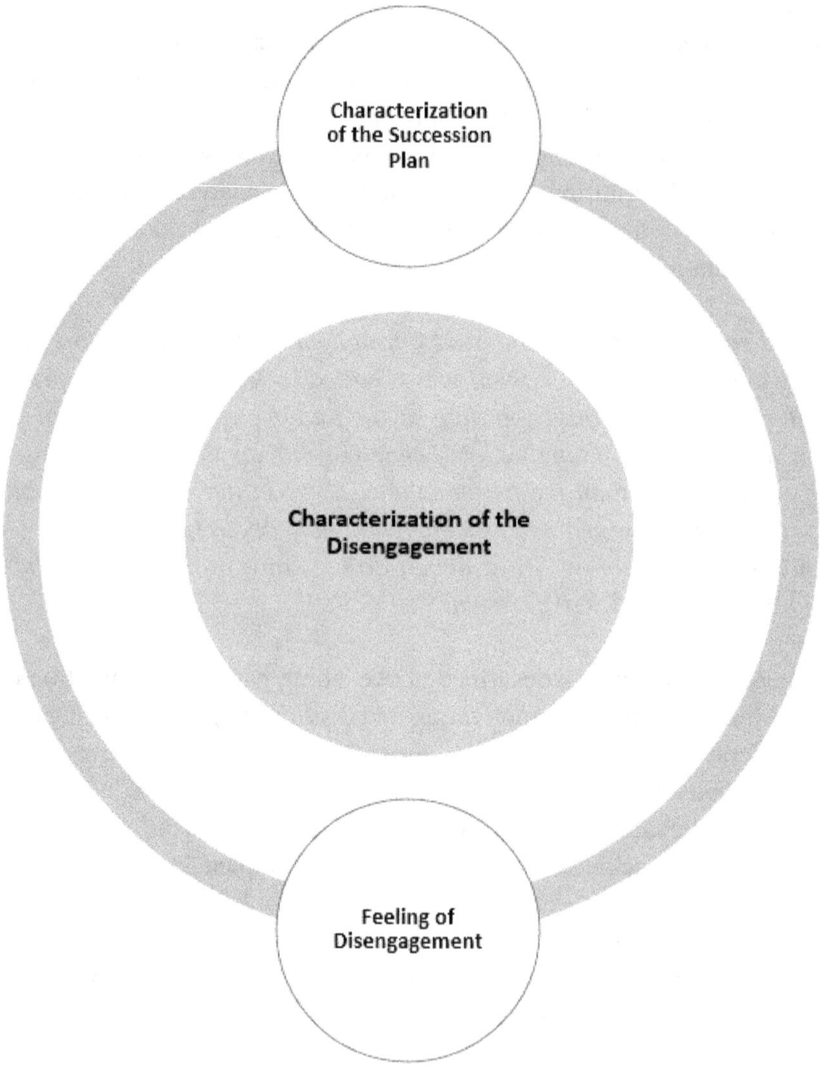

The first subcategory is the Characterization of the Succession Plan, which is characterized by the need that organizations denote in the transition of skills and knowledge of an employee to another who will replace him/her; likewise, in this process is analyzed the way passing on knowledge, the duration of the plan and how this process is managed, as such Participant 4 is an illustrative example about the importance given to this process. In order to obtain this code, the open code Duration of Succession Plan was obtained.

"There was that process because I told my boss a year before that I was going to be gone if he wanted me to pass my baton to someone, we will get someone, (...) and I went at least nine months with the person in the factory down wool, and then I went with someone else in the factory up here."

Parallel to the succession process gives the Feeling about the Disengagement at this point; in this subcategory, several ways are presented of how this process was approached and what the feeling had by the participants; most express contentment with their exit, Participant 6 serves as an example motto, as mentioned was also exemplified the Well-Being Referring to the Exit and the Well-Being with the Exit.

"My leaving was an excellent leaving; was a complete leaving was a leaving of friendship, a leaving of professionalism was a leaving of everything that could be that leads us to be satisfied and happy and with the feelings of friendship."

CONTRIBUTIONS, LIMITATIONS, AND FUTURE RESEARCH DIRECTION

This study aimed to provide an opportunity for reflection, increasing the understanding of the importance of studies regarding senior employees, being noticeable the scarcity of studies on the theme of career management, processes of disengagement, and adaptation to the retirement of senior workers, so this study has shown that we are facing a topic of great importance in today's society, whether at European, national or global level, and therefore deserves a more holistic approach by academics.

Since several processes and practices are identified in this chapter, it is hoped that this chapter will provide the necessary resources for decision-makers in the five-way helix to adopt solutions to a new social and economic reality with a direct impact on the workforce.

Inherent to research studies, some limitations to the study were identified, the main one being that only the experiences, perspectives, and emotions of senior employees who are already retired were analyzed, and there was no confrontation with the point of view and action of their respective organization or with other individuals in the same organization. It is crucial to analyze and understand these aspects and what might reveal that there are different forms and processes of career management, depending on the functions and the effective connection between people and the organization. The feeling of organizational recognition, which was not explored in this study, may be an influential factor in appealing to the sense of loyalty and seniority that different employees may have with the organization. Thus, future studies should explore not only the perspective of the senior employee but also that of the organization.

Another limitation was the fragility of the results regarding subjective interpretations of what was experienced by the participants of this study. Combining the qualitative methodology with a quantitative methodology through a mixed research or case study will ensure greater objectivity and generalization of the results obtained.

Data collection coincided with the outbreak of a global pandemic, COVID-19, making it difficult to access more participants with the desired profile. Being the profile of participants coincident with one of the risk groups of this pandemic, the fear of being physically present and the unfamiliarity with the use of distance communication technologies also proved to be a limitation of this study. Even though theoretical saturation was guaranteed, we believe this study could be enriched if the temporal context was not conditioned by the need for physical distance between interviewer and interviewee while preventing retirement participants from living a free social life. Revisiting these participants at a time of greater security and freedom of social movement may reveal new perspectives on retirement life, which was, for some, unexpectedly conditioned by this global pandemic.

CONCLUSION

Demographic aging has become a worldwide phenomenon of great importance and concern for modern societies, making it essential to evaluate an individual's career and especially the final phase since we will increasingly work later and investigate the impact of the transition between working life and retirement.

This study sought to study retirement and the transition to retirement as the final phase of an individual's working life. This phase has some specificities explored, namely the need for an effective transition between working life and retirement and the respective adaptation to this new social condition.

It is mentioned by the participants that the planning of this transition phase between both career stages may directly impact how this transition is experienced, which may result in negative or positive feelings, depending on the type of preparation and management that the organization does in this transition.

Allied with planning the transition to retirement, physical activities are considered by participants as one of the main ways to occupy their free time, thus allowing them to obtain a better quality of life and maintain their health status. However, one of the main factors for an effective and positive transition to retirement is the availability of time they can allocate to their time with their families by having time to spend with their children, grandchildren, or other loved ones. It is also mentioned as another way to occupy their free time and the opportunity to do household chores, personal development activities, and other activities to maintain mental activity.

When it comes to the factors that retirees consider most important during retirement, health preservation is the most important, as it is a stage of life generally characterized by several health problems. Financial independence is also seen as one of the most critical factors to value during retirement, as retirees consider it necessary to obtain a monetary return on their contributions during their working lives, but only for those who consider that their financial situation during retirement allows them to meet their basic needs.

Retirement can be perceived by the participants in this study as an important milestone in people's life transition, implying that they have to feel satisfied with retirement to avoid health problems, especially psychological ones. Additionally, satisfaction with retirement can generate a sense of accomplishment in terms of their working life.

Derived from the process of adaptation to retirement, it is essential to mention that several practices are adopted when an employee leaves for retirement but that many companies are not yet implementing them. This is a process that suggests greater care in order to avoid the development of feelings of uncertainty and fear. One of the processes most mentioned by the participants in this study is the definition of a good succession plan. Through this plan, it is possible to give the employee the necessary time to start changing his mindset to his new condition of "pre-retired," reinforced with practices that value the recognition of the career held by the person.

This transition consists of moving from the final career phase - leaving the organization - to a new phase of adaptation to retirement. When organizations have career development plans, providing over the years of their organizational life that the employee may wish to reach the top before retiring, the transition process may be reinforced by a feeling of greater satisfaction from the pre-retired employee. Otherwise, the employee tends to feel frustrated at the end of his working life, accelerating the early retirement process.

However, some individuals, as a result of feeling that the pension they receive is not enough for their needs, feel they need to re-enter the working world, although they prefer the part-time regime. As some participants said, it would be tough to return to an active life at 100% after entering their retirement phase. Similarly, if people feel satisfied with their professional path, they will find it easier to adapt to retirement.

REFERENCES

Alis, D., Des Horts, C.-H. B., Chevalier, F., Fabi, B., & Peretti, J.-M. (2012). *Gestão dos Recursos Humanos: Uma Abordagem Internacional* [Human Resource Management: An International Approach]. Edições Piaget.

Arthur, M. B., Khapova, S. N., & Wilderom, C. P. M. (2005). Career success in a boundaryless career world. *Journal of Organizational Behavior, 26*(2), 177–202. doi:10.1002/job.290

Baruch, Y. (2006). Career development in organizations and beyond: Balancing traditional and contemporary viewpoints. *Human Resource Management Review, 16*(2), 125–138. doi:10.1016/j.hrmr.2006.03.002

Cepellos, V. (2018). Envelhecimento Nas Organizações: Os Grandes Debates Sobre o Tema Nos Estudos De Administração De Empresas [Aging in Organizations: The Major Debates on the Topic in Business Administration Studies]. *Teoria e Prática em Administração, 8*(1), 138–159. doi:10.21714/2238-104X2018v8i1-37614

Charbonneau, D. H., & Freeman, J. L. (2016). Succession Planning for Libraries. *Journal of Library Administration, 56*(7), 884–892. doi:10.1080/01930826.2016.1216229

Charmaz, K. (2006). *Constructing Grounded Theory: A Practical Guide through Qualitative Analysis*. SAGE Publications, Ltd.

Corbin, J. L. (2020). Turnover is Coming: Strategies to Prepare for Impending Retirements. *Journal of Library Administration, 60*(4), 354–364. doi:10.1080/01930826.2020.1721942

Cunha, M. P., Rego, A., Cunha, R. C., Cabral-Cardoso, C., Marques, C. A., & Gomes, J. F. S. (2015). *Manual de Gestão de Pessoas e do Capital Humano (3ª Edição)* [Manual of People and Human Capital Management (3rd Edition)]. Edições Sílabo.

da Silva, C. R. (2019). Teorização em Educação Sexual a Partir da Grounded Theory [Theorizing in Sex Education from Grounded Theory]. *Revista Ibero-Americana de Estudos Em Educação, 14*(2), 1427–1440. doi:10.21723/riaee.v14iesp.2.12609

da Silva, R. C., Trevisan, L. N., Veloso, E. F. R., & Dutra, J. S. (2016). Career anchors and values from different career management perspectives. *Revista Brasileira de Gestão de Negócios, 18*(59), 145–162. doi:10.7819/rbgn.v17i58.2260

Daniel, F., Caetano, E., Monteiro, R., & Amaral, I. (2016). Representações sociais do envelhecimento ativo num olhar genderizado [Social representations of active aging in a gendered look]. *Análise Psicológica, 34*(4), 353–364. doi:10.14417/ap.1020 de Oliveira, P. I. D., & Anderson, M. I. P. (2020). Envelhecimento, finitude e morte [Aging, finitude and death]. *Revista Brasileira de Medicina de Família e Comunidade, 15*(42), 1–11. doi:10.5712/rbmfc15(42)2195

Domingues, A. C. G. E. (2011). *Comprometimento organizacional e intenções de abandono dos agentes em geriatria* [Organizational commitment and abandonment intentions of agents in geriatrics] [Master's thesis, Faculdade de Economia – Universidade do Porto]. Repository of Faculdade de Economia – Universidade do Porto. https://hdl.handle.net/10216/45733

Duh, M. (2015). Succession Process: A Chance for Rebirth or Failure of a Family Business. *International Journal of Business and Management, 10*(3), 45–56. doi:10.5539/ijbm.v10n3p45

Ekerdt, D. J. (2000). Retirement. In A. E. Kazdin (Ed.), *Encyclopaedia of Psychology* (Vol. 7, pp. 94–97). American Psychological Association.

EUR-Lex. (2006). *Livro Verde - Para uma futura política marítima da União: uma visão europeia para os oceanos e os mares "Que impróprio chamar Terra a este planeta de oceanos!"* [Green Paper - Towards a future Union maritime policy: a European vision for oceans and seas "How inappropriate to call this planet of oceans Earth!"]. Retrieved from https://eur-lex.europa.eu/legal-content/PT/TXT/?uri=CELEX%3A52006DC0275%2802%29

Euromonitor International. (2019). *How Ageing Population and Rising Longevity Drive Megatrends.* Retrieved from https://www.euromonitor.com/article/how-ageing-populations-and-rising-longevity-drive-megatrends

Eurostat. (2015). *International day of older persons: 1 out of every 8 persons in the EU could be 80 or above by 2080.* Retrieved from https://ec.europa.eu/eurostat/documents/2995521/7012459/3-29092015-AP-EN.pdf/0b823ac4-cbcb-46b0-a248-0acfb91626a7

Fàbregues, S., & Paré, M.-H. (2007). Constructing Grounded Theory: A Practical Guide Through Qualitative Analysis. *Papers - Revista de Sociologia, 86*, 284–287. doi:10.5565/rev/papers/v86n0.825

Fernandes, E.M., & Maia, Â. (2001). *Grounded Theory.* Universidade do Minho - Centro de Estudos em Educação e Psicologia (CEEP).

Finkelstein, L. M., Ryan, K. M., & King, E. B. (2013). What do the young (old) people think of me? Content and accuracy of age-based metastereotypes. *European Journal of Work and Organizational Psychology, 22*(6), 633–657. doi:10.1080/1359432X.2012.673279

Flick, U. (2007). *Managing Quality in Qualitative Research*. SAGE Publications, Ltd., doi:10.4135/9781849209441

Fonseca, A.M. (2012). Do trabalho à reforma: Quando os dias parecem mais longos. [From work to retirement: When the days seem longer]. *Sociologia: Revista da Faculdade de Letras da Universidade do Porto*, (2), 75–95.

Garg, A., & van Weele, E. (2012). Succession Planning and Its Impact on the Performance of Small Micro Medium Enterprises within the Manufacturing Sector in Johannesburg. *International Journal of Business and Management*, *7*(9), 96–107. doi:10.5539/ijbm.v7n9p96

Godinho, A. C. M. (2016). *Plano de sucessão na Delta Cafés* [Succession plan at Delta Cafés] [Master's thesis, ISCTE - Instituto Universitário de Lisboa]. Repository of ISCTE – Instituto Universitário de Lisboa. http://hdl.handle.net/10071/13725

Gonyea, J. G. (2009). *The Older Worker and the Changing Labor Market: New Challenges for the Workplace*. Routledge.

Government of Newfoundland and Labrador. (2008). *Succession Planning and Management Guide.* Retrieved from https://www.gov.nl.ca/exec/tbs/files/publications-succession-planning-and-management-guide.pdf

Greenhaus, J. H., Callanan, G. A., & Godshalk, V. M. (2018). *Career Management for Life*. Routledge. doi:10.4324/9781315205991

Gunz, H. P., & Peiperl, M. (2007). *Handbook of Career Studies*. SAGE Publications, Inc. doi:10.4135/9781412976107

Hanisch, K. A., & Hulin, C. L. (1990). Job attitudes and organizational withdrawal: An examination of retirement and other voluntary withdrawal behaviors. *Journal of Vocational Behavior*, *37*(1), 60–78. doi:10.1016/0001-8791(90)90007-O

Hedge, J. W., Borman, W. C., & Lammlein, S. E. (2006). *The aging workforce: Realities, myths, and implications for organizations*. American Psychological Association. doi:10.1037/11325-000

Ip, B., & Jacobs, G. (2006). Business succession planning: A review of the evidence. *Journal of Small Business and Enterprise Development*, *13*(3), 326–350. doi:10.1108/14626000610680235

Ivancevich, J. M. (2010). *Human Resource Management* (11th ed.). McGraw-Hill Irwin.

Johnson, J. A., & Lopes, J. (2008). The Intergenerational Workforce, Revisited. *Organization Development Journal, 26*(1), 31–36.

Kosterlitz, M., & Lewis, J. (2017). From Baby Boomer to Millennial: Succession Planning for the Future. *Nurse Leader, 15*(6), 396–398. doi:10.1016/j.mnl.2017.09.006

Lee, Y. G., Jasper, C. R., & Goebel, K. P. (2003). A Profile of Succession Planning among Family Business Owners. *Financial Counseling and Planning, 14*(2), 31–41.

Leibowitz, Z. B., Farren, C., & Kaye, B. L. (1991). *Designing Career Development Systems* (1st ed.). Pfeiffer.

Matour, S., & Prout, M. F. (2007). Psychological implications of retirement in the 21st century. *Journal of Financial Service Professionals, 61*(1), 57–63.

Moore, C., Gunz, H., & Hall, D. (2007). Tracing the historical roots of career theory in management and organization studies. In H. Gunz & M. Peiperl (Eds.), *Handbook of Career Studies* (pp. 13–38). SAGE Publications, Ltd. doi:10.4135/9781412976107.n2

Murty, S., Sassen, B., & Kammerdiener, M. (2016). Preparing for the passing of the baton: Leadership programs in senior living organizations. *Seniors Housing & Care Journal, 24*(1), 88–96.

Nazareth, J. M. (2009). *Crescer e envelhecer: Constrangimentos e Oportunidades do envelhecimento demográfico* [Growing and aging: Constraints and opportunities of demographic aging]. Editora Presença.

Nicholson, N., & West, M. (1989). Transitions, work histories, and careers. In Handbook of Career Theory (pp. 181–201). Cambridge University Press. doi:10.1017/CBO9780511625459.011

Osborne, J. W. (2012). Psychological effects of the transition to retirement. *Canadian Journal of Counselling and Psychotherapy, 46*(1), 45–58.

Painter, J. A., Allison, L., Dhingra, P., Daughtery, J., Cogdill, K., & Trujillo, L. G. (2012). Fear of Falling and Its Relationship With Anxiety, Depression, and Activity Engagement Among Community-Dwelling Older Adults. *The American Journal of Occupational Therapy, 66*(2), 169–176. doi:10.5014/ajot.2012.002535 PMID:22394526

Palade, A. (2010). Significant Aspects regarding Career Management: Means for a Better Career Planning and Development. *Economic Sciences Series, 62*(2), 124–134.

Pereira, M. A. da S. (2011). *Preditores do turnover organizacional: uma perspetiva multidimensional* [Predictors of organizational turnover: a multi-dimensional perspective] [Master's thesis, ISCTE - Instituto Universitário de Lisboa]. Repository of ISCTE – Instituto Universitário de Lisboa. http://hdl.handle.net/10071/7302

Pestana, N.N. (2003). *Trabalhadores Mais Velhos: Políticas Públicas e Práticas Empresariais* [Older Workers: Public Policies and Business Practices]. Ministério da Segurança Social e do Trabalho (MSST).

Pew Research Center. (2019). *Baby Boomers are staying in the labor force at rates not seen in generations for people their age*. Retrieved from https://www.pewresearch.org/fact-tank/2019/07/24/baby-boomers-us-labor-force/

Pimentel, D. (2019). *Planeamento de sucessão em equipas* [Succession planning in teams]. Academic Press.

Pitt-Catsouphes, M., & Smyer, M. A. (2006). *How Old are Today's Older Workers?* Boston College University Libraries.

Ramos, S. (2010). *Envelhecimento, trabalho e cognição: do laboratório para o terreno na construção de uma alternativa metodológica* [Aging, work and cognition: from the laboratory to the field in the construction of a methodological alternative]. Fundação Calouste Gulbenkian.

Riach, K. (2009). Managing 'difference': Understanding age diversity in practice. *Human Resource Management Journal, 19*(3), 319–335. doi:10.1111/j.1748-8583.2009.00096.x

Rosa, M.J.V. (2012). *O Envelhecimento da Sociedade Portuguesa* [The Aging of Portuguese Society]. Fundação Francisco Manuel dos Santos.

Rupp, D. E., Vodanovich, S. J., & Credé, M. (2006). Age Bias in the Workplace: The Impact of Ageism and Causal Attributions. *Journal of Applied Social Psychology, 36*(6), 1337–1364. doi:10.1111/j.0021-9029.2006.00062.x

Saad, P. M. (2016). Envelhecimento populacional: Demandas e possibilidades na área de saúde [Population aging: demands and possibilities in health care]. *Séries Demográficas, 3*, 153–166.

Schalk, R., van Veldhoven, M., de Lange, A. H., De Witte, H., Kraus, K., Stamov-Roßnagel, C., Tordera, N., van der Heijden, B., Zappalà, S., Bal, M., Bertrand, F., Claes, R., Crego, A., Dorenbosch, L., de Jonge, J., Desmette, D., Gellert, F. J., Hansez, I., Iller, C., ... Zacher, H. (2010). Moving European research on work and ageing forward: Overview and agenda. *European Journal of Work and Organizational Psychology*, *19*(1), 76–101. doi:10.1080/13594320802674629

Schmidt, J. A., & Lee, K. (2008). Voluntary Retirement and Organizational Turnover Intentions: The Differential Associations with Work and Non-Work Commitment Constructs. *Journal of Business and Psychology*, *22*(4), 297–309. doi:10.100710869-008-9068-y

Schreurs, B., De Cuyper, N., van Emmerik, I. J. H., Notelaers, G., & De Witte, H. (2011). Job demands and resources and their associations with early retirement intentions through recovery need and work enjoyment. *SA Journal of Industrial Psychology*, *37*(2), 1–11. doi:10.4102ajip.v37i2.859

Sharma, P., Chua, J. H., & Chrisman, J. J. (2000). Perceptions about the extent of succession planning in Canadian family firms. *Canadian Journal of Administrative Sciences*, *17*(3), 233–244. doi:10.1111/j.1936-4490.2000.tb00223.x

Smith, D. R., Holtom, B. C., & Mitchell, T. R. (2011). Enhancing precision in the prediction of voluntary turnover and retirement. *Journal of Vocational Behavior*, *79*(1), 290–302. doi:10.1016/j.jvb.2010.11.003

Sparkes, A. C., & Smith, B. (2013). *Qualitative Research Methods in Sport, Exercise and Health: From Process to Product*. Routledge. doi:10.4324/9780203852187

Statistics Portugal. (2014). *Projeções de população residente 2012-2060* [Projections of resident population 2012-2060]. Retrieved from https://www.ine.pt/xportal/xmain?xpid=INE&xpgid=ine_destaques&DESTAQUESdest_boui=208819970&DESTAQUESmodo=2&xlang=pt

Strauss, A., & Corbin, J. M. (1998). *Basics of Qualitative Research: Techniques and Procedures for Developing Grounded Theory*. Sage Publications, Inc.

Tavares, M. A. (2020). Envelhecimento e trabalho na sociedade capitalista [Aging and work in capitalist society]. *Revista Katálysis*, *23*(1), 143–151. doi:10.1590/1982-02592020v23n1p143

Tondo, C. (2008). *Desenvolvendo a empresa familiar e a família empresária (1ª Edição)* [Developing the family business and the entrepreneurial family (1st Edition)]. Editora Sulina.

Veloso, E. F. R., da Silva, R. C., & Dutra, J. S. (2012). Diferentes Gerações e Percepções sobre Carreiras Inteligentes e Crescimento Profissional nas Organizações [Different generations and perceptions of intelligent careers and career growth within organizations]. *Revista Brasileira de Orientação Profissional, 13*(2), 197–207.

Wang, M., & Shi, J. (2015). Work, Retirement, and Aging. In K. W. Schaie & S. Willis (Eds.), *Handbook of the Psychology of Aging* (pp. 339–359). Academic Press.

World Health Organization. (2012). *World Health Day 2012: ageing and health: Toolkit for event organizers*. Retrieved from https://apps.who.int/iris/handle/10665/70840

Xavier, B. G. L. (2004). Curso de Direito do Trabalho: Vol. I. *Introdução, Quadros Organizacionais e Fontes* [Labor Law Course - Volume I (Introduction, Organizational Frameworks and Sources)]. Editorial Verbo.

KEY TERMS AND DEFINITIONS

Aging: A worldwide phenomenon of aging (the world's population getting older) resulting from improved living conditions, better health services, increasing life expectancy, and declining birth and mortality rates, directly impacting the labor force nationally and globally.

Aging Workforce: Consists of a labor force for organizations that are older and closer to retirement.

Career: The entire journey within any organization, where an individual performs a specific task or function.

Career Management: Managing an individual's career within an organization.

Retirement: This is the final stage of an individual's career, where he/she leaves active life and enters a new phase.

Senior Collaborators: Those who are 65 years or older and have not yet retired.

Succession Plan: It is strategic planning for replacing an employee who will leave the organization, either to change the organization or to retire, where this employee will help his substitute orient himself in his new function for a complete transition without loss of knowledge.

Untying: The process of leaving an organization.

Chapter 8
Enterprise Architecture Solutions for an Aging Workforce

Raja Saravanan
University of Aveiro, Portugal

ABSTRACT

The aging workforce has been a topic of discussion for many years, and as we enter the fourth industrial revolution, it is clear that the issue will only become more pressing. In the past, it was believed that the older population would be unable to adapt to the increasingly technological world. However, as technology advances, many older workers are adapting and finding ways to remain competitive in the workplace. In this chapter, the authors examine how the aging workforce impacts economic and social development, and they discuss how Industry 4.0 and enterprise architecture can help address these challenges.

INTRODUCTION

The aging workforce is a worldwide challenge that affects all countries and industries. Understanding the aging workforce, its impact on economic and social development, and how to address its challenges to ensure sustainable long-term growth is essential. The aging workforce is a growing issue affecting many countries' economic and social development. As the population ages, fewer workers will replace retirees and help support the economy. This can lead to higher unemployment rates, slower economic growth, and lower tax revenues. To address the challenges of an aging workforce, countries must ensure that they have policies and programs to help them

DOI: 10.4018/978-1-6684-6351-2.ch008

attract, retain, and develop a skilled workforce. This can include improving education systems, increasing training opportunities, and providing better access to health care. It is important to note that a population's age structure can impact economic development. For example, countries with large youth or elderly populations may find it more challenging to achieve high levels of growth. This is because younger people generally have higher birth rates and are more likely than older generations to spend money on education and other goods and services that contribute to economic growth. Aging populations strain many countries' social services, such as health care and pensions. As life expectancy increases, the number of people over 65 will continue to grow in most countries. This will put pressure on social security systems, which have traditionally been based on the concept of "pay as you go," with contributions from current workers funding benefits for retirees.

The term aging workforce refers to workers who are older than 65 years old, as well as those who are close to retirement age. In some countries such as Japan, Germany, and Italy, more than half of all adults are members of this group—an indication that they are not just working longer hours or staying in the workforce past retirement age—they are staying on into their 60s and 70s! For many employers, this presents a problem: how to retain older workers and make them feel valued in an environment where they compete for jobs with younger people. It is a trend that has profound implications for employers around the world. As more and more workers enter retirement age, they will leave behind positions in their companies that need to be filled by novice younger staff. Businesses will have to compete harder than ever for skilled workers—especially those willing to relocate and work long hours in demanding environments.

The global aging workforce is projected to increase, as Figure 1 refers. The aging workforce statistics show that as many as 35% of the workforce will be 60 years or older by 2040, according to a report by the World Economic Forum (2019). This directly impacts businesses since they need experienced employees who can work with technology and adapt quickly to changing conditions or new technologies. There is no denying that the world's population is rapidly aging. By 2050, the number of people aged 60 or older will increase by almost a billion. By 2060, over 5 billion people aged 65 and older worldwide will be more than double what it was in 2015. Of these, about 1 billion are projected to be in developing countries.

Figure 1. Forecast aging workforce in enterprises
Source: Own elaboration, 2022

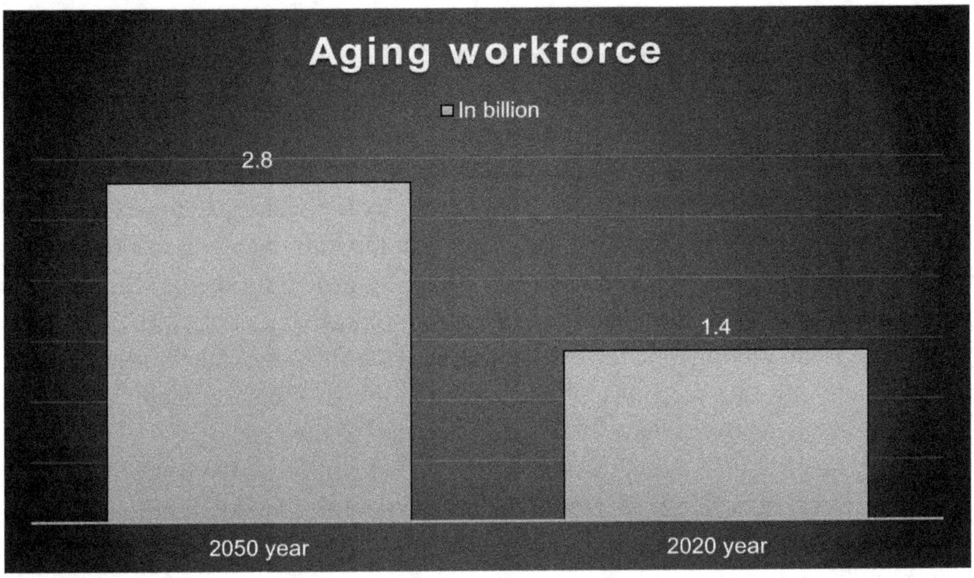

BACKGROUND

Impact and Challenges

The impact of the aging workforce on economic and social development has been well-documented, particularly in developed countries. It has been found that the aging workforce is a crucial driver of economic growth in developed countries, where most people will have to work longer due to reduced birth rates. In developing countries, however, aging populations are expected to be essential in slowing down their economic development. The aging workforce will have a significant impact on the global economy as well as society. On the economic side, it will cause productivity to decline and result in slower economic growth. The aging workforce also has implications for policymakers, who must plan for higher spending on pensions and health care for older people (Truxillo et al., 2015). The aging workforce presents significant challenges to businesses and governments, which must find new ways of generating growth and addressing issues such as increasing demand for healthcare.

The aging workforce is a challenge that needs to be addressed for businesses to stay competitive. The impact will be felt on economic development, social development, and the ability to provide quality services. Many industries are dependent on older workers (Silverstein, 2008). For example, in agriculture, farmers must have access to workers who can work with them and learn how their crops grow. This means that they need access to older people who have experience in this area so they can teach them about new developments in agriculture or even teach them how to do their jobs more efficiently. The same thing is true for other industries. Many professions require people with years of experience who can teach them how things must be done. If older workers were not around, this would cause a huge gap in the workforce that younger people could not quickly fill.

There will be a shortage of skilled individuals to fill the void created by retiring workers. The aging workforce is also an opportunity for businesses to reach out and tap into an untapped market. Businesses that can tap into the aging workforce will be in a position to better serve their customers by providing them with products and services that cater specifically to this group (Nagarajan et al., 2019). There is a growing trend among businesses today to provide more flexible working hours, offer on-site day-care facilities, create age-friendly work environments, and even hire individuals who may have been side-lined due to their age.

The influence of the aging workforce has not been fully explored yet. The global workforce is expected to shrink from 3.5 billion workers today to 2.8 billion in 2050. This will impact industries operating in different countries, especially those that rely heavily on young people for their workforce needs (Costa & Milia, 2008). In developed countries like Japan and Switzerland, where life expectancy is high, the impact of the aging population can be mitigated by designing enterprise architectures with mobility, flexibility, and agility features built into them. However, developing countries like India, where life expectancy is low, need more efforts to focus on innovative solutions like enterprise architecture frameworks to address issues related to workforce shortages due to high unemployment rates among young adults.

The impact of the aging workforce has been studied extensively. However, many people do not realize that it affects businesses in various ways, from reduced productivity to higher healthcare costs. The impact of the aging workforce can be felt in many ways. First, it affects productivity and efficiency at work because older workers tend to be less productive than younger ones (Wisse et al., 2018). Second, this trend negatively impacts society because fewer young people have access to good jobs as they grow up (Wisse et al., 2018). However, due to high unemployment rates, among other factors such as low birth rates and smaller families in recent years, there has been a decline in the number of young people entering job markets as well as an increase in older people leaving them because they cannot find work elsewhere (Minocha et al., 2015). Finally, there are serious challenges related to retirement savings and healthcare costs for older people who no longer have access to health insurance through their employers (Hertel & Zacher, 2017).

Older workers have historically faced discrimination due to their age, but this is no longer the case. According to research by economist Blanchflower (2021), employees over 50 earn as much as 10% more than those under 35. These findings suggest that there is less discrimination against older workers today than there used to be when they were younger. Despite this progress, there are still many challenges facing older workers today, such as lower wages than younger colleagues who perform similar tasks with equal skill levels (Blanchflower, 2021). One of the most common misconceptions about older workers is that they are less competent than younger colleagues. This is not true. Older workers can be just as effective and efficient as their younger counterparts, but this does not mean employers will give them the same opportunities or pay.

The aging population significantly impacts global economies since it leads to a decline in productivity levels due to increased absenteeism and other factors such as poor health (International Labour Organization, 2016). Various challenges arise from an aging workforce, including increased costs related to healthcare (International Labour Organization, 2016). In the past, many people assumed that technology would help to solve the problems associated with aging populations (Kumar & Srivastava, 2018). However, as we can see from the current situation, this is not the case. It has become a significant problem for society and the economy. The problem is that the elderly live longer than ever before but are not necessarily healthier. As a result, they need more care and attention than ever before. This means much more money needs to be spent on health care, which puts a strain on an already overburdened economy. In addition, employees need continuous training to ensure that they can adapt to new technologies that may be introduced into their work environment and keep up with technological changes (Wissemann et al., 2022). However, the aging population also allows companies to tap into this demographic. This is because older workers are more likely to have paid off their mortgages, have lower living costs, and may be less likely to relocate. This means they can work longer without worrying about replacing a lost income stream. The older population can be used as a source of labor and expertise in areas such as Research & Development, which may lead to increased innovation (International Labour Organization, 2016). In addition, companies can use their resources more efficiently by tapping into older workers' skills and knowledge base. Furthermore, many companies still rely on older workers because they believe they can provide quality services for extended periods without their skills deteriorating over time (Minocha et al., 2015).

Industry 4.0

Siemens asserts that Industry 4.0 is an industrial revolution driven by digitalization. It involves new technologies such as artificial intelligence (AI), robotics, automation systems, blockchain, and the Internet of Things (IoT). It refers to how businesses use technology to improve their processes and increase efficiency. Industry 4.0 is all about data; having access to the correct data can improve your business. It involves collecting, analyzing, and using the information to provide value for employees, customers, and other stakeholders. The goal is not just to make products but also to create experiences. The idea behind Industry 4.0 is that businesses can connect the physical and digital worlds, allowing them to create new value. This includes everything from manufacturing to customer service. It is not just about improving efficiency but also about creating new business models.

Industry 4.0 is helping to combat challenges caused by an aging workforce by using new technologies such as AI, robotics, and 3D printing to create solutions that help ease the burden on workers as they age while reducing costs associated with training new employees. Also, companies are exploring how they can help their aging workforce remain productive and engaged in the workplace. One way that companies are addressing this challenge is through Industry 4.0 (or IoT). This technology allows organizations to use data gathered from wearables like Fitbit or smartwatches, for example, for them to improve productivity and employee engagement by enhancing communication between co-workers or between workers and supervisors. For example, companies are using AI-based technologies capable of detecting patterns in data and making predictions based on this information without human intervention or supervision. The impact of technology on the workforce is a growing concern for many industries. The World Economic Forum (2019) estimated that around 5 million jobs would be lost to automation by 2020, with more than two-thirds of those in developing countries. For instance, companies need fewer workers in factories because machines can now perform many tasks instead of human labor (Calzavara et al., 2020). While automation is expected to cause a loss of jobs, it will also create new ones. The World Economic Forum (2019) estimated that adopting AI and robotics technologies would create an additional 28 million jobs. Industries such as healthcare, finance, and transportation are already incorporating these technologies into their business models.

The World Economic Forum (2019) also predicted that those aged between 65 and 69 will account for more than 20% of the global population in 2060. This means that more people in their early retirement age will still work while others have stopped altogether due to health issues or family responsibilities. Industry 4.0 is also expected to impact this age group since older workers may not be able to access advanced technology easily due to their physical limitations—yet they will still be needed in some cases because specific jobs require expertise or experience. This is why it is crucial to consider the needs of this group. The World Economic Forum (2019) recommends that companies adopt age-friendly practices to be more inclusive of people from all generations. This could mean creating flexible working schemes, providing training and mentorship opportunities, and ensuring that company policies accommodate older workers who may need more help than their younger colleagues. Companies should also be aware of the financial implications of an aging workforce. As people live longer, they will need to work for longer, which could pressure pension funds. The World Economic Forum (2019) recommends that companies consider how this will affect their business models and what steps can be taken to mitigate these impacts.

In today's world, the aging workforce is an issue that has been discussed in recent years. Industry 4.0 is particularly relevant to this discussion because it describes the use of information technology to enable smart manufacturing and smart services, both components of the aging workforce (Reiman et al., 2021).

Smart manufacturing means creating products with greater quality control and fewer defects, which is especially important for older workers with health issues or other conditions that make them more prone to injuries when working on-site. Smart services involve using digital tools to manage processes like scheduling, hiring, and training—essentially, anything a company needs to do but cannot do well enough.

The impact of these changes on economic development will vary by country depending on its labor laws, culture, and infrastructure. For example, in some countries, it would be easier for companies to hire older workers than in others because there are fewer legal restrictions on age discrimination based on nationality or religion; however, some countries might not have as many jobs available for older people as they do now due to automation technologies replacing traditional factory jobs like machine operators or assembly line workers.

Enterprise Architecture

Enterprise architecture is a comprehensive approach to managing an organization's information technology infrastructure across all departments—from the C-suite to the janitor's closet. It can be applied to any organization, regardless of size or industry. Enterprise architecture does not simply describe hardware and software systems but includes organizational processes, business goals, objectives, and information security controls. Enterprise architecture is the process of developing a holistic view of your organization and its current state. It allows you to create a plan to transform that current state into one that better aligns with your business goals and objectives.

The aging workforce has been a topic of concern for many years. The number of people over 65 in the United States has been increasing, and it is projected that by 2030, more than 85 million seniors will be participating in the workforce. The question that arises is, what does this mean for business? The answer to this question lies in business architecture. Business architecture is a set of processes that are used to manage an organization's resources and information in a way that optimizes performance. To examine how an organization can prepare itself for an aging workforce, we must first look at what makes up its business architecture.

The three components of the business architecture are data, application, and technology architectures. Data architecture consists of the organization's data storage system and management controls. Application architecture refers to all applications used by employees within an organization. Technology architectures refer to how information flows within and between systems within an organization and from external sources such as suppliers or vendors (Information technology knowledge-based). This allows us to examine how we can prepare ourselves for an aging workforce needing different skill sets than those traditionally needed by employees within large organizations such as Amazon.

As the workforce ages and the number of people in their prime working year's declines, businesses must develop new technologies to maximize efficiency. To keep up with changing economic conditions, businesses must constantly innovate and invest in new technology. Enterprise architecture (a framework for analyzing current systems and understanding the need for change) offers a way to manage business process change.

Enterprise architecture can help organizations address issues related to aging workers through better planning and data analysis, which allows them to make informed decisions that improve employee satisfaction and retention rates. Enterprise architecture can also help organizations prepare for the effects of aging workers by identifying and implementing tools that will allow them to remain competitive in an increasingly digital world. For example, companies may use AI-based tools to help workers with repetitive tasks or manual labor, allowing them to focus on more creative tasks that require human skills, such as problem-solving and communication.

Enterprise architecture is one-way business owners can address this aging workforce issue by creating an open-architecture framework that allows them to incorporate new technologies into existing systems without redesigning their entire system from scratch. This allows businesses to save time and money by incorporating new technologies without redesigning their entire system. Enterprise architecture can help companies avoid a complete overhaul when they need to incorporate new technologies into existing systems.

The aging workforce is a significant concern for organizations. As the population ages, the number of people working in organizations will also decrease. The aging workforce has caused several critical organizational issues, including lower productivity and higher employee turnover rates. One of the most significant impacts of the aging workforce is that it has caused organizations to rethink their hiring strategies. As organizations are unable to recruit new workers fast enough to replace those who retire, they are forced to consider several different options for replacing their retiring employees.

Companies must adopt new technologies and change their business processes to address these challenges. Enterprise architecture is one such technology that can help companies adapt to an aging workforce by allowing them to manage the adoption of new technologies across the organization. Enterprise architecture is a holistic, strategic approach to designing and implementing technology. It involves analyzing an organization's current state of technology, determining which parts of the business will benefit most from new technologies, and creating a roadmap for how those new technologies can be adopted. Enterprise architecture can also help companies assess their current workforce capabilities considering emerging technologies. For example, suppose a company is considering adopting AI into its operations but does not have enough data scientists on staff. In that case, it needs to determine how it will address that gap to successfully implement AI (Bauer et al., 2015). Enterprise architecture is an approach for aligning business and information technologies strategies, and it involves the creation of a roadmap that maps out an organization's future. This roadmap can identify gaps between where an organization currently stands and where it wants to be, and it helps companies prioritize projects that will close those gaps. With enterprise architecture in place, organizations can more effectively manage to adopt new technologies such as AI and automation.

The enterprise architecture provides several frameworks for analyzing current systems, identifying gaps between current business practices and desired outcomes, and determining how best to address those gaps through changes in technology or process re-engineering. Enterprise architecture is not a one-time project. It should be continually updated as the organization's needs change over time. For example, if an organization adopts AI, it must determine how best to implement the technology and train its workforce to achieve desired business outcomes. These decisions may require changes in processes and systems incorporated into the enterprise architecture.

Enterprise Architect

As the population ages, enterprise architects are responsible for examining the aging workforce and its impact on economic and social development. This is done by assessing an organization's current enterprise architecture maturity and long-term goals and objectives. The enterprise architect must also consider the implications of Industry 4.0 on the aging workforce. With the advent of robotics and AI, many jobs humans once performed are now being done by machines. This technology is also impacting how we live and work, as more and more people can work remotely. As a result, enterprise architects must be prepared to adapt their organizations' enterprise architectures to these changing demographics and technologies.

The enterprise architect must also consider the implications of technological advances on healthcare and their impact on an aging workforce. For example, new medical technologies are emerging that can detect health issues earlier in life, helping to reduce medical costs over time. In addition, these technologies can help employers proactively manage employee workloads and ensure that their employees remain healthy and productive at work.

Finally, the enterprise architect should evaluate how well the organization is leveraging digital transformation initiatives to serve an aging population better. By taking advantage of cloud computing, mobile applications, analytics platforms, and other digital tools, organizations can create a more efficient working environment that helps employees stay engaged and productive while they age. This includes providing resources for retirement planning and offering meaningful career opportunities, such as retraining and upskilling. Additionally, organizations may consider implementing solutions that promote flexibility in the workplace and make it easier for older workers to stay connected with their peers and colleagues.

In summary, enterprise architects must consider the implications of an aging workforce on economic development, healthcare, and digital transformation initiatives when developing their organization's enterprise architecture. By proactively addressing these issues, the enterprise architect can ensure that the organization can effectively meet an aging population's needs while positioning itself for long-term success. By considering these factors, organizations can ensure they are adequately prepared to meet the needs of an aging population and capitalize on the opportunity to increase productivity and efficiency. Ultimately, this will enable them to stay competitive in a rapidly changing world and remain successful for years. In conclusion, developing an effective enterprise architecture strategy for an aging workforce requires a deep understanding of how this demographic impacts your organization's operations.

Embracing Aging Workforce Ideas

The impact of the aging workforce on organizations can be seen in its impact on growth. Organizations that can maintain a strong workforce will be able to grow at a higher rate than those who are unable to do so. This is because younger generations view older workers as having more experience, which means they are more likely to be hired for jobs where their skillset is needed. The opposite also holds: if an organization does not have enough staff members with specific skill sets, then they will have trouble hiring new employees with those same skill sets because there are not enough available candidates who have them. The data shows that diversity is good for business. Companies with more diverse workforces tend to be more successful than those without because diverse teams are better able to tackle problems from various perspectives. They also tend to perform better in productivity because they have more creative thinking skills. This is where the problem with older workers comes in. They tend to have fewer skill sets than younger generations, which means they are less likely to be hired for jobs requiring those skill sets. Organizations will have a more challenging time hiring new employees to help grow their businesses.

Organizations must create new work models that meet aging workers' needs while minimizing costs. The aging worker challenge is an opportunity to rethink work models, but only if organizations are willing to think beyond their existing culture and processes (Heidemeier & Staudinger, 2015). There is no one-size-fits-all solution, but we can identify some of the most common approaches that organizations must consider as they adapt their work models for aging workers. The following are some of the most common work model adaptations for aging workers. The first step is to create a culture that values the contributions of all workers. Companies cannot afford to lose their most experienced workers and must make an effort to retain them. This requires companies to establish a work environment where older employees feel valued and supported as they age.

1. **Telecommuting:** Work from home and reduce time spent in a car or on public transportation. This approach can benefit aging workers and their employers by reducing traffic congestion, lowering carbon emissions, and improving worker health and productivity. Allows employees to work from home, which can help reduce employee stress and improve overall productivity. It also allows workers who live far away from the office to avoid long commutes.
2. **Remote work:** Like telecommuting, remote workers work from a different location instead of working from home. This approach allows for flexible working schedules and can be especially beneficial for aging workers by reducing the time spent traveling from home to work.
3. **Flexible Hours:** Allow employees to vary their daily start and end times based on personal needs. For example, an older worker may need to arrive at work later than younger colleagues so they can take care of morning errands before heading into the office.
4. **Inclusive Workspaces:** Many companies are making their offices more accessible by removing barriers such as staircases or cubicles that may make it difficult for seniors.
5. **Walking and Standing Breaks:** These breaks can help reduce the risk of high blood pressure, back pain, and other stress-related health problems.
6. **Wellness Programs:** These programs can be as simple as providing information on healthy living to more complex efforts, including gym memberships or team sports.

7. **Flexible Leave:** Allow employees to use their vacation and sick leave anytime during the year. This can be especially helpful for older workers who may have more flexibility in arranging caregiving arrangements.
8. **Shorter workdays:** Employers can offer employees the option to work fewer hours each day or week while still receiving full pay. While this approach may not be ideal for all workers and industries, it can benefit older workers by allowing them to spend more time with family members.
9. **Flexible Scheduling:** Allows employees to change their work schedule every week, typically on a day-by-day basis. This type of flexibility can give workers greater control over when they perform tasks and help reduce the stress associated with time management.

CONCLUSION

Ultimately, we believe that the impact of Industry 4.0 and enterprise architecture solutions will be substantial. As time goes on, the aging workforce will continue to occupy a more significant percentage of the workforce, and we expect this change to affect companies in every industry and sector of the economy. It may not necessarily be as dramatic as some projects predict, but it will be there.

Industry 4.0 can help organizations become more efficient as they work towards effectively implementing new technologies. Using enterprise architecture solutions can help organizations effectively implement these new technologies and minimize risk-taking on behalf of their employees.

For companies to be successful in this new era, they will need to adopt new strategies for recruiting, retaining, and motivating their employees—and these strategies will likely involve some training or education component. Older workers' knowledge about their careers and workplace environments could provide valuable insights into how younger workers should best be trained for the workplace today.

ACKNOWLEDGMENT

I would like to thank my family and friends for their support while I wrote this book chapter. I would also like to thank my editors for all their help in making this book chapter the best it can be.

REFERENCES

Bauer, W., Hämmerle, M., Schlund, S., & Vocke, C. (2015). Transforming to a Hyper-connected Society and Economy – Towards an "Industry 4.0". *Procedia Manufacturing, 3*, 417–424. doi:10.1016/j.promfg.2015.07.200

Blanchflower, D. G. (2021). Is Happiness U-shaped Everywhere? Age and Subjective Well-being in 145 countries. *Journal of Population Economics, 34*(2), 575–624. doi:10.100700148-020-00797-z PMID:32929308

Calzavara, M., Battini, D., Bogataj, D., Sgarbossa, F., & Zennaro, I. (2020). Ageing Workforce Management in Manufacturing Systems: State of the Art and Future Research Agenda. *International Journal of Production Research, 58*(3), 729–747. doi:10.1080/00207543.2019.1600759

Costa, G., & Milia, L. D. (2008). Aging and Shift Work: A Complex Problem to Face. *The Journal of Biological and Medical Rhythm Research, 25*(2-3), 165–181. Advance online publication. doi:10.1080/07420520802103410 PMID:18484359

Heidemeier, H., & Staudinger, U. M. (2015). Age differences in Achievement Goals and Motivational Characteristics of Work in an Ageing Workforce. *Ageing and Society, 35*(4), 809–836. doi:10.1017/S0144686X13001098

Hertel, G., & Zacher, H. (2017). Managing the Aging Workforce. In The SAGE Handbook of Industrial, Work, & Organizational Psychology (pp. 396-428). SAGE Publication.

International Labour Organization. (2016). *Towards a Framework for Fair and Effective Integration of Migrants into the Labour Market*. Retrieved from https://www.ilo.org/global/about-the-ilo/how-the-ilo-works/multilateral-system/g20/reports/WCMS_559139/lang--en/index.htm

Kumar, R., & Srivastava, U. R. (2018). Ageing Workforce: Negative Age Stereotypes and their Impact on Older Workers. *International Journal of Research in Social Sciences, 8*(5), 302–312.

Minocha, S., McNulty, C., & Evans, S. (2015). *Imparting digital skills to people aged 55 years and over in the UK*. The Open University.

Nagarajan, N. R., Wada, M., Fang, M. L., & Sixsmith, A. (2019). Defining Organizational Contributions to Sustaining an Ageing Workforce: A Bibliometric Review. *European Journal of Ageing, 16*(3), 337–361. doi:10.100710433-019-00499-w PMID:31543728

Reiman, A., Kaivo-oja, J., Parviainen, E., Takala, E.-P., & Lauraeus, T. (2021). Human factors and ergonomics in manufacturing in the industry 4.0 context – A scoping review. *Technology in Society*, *65*, 101572. doi:10.1016/j.techsoc.2021.101572

Silverstein, M. (2008). Meeting the Challenges of an Aging Workforce. *American Journal of Industrial Medicine*, *51*(4), 269–280. doi:10.1002/ajim.20569 PMID:18271000

Truxillo, D. M., Cadiz, D. M., & Hammer, L. B. (2015). Supporting the Aging Workforce: A Review and Recommendations for Workplace Intervention Research. *Annual Review of Organizational Psychology and Organizational Behavior*, *2*(1), 351–381. doi:10.1146/annurev-orgpsych-032414-111435

Wisse, B., van Eijbergen, R., Rietzschel, E. F., & Scheibe, S. (2018). Catering to the Needs of an Aging Workforce: The Role of Employee Age in the Relationship Between Corporate Social Responsibility and Employee Satisfaction. *Journal of Business Ethics*, *147*(4), 875–888. doi:10.100710551-015-2983-8

Wissemann, A. K., Pit, S. W., Serafin, P., & Gebhardt, H. (2022). Strategic Guidance and Technological Solutions for Human Resources Management to Sustain an Aging Workforce: Review of International Standards, Research, and Use Cases. *JMIR Human Factors*, *9*(3), e27250. doi:10.2196/27250 PMID:35862177

World Economic Forum. (2019, January 3). *An Ageing Workforce Isn't a Burden. It's an Opportunity.* Retrieved from https://www.weforum.org/agenda/2019/01/an-aging-workforce-isnt-a-burden-its-an-opportunity

KEY TERMS AND DEFINITIONS

Aging Workforce: The term refers to workers who are older than 50 years old, as well as those who are close to retirement age.

Digital Transformation: Process of transforming a company's products, services, processes, and business models to exploit opportunities in digital technologies fully.

Economic Development: Economic development often relies on government intervention to produce better public services, provide industry incentives, and increase the skills base.

Enterprise: It is an organization that has a specific goal. It usually has many employees, and it can be public or private.

Enterprise Architecture: It refers to what is fundamental for the organization of the enterprise and the principles underlying this entire organization.

Industry 4.0: Is all about data, and when you have access to the correct data, it can improve your business.

Social Development: Process of improving a group's social conditions and quality of life. It is a practice that involves learning, teaching, and changing attitudes toward others.

Glossary

Active Aging: Aging process with continuous participation in society's social, economic, cultural, and civil issues. It aims to increase healthy life expectancy and quality of life.

Age Bias or Age Prejudice: The prejudicial treatment of employees 40 years of age or older.

Ageism: The prejudgment or discrimination based on a person's age.

Aging: A worldwide phenomenon of aging (the world's population getting older) resulting from improved living conditions, better health services, increasing life expectancy, and declining birth and mortality rates, directly impacting the labor force nationally and globally; a continuous, gradual, irreversible process of molecular, cellular, and functional changes that begins in adulthood.

Aging in Place: *"the individual's ability to continue to live in his or her abode safely, as independently as possible, and comfortably, regardless of age, income, or ability level"* is observed so that older people can continue their lives with family and friends.

Aging Workforce: A labor force, i.e., available workforce for organizations that are older and closer to retirement; the term refers to workers who are older than 50 years old, as well as those who are close to retirement age.

Career: The entire journey within any organization, where an individual performs a specific task or function.

Career Management: Managing an individual's career within an organization.

Creativity: A competency described as the ability to imagine, produce, create or invent new ideas or concepts; such thinking is the predecessor of the innovation process through the creation of a new idea or way of looking at a problem or a new process.

Dependency Ratio: The ratio of those in employment to those outside of employment, usually represented by the ratio of the 15-64 years age group (those of working age) to those outside of working age.

Digital Transformation: The process of transforming a company's products, services, processes, and business models to exploit opportunities in digital technologies fully.

Discrimination: The practice of discriminating against marginalized groups.

Economic Development: Economic development often relies on government intervention to produce better public services, provide industry incentives, and increase the skills base.

Economic Growth: The increase in the production of one or several economic units over one or several periods. Such an increase presupposes the nation's enrichment and improving the standard of living.

Enterprise: An organization that has a specific goal. It usually has many employees, and it can be public or private.

Enterprise Architecture: What is fundamental for the organization of the enterprise and the principles underlying this entire organization.

Gender Equity Index (GEN): The index measures gender equity and estimates national gender gaps on economic, political, education, and health criteria.

Geriatric: A medical expression for analyzing, diagnosing, and treating diseases and health problems pertinent to older adults. Gerontology and geriatrics work to mitigate issues involving older adults by challenging how older adults are perceived in society.

Gerontology: The scientific analysis of aging that assesses the biological, psychological, and sociological factors correlated with aging.

Hearing: A sensory sense is related to hearing and processing sounds of different spectrums.

Hiring Practices: Companies hiring policies that govern their recruiting strategies.

Human Capital Index (HCI): Measures the extent to which a child who reaches 18 years of age has access to health and education.

Human Development Index (HDI): A measurement of a country's development trajectory based on measures of life expectancy, schooling, and Gross National Income per capita.

Human Resource (HR) Policies and Procedures: The policies and procedures employers use to handle affairs concerning employees.

Individual Aging: The biological, psychosocial, and other changes related to old age that depends on each individual. Each human being has an aging process accompanied by differentiated experiences.

Industry 4.0: Is all about data, and when you have access to the correct data, it can improve your business.

Informal Employment: Unregulated and unrecorded employment associated with family businesses, the self-employed, seasonal, and daily work.

Informal Sector: The component of the economy that is outside regulations and difficult to track.

Innovation: Its goal is to create something new or introduce novelties through the renewal or re-creation of a given product or way of producing. Such a process necessarily means changing or improving a given product or way of producing and is one of the engines of economic growth.

Innovative Work Behavior: The innovative behavior of an individual, applying his or her creativity, skills, and knowledge in a process capable of generating innovative ideas and elaborate projects that allow putting those ideas into practice regarding new products, new ways of producing, or reinventing a product.

Knowledge Transfer: The exchange of life experiences, technical knowledge, and practical knowledge among the various employees of the organization, either between age segments or within the same age segment.

Lifelong Learning: Learning that occurs outside a formal educational institute, such as a school, university, or others. Intentional learning that occurs throughout life focuses on personal development.

Mental Health: To feel great and healthy, personally and in relationships with others, providing the individuals with productivity, self-realization, satisfaction, and well-being.

Pancasli: Indonesian state philosophy is based on five principles: faith in God, respect for humankind, nationalism, and unity, democratic government, and social justice.

Pharmacodynamics: A drug's existent effect on the body.

Pharmacokinetics: The study of how drugs travel through the body over time.

Protected Classes: A group of employees or job seekers who received legal protection from employers based on age, race, color, national origin, sex, physical or mental disability, religion or creed, and veteran status.

Quality of Life (QoL): The physical, mental, and psychological well-being without the appearance of age-related diseases. This concept includes several domains: emotional state, social interaction, cultural, ethical, religious values, and satisfaction; this principle is understood from the individual's perspective and embodies feelings of well-being, basic needs are met, opportunities to achieve personal goals and challenges, autonomy, a sense of community, and multidimensionality.

Retirement: The final stage of an individual's career, where he/she leaves active life and enters a new phase.

Senior Collaborators: Those who are 65 years or older and have not yet retired.

Sensory Impairment: Gradual changes in structures and functioning of organs that constitute the sensory system, compromising the performance of daily life activities and social participation.

Sensory System: A set of organs endowed with specialized cells with the capacity to capture internal and external stimuli. It comprises sight, hearing, smell, taste, and touch.

Skills: The knowledge, skills, and attitudes inherent to an individual user in performing an individual's function.

Smell: A sensory sense that is related to the ability to sense and distinguish odors through the olfactory system.

Social Development: The process of improving a group's social conditions and quality of life. It is a practice that involves learning, teaching, and changing attitudes toward others.

Social Responses: Institutions and/or services provided to the population according to their needs. In aging, we have day centers, social centers, and nursing homes.

Sociocultural Animation: An area of social intervention for any age group, depending on the needs. It develops activities in several scenarios and organizations to occupy free time. It involves numerous art techniques; music; cognitive stimulation; games; etc.

Succession Plan: The strategic planning for replacing an employee who will leave the organization, either to change the organization or to retire, where this employee will help his substitute orient himself in his new function for a complete transition without loss of knowledge.

Taste: A sensory sense consisting of chemical sensations perceived by the taste buds. It allows the recognition of tastes.

Telomere Erosion Theory (TET): Age and cell mortality are caused by the gradual loss of the protective telomere nucleotide sequences at the ends of the DNA strands within chromosomes with each new cell division and the resultant inability of those cells to continue to divide.

Touch: A sensory sense allows the individual to feel the world around him, perceiving and distinguishing temperatures, textures, and sensations (pain).

Untying: The process of leaving an organization.

Vision: A sensory sense that allows, through the eyes, visualizing the external world.

Workforce: Physical, mental, and psychological capacity to perform organizational activities according to a specific function.

Compilation of References

AARP Foundation. (n.d.). *Compete with confidence for full-time jobs*. Retrieved from https://www.aarp.org/aarp-foundation/our-work/income/back-to-work-50-plus/?cmp=RDRCT-BCK2WK50PL_APR22_015

Achdut, N., & Refaeli, T. (2020). Unemployment and psychological distress among young people during the covid-19 pandemic: Psychological resources and risk factors. *International Journal of Environmental Research and Public Health*, *17*(19), 1–21. doi:10.3390/ijerph17197163 PMID:33007892

Adioetomo, S. M., & Mujahid, G. (2014). *Indonesia on the Threshold of Population Ageing*. United Nations Population Fund.

Afrianty, T. W., Artatanaya, I. G., & Burgess, J. (2022). Working from home effectiveness during Covid-19: Evidence from university staff in Indonesia. *Asia Pacific Management Review*, *27*(1), 50–57. doi:10.1016/j.apmrv.2021.05.002

Age-Friendly Institute. (n.d.). *About the Age-Friendly Institute*. Retrieved from https://institute.agefriendly.org/about/age-friendly-institute/

Alis, D., Des Horts, C.-H. B., Chevalier, F., Fabi, B., & Peretti, J.-M. (2012). *Gestão dos Recursos Humanos: Uma Abordagem Internacional* [Human Resource Management: An International Approach]. Edições Piaget.

Allen, E. R. (2016). *Analysis of Trends and Challenges in the Indonesian Labor Market - ADB Papers on Indonesia No. 16*. Asian Development Bank.

Allen, E. R., & Burgess, J. (2016). Using Targeted Jobs Programs to Support Local Communities: The Case of Indonesia. In M. F. Rola-Rubzen & J. Burgess (Eds.), *Human Development and Capacity Building: Asia Pacific Trends, Challenges, and Prospects* (pp. 117–139). Routledge.

Altmann, R. (2014). *Older workers benefit businesses and the economy*. Retrieved from http://search.proquest.com/docview/1747605274/citation/72F1F155507442E3PQ/1

Alves, T., Rodrigues, E., Neto, M., Mexia, R., & Dias, C. M. (2021). Acidentes domésticos e de lazer ocorridos em pessoas com 65 e mais anos durante a pandemia da COVID-19: comparação entre 2019 e 2020 [Home and leisure accidents in people aged 65 and over during the COVID-19 pandemic: comparison between 2019 and 2020]. *Instituto Nacional de Saúde Doutor Ricardo Jorge, 10*(30), 62-66. http://hdl.handle.net/10400.18/7768

Alzheimer Portugal. (n.d.). *A Doença de Alzheimer* [Alzheimer's Disease]. Retrieved from https://alzheimerportugal.org/a-doenca-de-alzheimer-2/

Amaro, M. M. G. (2013). *A Transformação da identidade em idosos institucionalizados - Um estudo de casos múltiplos* [Identity Transformation in Institutionalized Elderly People - A Multiple Case Study] [Master's thesis, Escola Superior de Educação - Instituto Politécnico de Bragança]. Repository of Instituto Politécnico de Bragança. http://hdl.handle.net/10198/8384

Ambrosini, D. L., Hirsch, C. H., & Hategan, A. (2018). Ethics, Mental Health Law, and Aging. In A. Hategan, J. Bourgeois, C. Hirsch, & C. Giroux (Eds.), *Geriatric Psychiatry* (pp. 201–216). Springer. doi:10.1007/978-3-319-67555-8_9

Ander-Egg, E. (1991). *Introduccion à la Planificación* [Introduction to Planning]. Siglo XXI.

Anzola-Román, P., Bayona-Saez, C., & García-Marco, T. (2018). Organizational innovation, internal R&D and externally sourced innovation practices: Effects on technological innovation outcomes. *Journal of Business Research, 91*, 233–247. doi:10.1016/j.jbusres.2018.06.014

Arifianto, A. (2006). *Public Policy Towards the Elderly in Indonesia: Current Policy and Future Directions*. SMERU Research Institute.

Arthur, M. B., Khapova, S. N., & Wilderom, C. P. M. (2005). Career success in a boundaryless career world. *Journal of Organizational Behavior, 26*(2), 177–202. doi:10.1002/job.290

Banks, J. A. (2016). Issues and concepts. In J. Banks & C. Banks (Eds.), *Multicultural education: Issues and perspectives* (9th ed., pp. 2–23). John Wiley & Sons.

Barken, R., & Lowndes, R. (2018). Supporting Family Involvement in Long-Term Residential Care: Promising Practices for Relational Care. *Qualitative Health Research, 28*(1), 60–72. doi:10.1177/1049732317730568 PMID:28918701

Barreto, T. M. C. (2020). *Fisiopatologia do envelhecimento cerebral e mecanismos anti-aging* [Pathophysiology of brain aging and anti-aging mechanisms] [Master's thesis, Universidade da Beira Interior]. Repository of Universidade da Beira Interior. http://hdl.handle.net/10400.6/10793

Barrington, L. (2015). Ageism and bias in the American workplace. *Generations, 39*(3), 34–38.

Barroca, A., Meireles, G., & Neto, C. (2014). *Estudo sobre Boas Práticas: Para o Aumento da Força de Trabalho Disponível em Portugal através da Manutenção e Reinserção de Seniores no Mercado de Trabalho* [Study on Best Practices: Towards Increasing the Available Workforce in Portugal by Retaining and Reintegrating Seniors into the Labor Market]. Advancis Business Services.

Baruch, Y. (2006). Career development in organizations and beyond: Balancing traditional and contemporary viewpoints. *Human Resource Management Review*, *16*(2), 125–138. doi:10.1016/j.hrmr.2006.03.002

Basrowi, R. W., Rahayu, E. M., Khoe, L. C., Wasito, E., & Sundjaya, T. (2021). The Road to Healthy Ageing: What Has Indonesia Achieved So Far? *Nutrients*, *13*(10), 3441. doi:10.3390/nu13103441 PMID:34684441

Batista, A. M. R. R. (2014). Animação Sociocultural: Imprecisões, ambiguidades, incertezas e controvérsias de uma ocupação professional [Sociocultural Animation: imprecisions, ambiguities, uncertainties and controversies of a professional occupation]. *Forum Sociológico*, *25*(1), 23–31. doi:10.4000ociologico.898

Bauer, W., Hämmerle, M., Schlund, S., & Vocke, C. (2015). Transforming to a Hyper-connected Society and Economy – Towards an "Industry 4.0". *Procedia Manufacturing*, *3*, 417–424. doi:10.1016/j.promfg.2015.07.200

Beers, H., & Butler, C. (2012). *Age related changes and safety critical work: Identification of tools and a review of the literature*. HSE Books Health and Safety Executive.

Belga, R. I. V. (2019). *Bem-estar e qualidade de vida em idosos institucionalizados com demência - Contributos da animação sociocultural* [Well-being and quality of life in institutionalized elderly with dementia - Contributions of sociocultural animation] [Master's thesis, Escola Superior de Educação - Instituto Politécnico de Beja]. Repository of Instituto Politécnico de Beja. http://hdl.handle.net/20.500.12207/5272

Berger, E. D. (2009). Managing age discrimination: An examination of the techniques used when seeking employment. *The Gerontologist*, *49*(3), 317–332. doi:10.1093/geront/gnp031 PMID:19377045

Berg, P., & Piszczek, M. M. (2022). Organizational Response to Workforce Aging: Tensions in Human Capital Perspectives. *Work, Aging and Retirement*, *8*(1), 7–24. doi:10.1093/workar/waab026

Bernardes, A., & Pinheiro, S. (2014). Anatomia do Envelhecimento [Anatomy of Aging]. In M. T. Veríssimo (Ed.), *Geriatria Fundamental, Saber e Praticar* [Fundamental Geriatrics, Knowledge and Practice] (pp. 41–48). LIDEL, Edições Técnicas, Lda.

Binnewies, C., Ohly, S., & Niessen, C. (2008). Age and creativity at work: The interplay between job resources, age and idea creativity. *Journal of Managerial Psychology*, *23*(4), 438–457. doi:10.1108/02683940810869042

Blanchflower, D. G. (2021). Is Happiness U-shaped Everywhere? Age and Subjective Well-being in 145 countries. *Journal of Population Economics*, *34*(2), 575–624. doi:10.100700148-020-00797-z PMID:32929308

Bouncken, R. B., Ratzmann, M., & Kraus, S. (2021). Anti-aging: How innovation is shaped by firm age and mutual knowledge creation in an alliance. *Journal of Business Research*, *137*, 422–429. doi:10.1016/j.jbusres.2021.08.056

Bousinakis, D., & Halkos, G. (2021). Creativity as the hidden development factor for organizations and employees. *Economic Analysis and Policy*, *71*, 645–659. doi:10.1016/j.eap.2021.07.003

Branson, S. M., Boss, L., Cron, S., & Turner, D. C. (2017). Depression, loneliness, and pet attachment in homebound older adult cat and dog owners. *Journal of Mind and Medical Sciences*, *4*(1), 38–48. doi:10.22543/7674.41.P3848

Brown, A. D., McMorris, C. A., Longman, R. S., Leigh, R., Hill, M. D., Friedenreich, C. M., & Poulin, M. J. (2010). Effects of Cardiorespiratory Fitness and Cerebral Blood Flow on Cognitive Outcomes in Older Women. *Neurobiology of Aging*, *31*(12), 2047–2057. doi:10.1016/j.neurobiolaging.2008.11.002 PMID:19111937

Burgess, J., Dayaram, K., Lambey, L., & Afrianty, T. W. (2020). The Challenges of Human Resource Development in Indonesia. In K. Dayaram, L. Lambey, J. Burgess, & T. Wulida Afrianty (Eds.), *Developing the Workforce in an Emerging Economy: The Case of Indonesia* (pp. 1–17). Routledge. doi:10.4324/9780429273353-1

Burn, I., Button, P., Corella, L. M., & Neumark, D. (2021). Does ageist language in job ads predict age discrimination in hiring? *Journal of Labor Economics*, *40*(3), 613–667. doi:10.1086/717730 PMID:35845105

Butler, R. N. (1989). Dispelling ageism: The cross-cutting intervention. *The Annals of the American Academy of Political and Social Science*, *503*(1), 138–147. doi:10.1177/0002716289503001011

Calzavara, M., Battini, D., Bogataj, D., Sgarbossa, F., & Zennaro, I. (2020). Ageing Workforce Management in Manufacturing Systems: State of the Art and Future Research Agenda. *International Journal of Production Research*, *58*(3), 729–747. doi:10.1080/00207543.2019.1600759

Capowski, G. (1994). Ageism: The new diversity issue. *Management Review*, *83*(10), 10–15.

Carlsson, M., & Eriksson, S. (2019). Age discrimination in hiring decisions: Evidence from a field experiment in the labor market. *Labour Economics*, *59*, 173–183. doi:10.1016/j.labeco.2019.03.002

Central Intelligence Agency. (2022). *The World Fact Book - Indonesia*. Retrieved from https://www.cia.gov/the-world-factbook/countries/indonesia/

Cepellos, V. (2018). Envelhecimento nas Organizações: Os Grandes Debates sobre o Tema nos Estudos de Administração de Empresas [Aging in Organizations: The Major Debates on the Topic in Business Administration Studies]. *Teoria e Prática em Administração*, *8*(1), 138–159. doi:10.21714/2238-104X2018v8i1-37614

Cerne, M., Bunjak, A., Wong, S.-I., & Moh'd, S. S. (2022). I'm creative and deserving! From self-rated creativity to creative recognition. *Creativity and Innovation Management*, *31*(4), 664–679. doi:10.1111/caim.12518

Chand, M., & Markova, G. (2019). The European Union's aging population: Challenges for human resource management. *Thunderbird International Business Review*, *61*(3), 519–529. doi:10.1002/tie.22023

Charbonneau, D. H., & Freeman, J. L. (2016). Succession Planning for Libraries. *Journal of Library Administration*, *56*(7), 884–892. doi:10.1080/01930826.2016.1216229

Charmaz, K. (2006). *Constructing Grounded Theory: A Practical Guide through Qualitative Analysis*. SAGE Publications, Ltd.

Chesbrough, H. W. (2006). *Open innovation: The new imperative for creating and profiting from technology*. Harvard Business Press.

Chomik, R., & Piggott, J. (2015). Population Ageing and Social Security in Asia. *Asian Economic Policy Review*, *10*(2), 199–222. doi:10.1111/aepr.12098

Cirillo, B., Brusoni, S., & Valentini, G. (2013). The rejuvenation of inventors through corporate spinouts. *Organization Science*, *25*(6), 1764–1784. doi:10.1287/orsc.2013.0868

Clark, K. A. (2012). *Long-term unemployment among the baby boom generation: An exploration of coping strategies and subjective well-being* [Ph.D. dissertation, Fielding Graduate University]. ProQuest Dissertations Publishing.

Columbia Public Health. (2022). *The advantages of older workers*. Retrieved from https://www.publichealth.columbia.edu/research/age-smart-employer/advantages-older-workers

Corbin, J. L. (2020). Turnover is Coming: Strategies to Prepare for Impending Retirements. *Journal of Library Administration*, *60*(4), 354–364. doi:10.1080/01930826.2020.1721942

Corodescu-Roşca, E., Hamdouch, A., & Iatu, C. (2023). Innovation in urban governance and economic resilience. The case of two Romanian regional metropolises: Timişoara and Cluj Napoca. *Cities (London, England)*, *132*, 104090. Advance online publication. doi:10.1016/j.cities.2022.104090

Correa-Velez, I., Gifford, S. M., & Barnett, A. G. (2010). Longing to belong: Social inclusion and wellbeing among youth with refugee backgrounds in the first three years in Melbourne, Australia. *Social Science & Medicine*, *71*(8), 1399–1408. doi:10.1016/j.socscimed.2010.07.018 PMID:20822841

Cortijo, V., McGinnis, L. P., & Şişli-Ciamarra, E. (2019). The AGE model: Addressing ageism in the workplace through corporate social responsibility. *Journal of Labor and Society*, *22*(1), 197–213. doi:10.1111/wusa.12387

Costa, G., & Milia, L. D. (2008). Aging and Shift Work: A Complex Problem to Face. *The Journal of Biological and Medical Rhythm Research*, *25*(2-3), 165–181. Advance online publication. doi:10.1080/07420520802103410 PMID:18484359

Cramês, L. (2012). *Envelhecimento activo no idoso institucionalizado* [Active aging in the institutionalized elderly] [Master's thesis, Escola Superior de Educação - Instituto Politécnico de Bragança]. Repository of Instituto Politécnico de Bragança. http://hdl.handle.net/10198/7645

Crawford, J. O., Graveling, R. A., Cowie, H. A., & Dixon, K. (2010). The health safety and health promotion needs of older workers. *Occupational Medicine*, *60*(3), 184–192. doi:10.1093/occmed/kqq028 PMID:20423949

Creswell, J. W. (2014). *Research design: Qualitative, quantitative, and mixed methods approaches* (4th ed.). Sage.

CUF. (2020). *AVC - Acidente vascular cerebral* [Stroke - Cerebrovascular Accident]. Retrieved from https://www.cuf.pt/saude-a-z/avc-acidente-vascular-cerebral

Cunha, M. P., Rego, A., Cunha, R. C., Cabral-Cardoso, C., Marques, C. A., & Gomes, J. F. S. (2015). *Manual de Gestão de Pessoas e do Capital Humano (3ª Edição)* [Manual of People and Human Capital Management (3rd Edition)]. Edições Sílabo.

Curnin, S., Brooks, B., & Brooks, O. (2022). Assessing the influence of individual creativity, perceptions of group decision-making and structured techniques on the quality of scenario planning. *Futures*, *144*, 103057. doi:10.1016/j.futures.2022.103057

Cypel, M. C., Salomão, S. R., Dantas, P. E. C., Lottenberg, C. L., Kasahara, N., & Ramos, L. R. (2017). Status da visão, avaliação oftalmológica e qualidade de vida em idosos [Vision status, ophthalmological assessment and quality of life in the elderly]. *Arquivos Brasileiros de Oftalmologia*, *8*(3), 159–164. PMID:28832732

da Silva, C. R. (2019). Teorização em Educação Sexual a Partir da Grounded Theory [Theorizing in Sex Education from Grounded Theory]. *Revista Ibero-Americana de Estudos Em Educação*, *14*(2), 1427–1440. doi:10.21723/riaee.v14iesp.2.12609

da Silva, R. C., Trevisan, L. N., Veloso, E. F. R., & Dutra, J. S. (2016). Career anchors and values from different career management perspectives. *Revista Brasileira de Gestão de Negócios*, *18*(59), 145–162. doi:10.7819/rbgn.v17i58.2260

Damasceno, N. A., Ventura, M. P., & Damasceno, E. F. (2015). Doenças oculares em clínicas geriátricas no Rio de Janeiro: Considerações sociais e epidemiológicas em pacientes com déficit de locomoção motora [Eye diseases in geriatric clinics in Rio de Janeiro: social and epidemiological considerations in patients with motor locomotion deficit]. *Arquivos Brasileiros de Oftalmologia*, *78*(1), 40–43. doi:10.5935/0004-2749.20150011 PMID:25714537

Daniel, F., Caetano, E., Monteiro, R., & Amaral, I. (2016). Representações sociais do envelhecimento ativo num olhar genderizado [Social representations of active aging in a gendered look]. *Análise Psicológica*, *34*(4), 353–364. doi:10.14417/ap.1020

Das, K., Patel, J. D., Sharma, A., & Shukla, Y. (2023). Creativity in marketing: Examining the intellectual structure using scientometric analysis and topic modeling. *Journal of Business Research*, *154*, 113384. doi:10.1016/j.jbusres.2022.113384

Davies, E. M. M., Hanley, K., Jenkins, A. K., & Chan, C. (2017). Learning and training for older workers. In M. Flynn, Y. Li, & A. Chiva (Eds.), *Managing the ageing workforce in the east and the west* (pp. 185–206). Emerald Publishing., doi:10.1108/978-1-78714-638-920171009

Davis, O., Fisher, B., & Radpour, G. (2020, October 20). *A first in nearly 50 years, older workers face higher unemployment than mid-career workers*. Retrieved from https://www.economicpolicyresearch.org/jobs-report/a-first-in-nearly-50-years-older-workers-face-higher-unemployment-than-mid-career-workers

de Oliveira, P. I. D., & Anderson, M. I. P. (2020). Envelhecimento, finitude e morte [Aging, finitude and death]. *Revista Brasileira de Medicina de Família e Comunidade*, *15*(42), 1–11. doi:10.5712/rbmfc15(42)2195

Delle Fave, A., Bassi, M., Boccaletti, E. S., Roncaglione, C., Bernardelli, G., & Mari, D. (2018). Promoting Well-Being in Old Age: The Psychological Benefits of Two Training Programs of Adapted Physical Activity. *Frontiers in Psychology*, *9*, 828. doi:10.3389/fpsyg.2018.00828 PMID:29910755

Deller, J., & Walwei, U. (2022). Workforce Age Trends and Projections 1. In H. Zacher & C. W. Rudolph (Eds.), *Age and Work: Advances in Theory, Methods, and Practice*. Routledge. doi:10.4324/9781003089674-3

Destiana, R., & Handayani, W. (2022). Exploring the Role of Levers of Control in a Work Environment That Supports Innovative Behavior (An Empirical Study at PT. SEMB). *Quality - Access to Success*, *23*(199), 253–265. doi:10.47750/QAS/23.191.30

Dhakal, S. P., Burgess, J., & Nankervis, A. (2022). Population Ageing: Challenges in the Asia Pacific and Beyond. In S. Dhakal, A. Nankervis, & J. Burgess (Eds.), *Ageing Asia and the Pacific in Changing Times* (pp. 3–17). Springer. doi:10.1007/978-981-16-6663-6_1

Dharmarajan, T. S. (2021). Physiology of Aging. In C. S. Pitchumoni & T. S. Dharmarajan (Eds.), *Geriatric Gastroenterology* (pp. 101–153). Springer. doi:10.1007/978-3-030-30192-7_5

Dias, S., Gonçalves, I., & Viegas, L. (2022). Risk Factors for Falls in the Elderly in a Day Care Center. *International Journal of Health Sciences (Qassim)*, *2*(62), 1–11.

Domingues, A. C. G. E. (2011). *Comprometimento organizacional e intenções de abandono dos agentes em geriatria* [Organizational commitment and abandonment intentions of agents in geriatrics] [Master's thesis, Faculdade de Economia – Universidade do Porto]. Repository of Faculdade de Economia – Universidade do Porto. https://hdl.handle.net/10216/45733

Duffy, B.E., & Hund, E. (2015). "Having it All" on Social Media: Entrepreneurial Femininity and Self-Branding Among Fashion Bloggers. *Social Media + Society*, *1*(2), 1–11. doi:10.1177/2056305115604337

Duh, M. (2015). Succession Process: A Chance for Rebirth or Failure of a Family Business. *International Journal of Business and Management*, *10*(3), 45–56. doi:10.5539/ijbm.v10n3p45

Ekerdt, D. J. (2000). Retirement. In A. E. Kazdin (Ed.), *Encyclopaedia of Psychology* (Vol. 7, pp. 94–97). American Psychological Association.

El-Amin, A. (2022a). Organizational Climate Change: Diversity, Equity, Inclusion, and Belonging. In A. El-Amin (Ed.), *Implementing Diversity, Equity, Inclusion, and Belonging Management in Organizational Change Initiatives* (pp. 1–23). IGI Global. doi:10.4018/978-1-6684-4023-0.ch001

El-Amin, A. (2022b). Do Board Member Duties of Care, Loyalty, and Obedience Matter in a Disaster? *Progress in Industrial Ecology, 15*(2-4), 268–276. doi:10.1504/PIE.2022.125577

Elias, S., & Noone, C. (2011). *The Growth and Development of the Indonesian Economy.* Retrieved from https://www.rba.gov.au/publications/bulletin/2011/dec/4.html

Enguita, M. F. (2001). *Educar en Tiempos Inciertos* [Educating in Uncertain Times]. Editorial Morata.

Ermida, J. G. (2014). Avaliação geriátrica global [Comprehensive geriatric assessment]. In M. T. Veríssimo (Ed.), *Geriatria Fundamental, Saber e Praticar* [Fundamental Geriatrics, Knowledge and Practice] (pp. 103–118). LIDEL, Edições Técnicas, Lda.

EU-OSHA, Cedefop, Eurofound, EIGE, Dubois, H., Jungblut, J-M., Wilkens, M., Vermeylen, G., & Vargas, O.L. (2017). *Towards age-friendly work in Europe: a life-course perspective on work and ageing from EU Agencies.* Retrieved from https://www.eurofound.europa.eu/publications/report/2017/towards-age-friendly-work-in-europe-a-life-course-perspective-on-work-and-ageing-from-eu-agencies

EUR-Lex. (2006). *Livro Verde - Para uma futura política marítima da União: uma visão europeia para os oceanos e os mares "Que impróprio chamar Terra a este planeta de oceanos!"* [Green Paper - Towards a future Union maritime policy: a European vision for oceans and seas "How inappropriate to call this planet of oceans Earth!"]. Retrieved from https://eur-lex.europa.eu/legal-content/PT/TXT/?uri=CELEX%3A52006DC0275%2802%29

Euromonitor International. (2019). *How Ageing Population and Rising Longevity Drive Megatrends.* Retrieved from https://www.euromonitor.com/article/how-ageing-populations-and-rising-longevity-drive-megatrends

Eurostat. (2015). *International day of older persons: 1 out of every 8 persons in the EU could be 80 or above by 2080.* Retrieved from https://ec.europa.eu/eurostat/documents/2995521/7012459/3-29092015-AP-EN.pdf/0b823ac4-cbcb-46b0-a248-0acfb91626a7

Fàbregues, S., & Paré, M.-H. (2007). Constructing Grounded Theory: A Practical Guide Through Qualitative Analysis. *Papers - Revista de Sociologia, 86*, 284–287. doi:10.5565/rev/papers/v86n0.825

Fernandes, E.M., & Maia, Â. (2001). *Grounded Theory.* Universidade do Minho - Centro de Estudos em Educação e Psicologia (CEEP).

Fernandes, M. H. (2016). A expressão plástica e a música erudita como recursos da animação sociocultural a idosos institucionalizados [Plastic expression and classical music as resources of sociocultural animation for institutionalized elderly people]. *Revista Kairós Gerontologia, 19*(4), 173–203.

Ferreira, P. M., Azevedo, A. B., & Garha, N. S. (2021). Envelhecimento e COVID-19: impactos e consequências [Aging and COVID-19: impacts and consequences]. In A. Delicado & J. Ferrão (Eds.), *Portugal Social em Mudança - Impactos Sociais da Pandemia COVID-19* [Social Portugal in Change - Social Impacts of the Pandemic COVID-19] (pp. 37–47). Instituto de Ciências Sociais da Universidade de Lisboa.

Ferreira, P. M., Cabral, M. V., & Moreira, A. (2017). Introdução [Introduction]. In P. M. Ferreira, M. V. Cabral, & A. Moreira (Eds.), *Envelhecimento na Sociedade Portuguesa. Pensões, Família e Cuidados* [Aging in Portuguese Society. Pensions, Family and Care] (pp. 19–26). Imprensa de Ciências Sociais.

Findsen, B. (2015). Older workers' learning within organizations: Issues and challenges. *Educational Gerontology*, *41*(8), 582–589. doi:10.1080/03601277.2015.1011582

Finkelstein, L. M., Ryan, K. M., & King, E. B. (2013). What do the young (old) people think of me? Content and accuracy of age-based metastereotypes. *European Journal of Work and Organizational Psychology*, *22*(6), 633–657. doi:10.1080/1359432X.2012.673279

Flick, U. (2007). *Managing Quality in Qualitative Research*. SAGE Publications, Ltd., doi:10.4135/9781849209441

Fonseca, A.M. (2012). Do trabalho à reforma: Quando os dias parecem mais longos. [From work to retirement: When the days seem longer]. *Sociologia: Revista da Faculdade de Letras da Universidade do Porto*, (2), 75–95.

Forner, F. C., & Alves, C. F. (2019). Uma revisão de literatura sobre os fatores que contribuem para o envelhecimento ativo na atualidade [A literature review on the factors contributing to active aging today]. *Revista Universo Psi*, *1*(1), 150–174.

Fraher, E., & Brandt, B. (2019). Toward a System where Workforce Planning and Interprofessional Practice and Education are Designed around Patients and Populations not Professions. *Journal of Interprofessional Care*, *33*(4), 389–397. doi:10.1080/13561820.2018.1564252 PMID:30669922

Franz, N. E. (2021). *A phenomenological case study to describe the ageism-induced anxiety of job seekers aged 50–83* [Ed.D. Problem of Practice Dissertation]. Baylor University.

Franz, N. E., Werse, N. R., & Talbert, T. L. (2022). Ageism-induced anxiety of job seekers aged 50–83: Preliminary findings from a phenomenological case study problem of practice dissertation. *Impacting Education: Journal on Transforming Professional Practice*, *7*(2), 11–18. doi:10.5195/ie.2022.199

Fried, L. P. (2000). Epidemiology of Aging. *Epidemiologic Reviews*, *22*(1), 95–106. doi:10.1093/oxfordjournals.epirev.a018031 PMID:10939013

Friedman, H., & Friedman, L., & Leverton. (2016). Increase diversity to boost creativity and enhance problem solving. *Psychological Issues in Human Resource Management*, *4*(2), 7–33.

Galinha, S. A. (2010). *Sociedades Empáticas e Organizativas: Contributos Psicossociológicos em Educação* [Empathic and Organizational Societies: Psychosociological Contributions in Education]. Imprinove.

Garg, A., & van Weele, E. (2012). Succession Planning and Its Impact on the Performance of Small Micro Medium Enterprises within the Manufacturing Sector in Johannesburg. *International Journal of Business and Management, 7*(9), 96–107. doi:10.5539/ijbm.v7n9p96

Gaspar, D., & Mabic, M. (2015). Creativity in Higher Education. *Universal Journal of Educational Research, 3*(9), 598–605. doi:10.13189/ujer.2015.030903

General Direction of Health. (2011). *Norma da Direção-Geral da Saúde - Acidente Vascular Cerebral: Prescrição de Medicina Física e de Reabilitação* [Norm from the General Direction of Health - Stroke: Prescription of Physical Medicine and Rehabilitation]. Retrieved from https://www.dgs.pt/directrizes-da-dgs/normas-e-circulares-normativas/norma-n-0542011-de-27122011-jpg.aspx

Gibson, J. W., Jones, J. P., Cella, J., Clark, C., Epstein, A., & Haselberger, J. (2010). Ageism and the baby boomers: Issues, challenges and the team approach. *Contemporary Issues in Education Research, 3*(1), 53–60. doi:10.19030/cier.v3i1.161

Giddens, A. (2001). *Sociologia* [Sociology] (6th ed.). Fundação Calouste Gulbenkian.

Gilles, M. A., Gaudez, C., Savin, J., Remy, A., Remy, O., & Wild, P. (2022). Do Age and Work Pace Affect Variability when Performing a Repetitive Light Assembly Task? *Applied Ergonomics, 98*, 103601. doi:10.1016/j.apergo.2021.103601 PMID:34634583

Ginting, E., & Aji, P. (2015). *Summary of Indonesia's Economic Analysis - ADB Papers on Indonesia No. 2*. Asian Development Bank.

Godinho, A. C. M. (2016). *Plano de sucessão na Delta Cafés* [Succession plan at Delta Cafés] [Master's thesis, ISCTE - Instituto Universitário de Lisboa]. Repository of ISCTE – Instituto Universitário de Lisboa. http://hdl.handle.net/10071/13725

Gohn, M. G. (2014). Educação Não Formal, Aprendizagens e Saberes em Processos Participativos [Non-Formal Education, Learning and Knowledge in Participatory Participatory Processes]. *Investigar em Educação, 2*(1), 35–50.

Gomes, A. M. (2011). O tempo do envelhecimento [The time of aging]. In J. Saraiva (Ed.), *Otorrinolaringologia e Envelhecimento* [Otorhinolaryngology and Aging] (pp. 1–13). LIDEL Edições Técnicas, Lda.

Gonyea, J. G. (2009). *The Older Worker and the Changing Labor Market: New Challenges for the Workplace*. Routledge.

Government of Newfoundland and Labrador. (2008). *Succession Planning and Management Guide*. Retrieved from https://www.gov.nl.ca/exec/tbs/files/publications-succession-planning-and-management-guide.pdf

Greenhaus, J. H., Callanan, G. A., & Godshalk, V. M. (2018). *Career Management for Life*. Routledge. doi:10.4324/9781315205991

Gringart, E., Helmes, E., & Speelman, C. P. (2005). Exploring attitudes toward older workers among Australian employers. *Journal of Aging & Social Policy*, *17*(3), 85–103. doi:10.1300/J031v17n03_05 PMID:16219595

Grossman, R. J. (2013). Invest in older workers. *HRMagazine*, *58*(8), 20–25.

Guillén, L., & Kunze, F. (2019). When age does not harm innovative behavior and perceptions of competence: Testing interdepartmental collaboration as a social buffer. *Human Resource Management*, *58*(3), 301–316. doi:10.1002/hrm.21953

Gunz, H. P., & Peiperl, M. (2007). *Handbook of Career Studies*. SAGE Publications, Inc. doi:10.4135/9781412976107

Hackenberger, B. K. (2020). R software: Unfriendly but probably the best. *Croatian Medical Journal*, *61*(1), 66–68. doi:10.3325/cmj.2020.61.66 PMID:32118381

Hanisch, K. A., & Hulin, C. L. (1990). Job attitudes and organizational withdrawal: An examination of retirement and other voluntary withdrawal behaviors. *Journal of Vocational Behavior*, *37*(1), 60–78. doi:10.1016/0001-8791(90)90007-O

Hargadon, A. B., & Bechky, B. A. (2006). When collections of creatives become creative collectives: A field study of problem solving at work. *Organization Science*, *17*(4), 484–500. doi:10.1287/orsc.1060.0200

Harris, K., Krygsman, S., Waschenko, J., & Laliberte Rudman, D. (2018). Ageism and the older worker: A scoping review. *The Gerontologist*, *58*(2), e1–e14. doi:10.1093/geront/gnw194 PMID:28082278

Hedge, J. W., Borman, W. C., & Lammlein, S. E. (2006). *The aging workforce: Realities, myths, and implications for organizations*. American Psychological Association. doi:10.1037/11325-000

Heidemeier, H., & Staudinger, U. M. (2015). Age differences in Achievement Goals and Motivational Characteristics of Work in an Ageing Workforce. *Ageing and Society*, *35*(4), 809–836. doi:10.1017/S0144686X13001098

Hekmat-Panah, J. (2019). The "Elderly" in Medicine: Ethical Issues Surrounding This Outdated and Discriminatory Term. *Inquiry: A Journal of Medical Care Organization. Provision and Financing*, *56*, 46958019856975. doi:10.1177/0046958019856975 PMID:31189387

Help Age Global Network. (n.d.). *Ageing population in Indonesia.* Retrieved from https://ageingasia.org/ageing-population-indonesia/

Hernaus, T., Maric, M., & Černe, M. (2019). Age-sensitive job design antecedents of innovative work behavior: The role of cognitive job demands. *Journal of Managerial Psychology*, *34*(5), 368–382. doi:10.1108/JMP-10-2018-0478

Hertel, G., & Zacher, H. (2017). Managing the Aging Workforce. In The SAGE Handbook of Industrial, Work, & Organizational Psychology (pp. 396-428). SAGE Publication.

Hirsch, B. T., Macpherson, D. A., & Hardy, M. A. (2000). Occupational age structure and access for older workers. *Industrial & Labor Relations Review*, *53*(3), 401–418. doi:10.1177/001979390005300303

Hollis, J. L., Collins, C. E., DeClerck, F., Chai, L. K., McColl, K., & Demaio, A. R. (2020). Defining Healthy and Sustainable Diets for Infants, Children and Adolescents. *Global Food Security*, *27*, 100401. doi:10.1016/j.gfs.2020.100401

Hooper, C. R., & Bello-Haas, V. D. (2009). Sensory Function. In B. R. Bonder & V. D. Bello-Haas (Eds.), *Functional Performance in Older Adults* (pp. 101–129). F. A. Davis Company.

Hosain, S., Manzurul Arefin, A. H. M., & Hossin, M. A. (2020). E-recruitment: A social media perspective. Asian Journal of Economics. *Business and Accounting*, *16*(4), 51–62.

Hujsak, J. (2015). Older workers: The value proposition-A sustainable enterprise imperative. *Cost and Management*, *29*(6), 6–15.

Huot, C., Cruz-Knight, W., Jester, D. J., Wenders, A., Andel, R., & Hyer, K. (2022). Impact of Establishing a Geriatrics Workforce Enhancement Program Clinic on Preventive Health and Medicare Annual Wellness Visits. *Gerontology & Geriatrics Education*, *43*(2), 285–294. doi:10.1080/02701960.2020.1854247 PMID:33272147

International Labour Organization. (2016). *Towards a Framework for Fair and Effective Integration of Migrants into the Labour Market*. Retrieved from https://www.ilo.org/global/about-the-ilo/how-the-ilo-works/multilateral-system/g20/reports/WCMS_559139/lang--en/index.htm

Ip, B., & Jacobs, G. (2006). Business succession planning: A review of the evidence. *Journal of Small Business and Enterprise Development*, *13*(3), 326–350. doi:10.1108/14626000610680235

Islam, M. S., Ng, T. K. S., Manierre, M., Hamiduzzaman, M., & Tareque, M. I. (2022). Modifications of Traditional Formulas to Estimate and Project Dependency Ratios and Their Implications in a Developing Country, Bangladesh. *Population Research and Policy Review*, *41*(5), 1931–1949. doi:10.100711113-022-09720-8 PMID:35572094

Ivancevich, J. M. (2010). *Human Resource Management* (11th ed.). McGraw-Hill Irwin.

Jacob, L. (2002). *O Idoso e a Comunidade-respostas Sociais* [The Elderly and the Community-Social Responses]. Academic Press.

Jacob, L., Santos, E., Pocinho, R., & Fernandes, H. (2013). *Envelhecimento e Economia Social: Perspetivas Atuais* [Aging and Social Economy: Current Perspectives]. PsicoSoma.

Jakovljevic, D. G. (2018). Physical Activity and Cardiovascular Aging: Physiological and Molecular Insights. *Experimental Gerontology*, *109*, 67–74. doi:10.1016/j.exger.2017.05.016 PMID:28546086

Jankelová, N., Joniaková, Z., & Mišún, J. (2021). Innovative Work Behavior—A Key Factor in Business Performance? The Role of Team Cognitive Diversity and Teamwork Climate in This Relationship. *Journal of Risk and Financial Management, 14*(4), 1–16. doi:10.3390/jrfm14040185

Johnson, J. A., & Lopes, J. (2008). The Intergenerational Workforce, Revisited. *Organization Development Journal, 26*(1), 31–36.

Johnson, J. H. Jr, Parnell, A. M., & Lian, H. (2018). Aging as an Engine of Innovation, Business Development, and Employment Growth. *Economic Development Journal, 17*(3), 32–42.

Jones, G.W. (2014). *The 2010-2035 Indonesian Population Projection - Understanding the Causes, Consequences and Policy Options for Population and Development.* United Nations Population Fund (UNFPA).

Kapp, M. B. (2020). Legal Issues in Older Adults. In R. Rosenthal, M. Zenilman, & M. Katlic (Eds.), *Principles and Practice of Geriatric Surgery* (pp. 313–338). Springer. doi:10.1007/978-3-319-47771-8_20

Karmel, T., & Woods, D. (2004). *Lifelong learning and older workers.* Retrieved from https://eric.ed.gov/?id=ED494053

Katz, J. H., Mann, T. C., Shen, X., Goncalo, J. A., & Ferguson, M. J. (2022). Implicit impressions of creative people: Creativity evaluation in a stigmatized domain. *Organizational Behavior and Human Decision Processes, 169*, 104116. doi:10.1016/j.obhdp.2021.104116

Kirkwood, T. B. L. (2005). Understanding the odd science of aging. *Cell, 120*(4), 437–447. doi:10.1016/j.cell.2005.01.027 PMID:15734677

Kitwood, T. (1997). *Dementia Reconsidered Revisited: The Person Still Comes First* (1st ed.). Open University Press.

Kleineidam, L., Thoma, M. V., Maercker, A., Bickel, H., Mösch, E., Hajek, A., König, H. H., Eisele, M., Mallon, T., Luck, T., Röhr, S., Weyerer, S., Werle, J., Pentzek, M., Fuchs, A., Wiese, B., Mamone, S., Scherer, M., Maier, W., ... Wagner, M. (2019). What Is Successful Aging? A Psychometric Validation Study of Different Construct Definitions. *The Gerontologist, 59*(4), 738–748. doi:10.1093/geront/gny083 PMID:30016435

Knezovic, E., & Drkic, A. (2020). Innovative work behavior in SMEs: The role of transformational leadership. *Employee Relations: The International Journal, 43*(2), 398–415. doi:10.1108/ER-03-2020-0124

Kosterlitz, M., & Lewis, J. (2017). From Baby Boomer to Millennial: Succession Planning for the Future. *Nurse Leader, 15*(6), 396–398. doi:10.1016/j.mnl.2017.09.006

Kudrna, G., Le, T., & Piggott, J. (2020*). Review report on demographics, labor force and older people in Indonesia.* Retrieved from https://www.cepar.edu.au/publications/working-papers/review-report-demographics-labour-force-and-older-people-indonesia

Kudrna, G., Le, T., & Piggott, J. (2022). Macro-Demographics and Ageing in Emerging Asia: The Case of Indonesia. *Journal of Population Ageing, 15*(1), 7–38. doi:10.100712062-022-09358-6 PMID:35399208

Kulik, C. T., Ryan, S., Harper, S., & George, G. (2014). Aging populations and management. *Academy of Management Journal, 57*(4), 929–935. doi:10.5465/amj.2014.4004

Kumar, R., & Srivastava, U. R. (2018). Ageing Workforce: Negative Age Stereotypes and their Impact on Older Workers. *International Journal of Research in Social Sciences, 8*(5), 302–312.

Kurtz, S. M., Ong, K. L., Lau, E., & Bozic, K. J. (2014). Impact of the Economic Downturn on Total Joint Replacement Demand in the United States: Updated Projections to 2021. *The Journal of Bone & Joint Surgery, 96*(8), 624–630. doi:10.2106/JBJS.M.00285 PMID:24740658

Lahey, J. N. (2005). *Do older workers face discrimination? (Issue Brief No. 33).* Retrieved from https://crr.bc.edu/briefs/do-older-workers-face-discrimination/

Lalwani, A. K., & Snow, J. B. (2002). Distúrbios do olfato, da gustação e da audição [Disturbance of smell, taste and hearing]. In E. Braunwald, A. S. Fauci, D. L. Kasper, S. L. Hauser, D. L. Longo & J. L. Jameson (Eds.), Medicina Interna de Harrison [Harrison's Internal Medicine] (pp. 192-208). McGraw-Hill.

Lamas, M.C.R., & Paúl, C. (2013). O envelhecimento do sistema sensorial: implicações na funcionalidade e qualidade de vida [The ageing sensory system: implications on functionality and quality of life]. *Atas de Gerontologia - Congresso Português de Avaliacão Intervencão em Gerontologia Social, 1*, 1-11.

Lee, Y. G., Jasper, C. R., & Goebel, K. P. (2003). A Profile of Succession Planning among Family Business Owners. *Financial Counseling and Planning, 14*(2), 31–41.

Leibowitz, Z. B., Farren, C., & Kaye, B. L. (1991). *Designing Career Development Systems* (1st ed.). Pfeiffer.

Lesonsky, R. (2017). *Small business trends: 8 signs of ageism in the workplace and what to do about them.* Retrieved from http://search.proquest.com/docview/1939712583/citation/D3A138FA00F54167PQ/1

Lestari, M., Stephens, C., & Morison, T. (2022). Constructions of older people's identities in Indonesian regional ageing policies: The impacts on micro and macro experiences of ageing. *Ageing and Society, 42*(9), 2046–2066. doi:10.1017/S0144686X20001907

Libertini, G., Rengo, G., & Ferrara, N. (2017). Aging and Aging Theories. *Journal of Gerontology and Geriatrics, 65*(1), 59–77.

Lippmann, S. (2008). Rethinking risk in the new economy: Age and cohort effects on unemployment and re-employment. *Human Relations, 61*(9), 1259–1292. doi:10.1177/0018726708094912

Liu-Ambrose, T., Barha, C., & Falck, R. S. (2019). Active body, healthy brain: Exercise for healthy cognitive aging. *International Review of Neurobiology, 147*, 95–120. doi:10.1016/bs.irn.2019.07.004 PMID:31607364

Lopes, A. A., Jayme, D. H. C., Abreu, I. L. V., Silva, I. E., Lobo, M. H. S., Oliveira, M. C., & Pinheiro, I. F. (2020). Avaliação das funções visuais e sua relação com a visão funcional e quedas em idosos ativos da comunidade [Assessment of visual functions and its relation to functional vision and falls in active community-dwelling elderly]. *Revista Brasileira de Oftalmologia, 79*(4), 236–241.

Lopes, M. S. (2006). *Animação Sociocultural em Portugal* [Sociocultural Animation in Portugal]. Editorial Intervenção.

Lourenço, P. M. R. (2014). *Institucionalização do idoso e identidade: estudo de caso de idosos institucionalizados* [Institutionalization of the elderly and identity: a case study of institutionalized elderly people] [Master's thesis, Escola Superior de Educação e Ciências Sociais - Instituto Politécnico de Portalegre]. Repository of Instituto Politécnico de Portalegre. http://hdl.handle.net/10400.26/9205

Lu, Z., Daneman, M., & Schneider, B. A. (2016). Does increasing the intelligibility of a competing sound source interfere more with speech comprehension in older adults than it does in younger adults? *Attention, Perception & Psychophysics, 78*(8), 2655–2677. doi:10.375813414-016-1193-5 PMID:27566326

Lyons, B. J., Wessel, J. L., Tai, Y. C., & Ryan, A. M. (2014). Strategies of job seekers related to age-related stereotypes. *Journal of Managerial Psychology, 29*(8), 1009–1027. doi:10.1108/JMP-03-2013-0078

Makridis, C. A., & McGuire, E. (2023). The quality of innovation "Booms" during "Busts.". *Research Policy, 52*(1), 104657. doi:10.1016/j.respol.2022.104657

Malinen, S., & Johnston, L. (2013). Workplace ageism: Discovering hidden bias. *Experimental Aging Research, 39*(4), 445–465. doi:10.1080/0361073X.2013.808111 PMID:23875840

Mandal, B., Ayyagari, P., & Gallo, W. T. (2011). Job loss and depression: The role of subjective expectations. *Social Science & Medicine, 72*(4), 576–583. doi:10.1016/j.socscimed.2010.11.014 PMID:21183267

Marinho, H. I. R. (2013). *Serviço de Apoio Domiciliário: práticas e dinâmicas na ótica do utente* [Home Support Service: practices and dynamics from the user's point of view] [Master's thesis, Fundação Bissaya Barreto]. Repository of Fundação Bissaya Barreto. http://hdl.handle.net/10400.26/29499

Martins, E. C. (2013). *Gerontologia & Gerontagogia – Animação Sociocultural em Idosos* [Gerontology & Gerontagogy - Sociocultural Animation in the Elderly]. Editorial Cáritas.

Matour, S., & Prout, M. F. (2007). Psychological implications of retirement in the 21st century. *Journal of Financial Service Professionals, 61*(1), 57–63.

McPhee, J. S., French, D. P., Jackson, D., Nazroo, J., Pendleton, N., & Degens, H. (2016). Physical Activity in Older Age: Perspectives for Healthy Ageing and Frailty. *Biogerontology*, *17*(3), 567–580. doi:10.100710522-016-9641-0 PMID:26936444

Meléndez, J. C., Deholm, I., & Satorres, E. (2022). Emotions and Emotional Intelligence in the Field of Gerontology. In Promoting Good Care of Older People in Institutions (pp. 67-82). doi:10.2307/j.ctv2gz3tp3.9

Midtsundstad, T. I. (2011). Inclusive workplaces and older employees: An analysis of companies' investment in retaining senior workers. *International Journal of Human Resource Management*, *22*(6), 1277–1293. doi:10.1080/09585192.2011.559099

Miguel, I. (2014). Envelhecimento e Desenvolvimento Psicológico: Entre Mitos e Factos [Aging and psychological development: Between myths and facts]. In H. R. Amaro da Luz & I. Miguel (Eds.), Gerontologia Social: Perspetivas de Análise e Intervenção [Social Gerontology: Perspectives of Analysis and Intervention] (pp. 53-67). Center for Research in Social and Organizational Innovation - Instituto Superior Bissaya Barreto.

Miller, D. I., Taler, V., Davidson, P. S., & Messier, C. (2012). Measuring the Impact of Exercise on Cognitive Aging: Methodological Issues. *Neurobiology of Aging, 33*(3). doi:10.1016/j.neurobiolaging.2011.02.020

Minocha, S., McNulty, C., & Evans, S. (2015). *Imparting digital skills to people aged 55 years and over in the UK*. The Open University.

Moore, C., Gunz, H., & Hall, D. (2007). Tracing the historical roots of career theory in management and organization studies. In H. Gunz & M. Peiperl (Eds.), *Handbook of Career Studies* (pp. 13–38). SAGE Publications, Ltd. doi:10.4135/9781412976107.n2

Morfit, M. (1981). Pancasila: The Indonesian State Ideology According to the New Order Government. *Asian Survey*, *21*(8), 838–851. doi:10.2307/2643886

Murty, S., Sassen, B., & Kammerdiener, M. (2016). Preparing for the passing of the baton: Leadership programs in senior living organizations. *Seniors Housing & Care Journal*, *24*(1), 88–96.

Nagarajan, N. R., Wada, M., Fang, M. L., & Sixsmith, A. (2019). Defining Organizational Contributions to Sustaining an Ageing Workforce: A Bibliometric Review. *European Journal of Ageing*, *16*(3), 337–361. doi:10.100710433-019-00499-w PMID:31543728

Nazareth, J. M. (2009). *Crescer e envelhecer: Constrangimentos e Oportunidades do envelhecimento demográfico* [Growing and aging: Constraints and opportunities of demographic aging]. Editora Presença.

Netz, Y., Wu, M. J., Becker, B. J., & Tenenbaum, G. (2005). Physical Activity and Psychological Well-being in Advanced Age: A Meta-analysis of Intervention Studies. *Psychology and Aging*, *20*(2), 272–284. doi:10.1037/0882-7974.20.2.272 PMID:16029091

Neumark, D. (2021). Age discrimination in hiring: Evidence from age-blind vs. non-age-blind hiring procedures. *The Journal of Human Resources*, 0420-10831R1. Advance online publication. doi:10.3368/jhr.0420-10831R1

Ng, R., & Lim-Soh, J. W. (2021). Ageism linked to culture, not demographics: Evidence from an 8-billion-word corpus across 20 countries. *The Journals of Gerontology: Series B*, *76*(9), 1791–1798. doi:10.1093/geronb/gbaa181 PMID:33099600

Ng, T. W. H., & Feldman, D. C. (2012). Evaluating six common stereotypes about older workers with meta-analytical data. *Personnel Psychology*, *65*(4), 821–858. doi:10.1111/peps.12003

Nicholson, N., & West, M. (1989). Transitions, work histories, and careers. In Handbook of Career Theory (pp. 181–201). Cambridge University Press. doi:10.1017/CBO9780511625459.011

Nolan, L. C. (2011). Dimensions of aging and belonging for the older person and the effects of ageism. *BYU Journal of Public Law*, *25*(2), 317–339.

Nomaan, M., & Nayantara, S. (2018). *Employment and Growth in Indonesia (1990-2015)*. International Labour Organization.

North, M., & Hershfield, H. (2014). *Four ways to adapt to an aging workforce*. Retrieved from https://hbr.org/2014/04/four-ways-to-adapt-to-an-aging-workforce

North, M. S., & Fiske, S. T. (2013). Subtyping ageism: Policy issues in succession and consumption. *Social Issues and Policy Review*, *7*(1), 36–57. doi:10.1111/j.1751-2409.2012.01042.x PMID:24523829

Noveria, M. (2006, June 7-9). *Challenges of Population aging in Indonesia* [Paper Presentation]. Conference on Impact of Ageing: A Common Challenge for Europe and Asia, Vienna, Austria.

OECD. (2022). *Indonesia Economic Snapshot*. Retrieved from https://www.oecd.org/economy/indonesia-economic-snapshot/

Oliveira, E. A. da S. (2017). *Ageism in the workplace: Stereotype threat, work disengagement and organizational disidentification among older workers* [Doctoral dissertation, Universidade do Porto]. ProQuest Dissertations Publishing.

Oliveira, C. R., & Pinto, A. M. (2014). Biologia e fisiopatologia do envelhecimento [Biology and pathophysiology of Ageing]. In M. T. Veríssimo (Ed.), *Geriatria Fundamental, Saber e Praticar* [Fundamental Geriatrics, Knowledge and Practice] (pp. 17–28). LIDEL, Edições Técnicas, Lda.

Oliveira, T., Baixinho, C. L., & Henriques, M. A. (2018). Risco Multidimensional de Queda em Idosos [Multidimensional risk of falls in elderly]. *Revista Brasileira em Promoção da Saúde*, *31*(2), 1–9. doi:10.5020/18061230.2018.7058

Ortiz-Barrios, M., Silvera-Natera, E., Petrillo, A., Gul, M., & Yucesan, M. (2022). A Multicriteria Approach to Integrating Occupational Safety & Health Performance and Industry Systems Productivity in the Context of Aging Workforce: A Case Study. *Safety Science*, *152*, 105764. doi:10.1016/j.ssci.2022.105764

Osborne, J. W. (2012). Psychological effects of the transition to retirement. *Canadian Journal of Counselling and Psychotherapy*, *46*(1), 45–58.

Osborne, T., & McCann, L. A. (2004). Forced ranking and age-related employment discrimination. *Human Rights (Chicago, Ill.)*, *31*(2), 6.

Painter, J. A., Allison, L., Dhingra, P., Daughtery, J., Cogdill, K., & Trujillo, L. G. (2012). Fear of Falling and Its Relationship With Anxiety, Depression, and Activity Engagement Among Community-Dwelling Older Adults. *The American Journal of Occupational Therapy*, *66*(2), 169–176. doi:10.5014/ajot.2012.002535 PMID:22394526

Paiva, A., & Paiva, S. (2014). Patologia otorrinolaringológica e envelhecimento [Otorhinolaryngological pathology and ageing]. In M. T. Veríssimo (Ed.), *Geriatria Fundamental, Saber e Praticar* [Fundamental Geriatrics, Knowledge and Practice] (pp. 245–253). LIDEL, Edições Técnicas, Lda.

Palade, A. (2010). Significant Aspects regarding Career Management: Means for a Better Career Planning and Development. *Economic Sciences Series*, *62*(2), 124–134.

Palmer, W., & Missbach, A. (2019). Enforcing Labour Rights of Irregular Migrants in Indonesia. *Third World Quarterly*, *40*(5), 908–925. doi:10.1080/01436597.2018.1522586

Paterson, D. H., & Warburton, D. E. (2010). Physical Activity and Functional Limitations in Older Adults: A Systematic Review Related to Canada's Physical Activity Guidelines. *The International Journal of Behavioral Nutrition and Physical Activity*, *7*(38), 1–22. doi:10.1186/1479-5868-7-38 PMID:20459782

Pedersen, K. M., Andersen, J. S., & Søndergaard, J. (2012). General practice and primary health care in Denmark. *Journal of the American Board of Family Medicine*, *25*(Suppl 1), S34–S38. doi:10.3122/jabfm.2012.02.110216 PMID:22403249

Pedota, M., & Piscitello, L. (2022). A new perspective on technology-driven creativity enhancement in the Fourth Industrial Revolution. *Creativity and Innovation Management*, *31*(1), 109–122. doi:10.1111/caim.12468

Pereira, C. I. P. S. (2015). *A relevância do desenvolvimento humano versus desenvolvimento comunitário: uma nova perspetiva do apoio ao envelhecimento ativo no centro dia* [The relevance of human development versus community development: a new perspective on supporting active aging in the day center] [Master's thesis, Escola Superior de Educação e Ciências Sociais – Instituto Politécnico de Leiria]. Repository of Instituto Politécnico de Leiria. http://hdl.handle.net/10400.8/1683

Pereira, M. A. da S. (2011). *Preditores do turnover organizacional: uma perspetiva multidimensional* [Predictors of organizational turnover: a multi-dimensional perspective] [Master's thesis, ISCTE - Instituto Universitário de Lisboa]. Repository of ISCTE – Instituto Universitário de Lisboa. http://hdl.handle.net/10071/7302

Perron, R. (2013). *Staying ahead of the curve 2013: AARP multicultural work and career study.* Retrieved from https://www.aarp.org/research/topics/economics/info-2014/staying-ahead-curve-work.html

Pestana, N.N. (2003). *Trabalhadores Mais Velhos: Políticas Públicas e Práticas Empresariais* [Older Workers: Public Policies and Business Practices]. Ministério da Segurança Social e do Trabalho (MSST).

Petery, G. A., & Grosch, J. W. (2022). Broadening the view of workplace ageism. *Work, Aging and Retirement, 8*(4), 379–382. doi:10.1093/workar/waac015 PMID:35923432

Pew Research Center. (2019). *Baby Boomers are staying in the labor force at rates not seen in generations for people their age.* Retrieved from https://www.pewresearch.org/fact-tank/2019/07/24/baby-boomers-us-labor-force/

Pimentel, D. (2019). *Planeamento de sucessão em equipas* [Succession planning in teams]. Academic Press.

Pindado, E., Sánchez, M., & Martínez, M. G. (2023). Entrepreneurial innovativeness: When too little or too much agglomeration hurts. *Research Policy, 52*(1), 104625. doi:10.1016/j.respol.2022.104625

Pinto, A. M. G. L. R. S., da Silva Ramos, S. C. M., & Nunes, S. M. M. D. (2015). Managing an Aging Workforce: What is the Value of Human Resource Management Practices for Different Age Groups of Workers? *Tékhne (Instituto Politécnico do Cávado e do Ave), 12*, 58–68. doi:10.1016/j.tekhne.2015.01.007

Pitt-Catsouphes, M., & Smyer, M. A. (2006). *How Old are Today's Older Workers?* Boston College University Libraries.

PORDATA. (2022, June 15). *Indicadores de Envelhecimento* [Aging Indicators]. Retrieved from https://www.pordata.pt/Portugal/Indicadores+de+envelhecimento-526

Portuguese Association for the Development of Sociocultural Animation. (2019). *Estatuto da Carreira Profissional de Animador/a Sociocultural* [Statute of the Professional Career of Sociocultural Animator]. Retrieved from shorturl.at/jPUW1

Powell, T., & Bonito, O. (2015). *Attitudes of the over 50s to fuller working lives.* Retrieved from https://www.gov.uk/government/publications/attitudes-of-the-over-50s-to-fuller-working-lives

Powell, M. (2010). Ageism and abuse in the workplace: A new frontier. *Journal of Gerontological Social Work, 53*(7), 654–658. doi:10.1080/01634372.2010.508510 PMID:20865626

Priebe, J., & Howell, F. (2014). *Old-age Poverty in Indonesia: Empirical evidence and policy options - A role for social pensions.* TNP2K Working Paper.

Prihatiningtyastuti, E., Dayaram, K., & Burgess, J. (2020). Skills development and challenges for regional women. In K. Dayaram, L. Lambey, J. Burgess, & T. W. Afrianty (Eds.), *Developing the Workforce in an Emerging Economy: The Case of Indonesia* (pp. 53–67). Routledge. doi:10.4324/9780429273353-5

Priyono, S., & Nankervis, A. (2020). Graduate work readiness in Indonesia: challenges and opportunities. In K. Dayaram, L. Lambey, J. Burgess, & T. W. Afrianty (Eds.), *Developing the Workforce in an Emerging Economy: The Case of Indonesia* (pp. 110–124). Routledge. doi:10.4324/9780429273353-9

Puvill, T., Lindenberg, J., de Craen, A. J., Slaets, J. P., & Westendorp, R. G. (2016). Impact of Physical and Mental Health on Life Satisfaction in Old Age: A Population based Observational Study. *BMC Geriatrics*, *16*(1), 194. doi:10.118612877-016-0365-4 PMID:27887583

Qualls, K. E. (2022). Pharmacokinetics and Pharmacodynamics. In P. C. Bollu (Ed.), *Neurochemistry in Clinical Practice* (pp. 313–316). Springer. doi:10.1007/978-3-031-07897-2_16

Rafique, T., Asif, F., Afridi, J., & Mahmood, K. (2021). Credibility of social networking sites: Impact on organizational attraction in recruitment field. *Sarhad Journal of Management Sciences*, *6*(2), 2414–2336.

Ramos, S. (2010). *Envelhecimento, trabalho e cognição: do laboratório para o terreno na construção de uma alternativa metodológica* [Aging, work and cognition: from the laboratory to the field in the construction of a methodological alternative]. Fundação Calouste Gulbenkian.

Ranzijn, R. (2002). The Potential of Older Adults to Enhance Community Quality of Life: Links between Positive Psychology and Productive Aging. *Ageing International*, *27*(2), 30–55. doi:10.100712126-002-1001-5

Reiman, A., Kaivo-oja, J., Parviainen, E., Takala, E.-P., & Lauraeus, T. (2021). Human factors and ergonomics in manufacturing in the industry 4.0 context – A scoping review. *Technology in Society*, *65*, 101572. doi:10.1016/j.techsoc.2021.101572

Reitz, S. M., Scaffa, M. E., & Dorsey, J. (2020). Occupational Therapy in the Promotion of Health and Well-Being. *The American Journal of Occupational Therapy, 74*(3). doi:10.5014/ajot.2020.743003

Riach, K. (2009). Managing 'difference': Understanding age diversity in practice. *Human Resource Management Journal*, *19*(3), 319–335. doi:10.1111/j.1748-8583.2009.00096.x

Richardson, B., Webb, J., Webber, L., & Smith, K. (2013). Age discrimination in the evaluation of job applicants. *Journal of Applied Social Psychology*, *43*(1), 35–44. doi:10.1111/j.1559-1816.2012.00979.x

Rinsky-Halivni, L., Hovav, B., Christiani, D. C., & Brammli-Grinberg, S. (2022). Aging workforce with reduced work capacity: From organizational challenges to successful accommodations sustaining productivity and well-being. *Social Science & Medicine*, *312*, 115369. doi:10.1016/j.socscimed.2022.115369 PMID:36162364

Rippon, I., Kneale, D., de Oliveira, C., Demakakos, P., & Steptoe, A. (2014). Perceived age discrimination in older adults. *Age and Ageing*, *43*(3), 379–386. doi:10.1093/ageing/aft146 PMID:24077751

Robnett, R. H., & Chop, W. C. (2013). *Gerontology for the Health Care Professional*. Jones & Bartlett Publishers.

Rocha, M. F. (2018). *Envelhecer ativamente em Centro de Dia* [Active aging in the Day Center] [Master's thesis, Instituto Superior de Serviço Social do Porto]. Repository of Instituto Superior de Serviço Social do Porto. http://hdl.handle.net/10400.26/26005

Rodriguez, F. S., & Saenz, J. (2022). Working in old age in Mexico: Implications for cognitive functioning. *Ageing and Society*, *42*(11), 1–21. doi:10.1017/S0144686X2100012X

Rogers, C. S., & Peelle, J. E. (2022). Interactions Between Audition and Cognition in Hearing Loss and Aging. In L. L. Holt, J. E. Peelle, A. B. Coffin, A. N. Popper, & R. R. Fay (Eds.), *Speech Perception* (pp. 227–252). Springer. doi:10.1007/978-3-030-81542-4_9

Rosa, M.J.V. (2012). *O Envelhecimento da Sociedade Portuguesa* [The Aging of Portuguese Society]. Fundação Francisco Manuel dos Santos.

Roscigno, V. J. (2010). Ageism in the American workplace. *American Sociological Association*, *9*(1), 16–21. doi:10.1525/ctx.2010.9.1.16

Roser, M., & Rodés-Guirão, L. (2019). *Future Population Growth*. Retrieved from https://ourworldindata.org/future-population-growth

Rupp, D. E., Vodanovich, S. J., & Credé, M. (2006). Age Bias in the Workplace: The Impact of Ageism and Causal Attributions. *Journal of Applied Social Psychology*, *36*(6), 1337–1364. doi:10.1111/j.0021-9029.2006.00062.x

Saad, P. M. (2016). Envelhecimento populacional: Demandas e possibilidades na área de saúde [Population aging: demands and possibilities in health care]. *Séries Demográficas*, *3*, 153–166.

Santos, M., & Almeida, A. (2017). Saúde ocupacional aplicada a trabalhadores menos jovens [Occupational health applied to younger workers]. *Revista Portuguesa de Saúde Ocupacional*, *3*, 39–52. doi:10.31252/RPSO.15.03.2017

Sanusi, M. (2014, October 21-23). *Inter-generational family and community support: implication to social participation and contribution of older persons* [Paper Presentation]. *12th ASEAN and Japan Meeting on Caring Societies*, Tokyo, Japan.

Saraiva, J. (2011). Olfacto e envelhecimento [Smell and ageing]. In J. Saraiva (Ed.), *Otorrinolaringologia e Envelhecimento* [Otorhinolaryngology and Aging] (pp. 101–107). LIDEL Edições Técnicas, Lda.

Savioli, G., Ceresa, I. F., Novelli, V., Ricevuti, G., Bressan, M. A., & Oddone, E. (2022). How the coronavirus disease 2019 pandemic changed the patterns of healthcare utilization by geriatric patients and the crowding: A call to action for effective solutions to the access block. *Internal and Emergency Medicine*, *17*(2), 503–514. doi:10.100711739-021-02732-w PMID:34106397

Schalk, R., van Veldhoven, M., de Lange, A. H., De Witte, H., Kraus, K., Stamov-Roßnagel, C., Tordera, N., van der Heijden, B., Zappalà, S., Bal, M., Bertrand, F., Claes, R., Crego, A., Dorenbosch, L., de Jonge, J., Desmette, D., Gellert, F. J., Hansez, I., Iller, C., ... Zacher, H. (2010). Moving European research on work and ageing forward: Overview and agenda. *European Journal of Work and Organizational Psychology*, *19*(1), 76–101. doi:10.1080/13594320802674629

Schlicht, N. (2008). Body and memory – Physical diseases and cognitive disorders. *Zeitschrift für Gerontologie und Geriatrie*, *41*(3), 156–161. doi:10.100700391-008-0541-z PMID:18446304

Schmidt, J. A., & Lee, K. (2008). Voluntary Retirement and Organizational Turnover Intentions: The Differential Associations with Work and Non-Work Commitment Constructs. *Journal of Business and Psychology*, *22*(4), 297–309. doi:10.100710869-008-9068-y

Schor, E. L., & American Academy of Pediatrics Task Force on the Family. (2003). Family pediatrics: Report of the Task Force on the Family. *Pediatrics*, *111*(6 Pt 2), 1541–1571. PMID:12777595

Schreurs, B., De Cuyper, N., van Emmerik, I. J. H., Notelaers, G., & De Witte, H. (2011). Job demands and resources and their associations with early retirement intentions through recovery need and work enjoyment. *SA Journal of Industrial Psychology*, *37*(2), 1–11. doi:10.4102ajip.v37i2.859

Schulte, P. A., Grosch, J., Scholl, J. C., & Tamers, S. L. (2018). Framework for considering productive aging and work. *Journal of Occupational and Environmental Medicine*, *60*(5), 440–448. doi:10.1097/JOM.0000000000001295 PMID:29420331

Schumacher, K., Beck, C. A., & Marren, J. M. (2006). Family Caregivers: Caring for Older Adults, Working with their Families. *The American Journal of Nursing*, *106*(8), 40–50. doi:10.1097/00000446-200608000-00020 PMID:16905931

Settels, J. (2022). The Health Effects of Workforce Involvement and Transitions for Europeans 50–75 Years of Age: Heterogeneity by Financial Difficulties and Gender. *Canadian Journal on Aging*, *41*(3), 304–319. doi:10.1017/S0714980821000556 PMID:35859357

Sharma, P., Chua, J. H., & Chrisman, J. J. (2000). Perceptions about the extent of succession planning in Canadian family firms. *Canadian Journal of Administrative Sciences*, *17*(3), 233–244. doi:10.1111/j.1936-4490.2000.tb00223.x

Silva, B. C., & Moreira, A. C. (2022). Entrepreneurship and the gig economy: A bibliometric analysis. *Management Letters. Cuadernos de Gestión*, *22*(2), 23–22. doi:10.5295/cdg.211580am

Silverstein, M. (2008). Meeting the Challenges of an Aging Workforce. *American Journal of Industrial Medicine*, *51*(4), 269–280. doi:10.1002/ajim.20569 PMID:18271000

SMERU Research Report. (2020). *The Situation of the Elderly in Indonesia and Access to Social Protection Programs: Secondary Data Analysis.* The National Team for The Acceleration of Poverty Reduction.

Smith, D. R., Holtom, B. C., & Mitchell, T. R. (2011). Enhancing precision in the prediction of voluntary turnover and retirement. *Journal of Vocational Behavior*, *79*(1), 290–302. doi:10.1016/j.jvb.2010.11.003

Social Security Institute. (2021). *Objetivos e princípios* [Objectives and principles]. Retrieved from https://www.seg-social.pt/objectivos-e-principios

Social Security Institute. (n.d). *Quem pode desenvolver respostas sociais* [Who can develop social answers]. Retrieved from https://www.seg-social.pt/como-desenvolver-respostas-sociais

Sparkes, A. C., & Smith, B. (2013). *Qualitative Research Methods in Sport, Exercise and Health: From Process to Product.* Routledge. doi:10.4324/9780203852187

Spitzer, W. J., & Davidson, K. W. (2013). Future Trends in Health and Health care: Implications for Social Work Practice in an Aging Society. *Social Work in Health Care*, *52*(10), 959–986. doi:10.1080/00981389.2013.834028 PMID:24255978

Statistics Portugal. (2002). *Censos 2001 - Resultados Definitivos* [2001 Census - Definitive Results]. Statistics Portugal.

Statistics Portugal. (2009). *Aprendizagem ao Longo da Vida - Inquérito à Educação e Formação de Adultos 2007* [Lifelong Learning - Adult Education and Training Survey 2007]. Statistics Portugal.

Statistics Portugal. (2014). *Projeções de população residente 2012-2060* [Projections of resident population 2012-2060]. Retrieved from https://www.ine.pt/xportal/xmain?xpid=INE&xpgid=ine_destaques&DESTAQUESdest_boui=208819970&DESTAQUESmodo=2&xlang=pt

Statistics Portugal. (2015). *Envelhecimento da população residente em Portugal e na União Europeia* [Aging of the resident population in Portugal and in the European Union]. Retrieved from https://www.ine.pt/xportal/xmain?xpid=INE&xpgid=ine_destaques&DESTAQUESdest_boui=224679354&DESTAQUESmodo=2&xlang=pt

Statistics Times. (2021). *Projected GDP Ranking*. Retrieved from http://statisticstimes.com/economy/projected-world-gdp-ranking.php

Staudinger, U. M., Finkelstein, R., Calvo, E., & Sivaramakrishnan, K. (2016). A Global View on the Effects of Work on Health in Later Life. *The Gerontologist*, *56*(Supplement 2), S281–S292. doi:10.1093/geront/gnw032 PMID:26994267

Stengård, J., Leineweber, C., Virtanen, M., Westerlund, H., & Wang, H.-X. (2022). Do good psychosocial working conditions prolong working lives? Findings from a prospective study in Sweden. *European Journal of Ageing*, *19*(3), 1–12. doi:10.100710433-021-00672-0 PMID:36052189

Stone, A., & Harkiolakis, N. (2022). Technology Boom(ers): How US Multinational Technology Companies Are Preparing for an Ageing Workforce. *Administrative Sciences*, *12*(3), 1–14. doi:10.3390/admsci12030091

Stones, D., & Gullifer, J. (2016). 'At home it's just so much easier to be yourself': Older adults' perceptions of ageing in place. *Ageing and Society*, *36*(3), 449–481. doi:10.1017/S0144686X14001214

Strauss, A., & Corbin, J. M. (1998). *Basics of Qualitative Research: Techniques and Procedures for Developing Grounded Theory*. Sage Publications, Inc.

Stypinska, J., & Turek, K. (2017). Hard and soft age discrimination: The dual nature of workplace discrimination. *European Journal of Ageing*, *14*(1), 49–61. doi:10.100710433-016-0407-y PMID:28804394

Taskforce on the Aging of the American Workforce. (n.d.). *Older worker initiative*. Retrieved from https://www.dol.gov/agencies/eta/reports/older-worker-initiative

Tavares, M. A. (2020). Envelhecimento e trabalho na sociedade capitalista [Aging and work in capitalist society]. *Revista Katálysis*, *23*(1), 143–151. doi:10.1590/1982-02592020v23n1p143

Taylor, P., & Walker, A. (1998). Employers and older workers: Attitudes and employment practices. *Ageing and Society*, *18*(6), 641–658. doi:10.1017/S0144686X98007119

Tekles, A., & Bornmann, L. (2020). Author name disambiguation of bibliometric data: A comparison of several unsupervised approaches. *Quantitative Science Studies*, *1*(4), 1510–1528. doi:10.1162/qss_a_00081

The Organization for Economic Cooperation and Development. (2020). *OECD Data: Labour Force Participation Rate*. Retrieved from https://data.oecd.org/searchresults/?q=labour+force +participation+rate

The Tobacco Atlas. (2019). *State of global tobacco*. Retrieved from https://tobaccoatlas.org/

The World Bank. (2017). *Indonesia's Global Workers: Juggling Opportunities and Risks*. The World Bank.

The World Bank. (2018). *The World Bank In Indonesia*. Retrieved from https://www.worldbank.org/en/country/indonesia/overview

The World Bank. (2019). *Human Capital Index*. Retrieved from https://databank.worldbank.org/reports.aspx?source=3698&series=HD.HCI.EYRS

Thompson, L. F., & Mayhorn, C. B. (2012). Aging workers and technology. In W. Borman & T. Hedge (Eds.), *The Oxford handbook of work and aging* (pp. 341–361). Oxford University Press. doi:10.1093/oxfordhb/9780195385052.013.0113

Tondo, C. (2008). *Desenvolvendo a empresa familiar e a família empresária (1ª Edição)* [Developing the family business and the entrepreneurial family (1st Edition)]. Editora Sulina.

Troger, H. (2021). *Human resource management in a post Covid-19 world: New distribution of power, individualization, digitalization and demographic developments*. Springer. https://link.springer.com/book/10.1007/978-3-030-67470-0

Truxillo, D., Cadiz, D., & Hammer, L. (2015). Supporting the aging workforce: A research review and recommendations for workplace intervention research. *Annual Review of Organizational Psychology and Organizational Behavior*, *2*(1), 351–381. doi:10.1146/annurev-orgpsych-032414-111435

U.S. Department of Labor, Bureau of Labor Statistics. (2018). *Age discrimination*. Retrieved from https://www.dol.gov/general/topic/discrimination/agedisc

U.S. Equal Employment Opportunity Commission. (2019). *Home*. Retrieved from https://www.eeoc.gov/

United Nations Department of Economic and Social Affairs. (2017). *Population Aging and Sustainable Development*. United Nations.

United Nations Department of Economic and Social Affairs. (2019). *World Population Prospects 2019: Highlights*. United Nations.

United Nations Development Program. (2018). *Human Development Index (HDI)*. Retrieved from https://hdr.undp.org/data-center/human-development-index#/indicies/HDI

United Nations Population Fund. (2012). *Envelhecimento no Século XXI: Celebração e Desafio - Resumo Executivo* [Aging in the 21st Century: Celebration and Challenge - Executive Summary]. Retrieved from https://www.unfpa.org/sites/default/files/pub-pdf/Portuguese-Exec-Summary_0.pdf

United Nations. (2019). *Global Issues - Ageing*. Retrieved from https://www.un.org/en/global-issues/ageing

United Nations. (2022). *Envelhecimento* [Ageing]. Retrieved from https://unric.org/pt/envelhecimento/

Urabe, K., Child, J., & Kagono, T. (2018). *Innovation and Management: International Comparisons* (13th ed.). De Gruyter.

van den Anker, J., Reed, M. D., Allegaert, K., & Kearns, G. L. (2018). Developmental Changes in Pharmacokinetics and Pharmacodynamics. *Journal of Clinical Pharmacology*, *58*, S10–S25. doi:10.1002/jcph.1284 PMID:30248190

Vanleerberghe, P., De Witte, N., Claes, C., Schalock, R. L., & Verté, D. (2017). The Quality of Life of Older People Aging in Place: A Literature Review. *Quality of Life Research: An International Journal of Quality of Life Aspects of Treatment, Care and Rehabilitation*, *26*(11), 2899–2907. doi:10.100711136-017-1651-0 PMID:28707047

Vasconcelos, A. F. (2018). Older workers as a source of wisdom capital: Broadening perspectives. *Revista de Gestão*, *25*(1), 102–118. doi:10.1108/REGE-11-2017-002

Veldon, B. (2013). Ageism and age discrimination in the workplace. *CRIS-Bulletin of the Centre for Research and Interdisciplinary Study, 2013*(2), 33–41. doi:10.2478/cris-2013-0008

Veloso, E. F. R., da Silva, R. C., & Dutra, J. S. (2012). Diferentes Gerações e Percepções sobre Carreiras Inteligentes e Crescimento Profissional nas Organizações [Different generations and perceptions of intelligent careers and career growth within organizations]. *Revista Brasileira de Orientação Profissional, 13*(2), 197–207.

Verworn, B., & Hipp, C. (2009). Does the ageing workforce hamper the innovativeness of firms? (No) evidence from Germany. *International Journal of Human Resources Development and Management, 9*(2/3), 180–197. doi:10.1504/IJHRDM.2009.023452

Vilardouro, C. F. (2013). *O contributo da animação sociocultural para o desenvolvimento pessoal e social de alunos com Necessidades Educativas Especiais no 1º ciclo do ensino básico* [The contribution of sociocultural animation to the personal and social development of students with Special Educational Needs in the 1st cycle of basic education] [Master's thesis, Universidade Católica Portuguesa]. Repository of, Universidade Católica Portuguesa. http://hdl.handle.net/10400.14/13639

Viswanathan, M., & Sridharan, S. (2011). Product Development for the BoP: Insights on Concept and Prototype Development from University-Based Student Projects in India. *Journal of Product Innovation Management, 29*(1), 52–69. doi:10.1111/j.1540-5885.2011.00878.x

Viviani, C. A., Bravo, G., Lavallière, M., Arezes, P. M., Martínez, M., Dianat, I., Bragança, S., & Castellucci, H. I. (2021). Productivity in older versus younger workers: A systematic literature review. *Work (Reading, Mass.), 68*(3), 577–618. doi:10.3233/WOR-203396 PMID:33612506

Wanberg, C. R., Kanfer, R., Hamann, D. J., & Zhang, Z. (2016). Age and reemployment success after job loss: An integrative model and meta-analysis. *Psychological Bulletin, 142*(4), 400–426. doi:10.1037/bul0000019 PMID:26011790

Wang, M., & Fang, Y. (2020). Age diversity in the workplace: Facilitating opportunities with organizational practices. *The Public Policy and Aging Report, 30*(3), 119–123. doi:10.1093/ppar/praa015

Wang, M., & Shi, J. (2015). Work, Retirement, and Aging. In K. W. Schaie & S. Willis (Eds.), *Handbook of the Psychology of Aging* (pp. 339–359). Academic Press.

Wegge, J., & Meyer, B. (2020). Age diversity and age-based faultlines in teams: Understanding a Brezel phenomenon requires a Brezel theory. *Work, Aging and Retirement, 6*(1), 8–14. doi:10.1093/workar/waz017

Weyman, A., Meadows, P., & Buckingham, A. (2013). *Extending Working Life: Audit of research relating to impacts on NHS employees.* NHS Confederation.

Whillans, J., Nazroo, J., & Matthews, K. (2016). Trajectories of vision in older people: The role of age and social position. *European Journal of Ageing*, *13*(2), 171–184. doi:10.100710433-015-0360-1 PMID:27358606

Williams van Rooij, S. (2012). Training older workers: Lessons learned, unlearned, and relearned from the field of instructional design. *Human Resource Management*, *51*(2), 281–298. doi:10.1002/hrm.21466

Wisse, B., van Eijbergen, R., Rietzschel, E. F., & Scheibe, S. (2018). Catering to the Needs of an Aging Workforce: The Role of Employee Age in the Relationship Between Corporate Social Responsibility and Employee Satisfaction. *Journal of Business Ethics*, *147*(4), 875–888. doi:10.100710551-015-2983-8

Wissemann, A. K., Pit, S. W., Serafin, P., & Gebhardt, H. (2022). Strategic Guidance and Technological Solutions for Human Resources Management to Sustain an Aging Workforce: Review of International Standards, Research, and Use Cases. *JMIR Human Factors*, *9*(3), e27250. doi:10.2196/27250 PMID:35862177

World Economic Forum. (2015). *The Global Gender Gap Report 2015*. Retrieved from https://www.weforum.org/reports/global-gender-gap-report-2015/

World Economic Forum. (2019, January 3). *An Ageing Workforce Isn't a Burden. It's an Opportunity*. Retrieved from https://www.weforum.org/agenda/2019/01/an-aging-workforce-isnt-a-burden-its-an-opportunity

World Health Organization. (2005). *Envelhecimento Ativo: Uma Política de Saúde* [Active Aging: A Health Policy]. Retrieved from https://bvsms.saude.gov.br/bvs/publicacoes/envelhecimento_ativo.pdf

World Health Organization. (2012)‎. *World Health Day 2012: ageing and health: toolkit for event organizers*. Retrieved from https://apps.who.int/iris/handle/10665/70840

World Health Organization. (2012)‎. *World Health Day 2012: ageing and health: Toolkit for event organizers*. Retrieved from https://apps.who.int/iris/handle/10665/70840

World Health Organization. (2021a). *Comprehensive Mental Health Action Plan 2013–2030*. Retrieved from https://apps.who.int/iris/bitstream/handle/10665/345301/9789240031029-eng.pdf?sequence=1&isAllowed=y

World Health Organization. (2021b). *Strategies for preventing and managing falls across the life-course*. World Health Organization.

Worldometers. (2022). *Indonesia Population*. Retrieved from https://www.worldometers.info/world-population/indonesia-population/

Xavier, B. G. L. (2004). Curso de Direito do Trabalho: Vol. I. *Introdução, Quadros Organizacionais e Fontes* [Labor Law Course - Volume I (Introduction, Organizational Frameworks and Sources)]. Editorial Verbo.

Yates, L. A., Ziser, S., Spector, A., & Orrell, M. (2016). Cognitive leisure activities and future risk of cognitive impairment and dementia: Systematic review and meta-analysis. *International Psychogeriatrics*, *28*(11), 1791–1806. doi:10.1017/S1041610216001137 PMID:27502691

Yeomans, L. (2011). *An update of the literature on age and employment*. HSE Books Health and Safety Executive.

Zhang, W., & Wood, S. (2022). Awareness of age-related change, chronological age, subjective age and proactivity: An empirical study in China. *Frontiers in Psychiatry*, *13*, 915673. doi:10.3389/fpsyt.2022.915673 PMID:36245881

Zhang, Z., Jin, J., Li, S., & Zhang, Y. (2023). Digital transformation of incumbent firms from the perspective of portfolios of innovation. *Technology in Society*, *72*, 102149. doi:10.1016/j.techsoc.2022.102149

About the Contributors

Bruno de Sousa Lopes is a Business and Economics Ph.D. student at the University of Aveiro - Portugal. He has a master's in Human Resource Management and Development and a bachelor's degree in Human Resources from the Institute Polytechnic of Porto, Portugal. His main research interests are Human Resources, Ageing, Career Management, and Business Management.

Maria do Céu Lamas is a Professor at the School of Health I IPP (ESS IPP) in the technical and scientific area of Clinical Analysis and Public Health. Member of the Center for Research in Health and Environment (CISA), ESS IPP, and collaborator of the Research Center in Technologies and Health Services (CINTESIS) - University of Porto (UP), Portugal, in the line of research on aging. She is the author and co-author of several scientific papers. She has a Bachelor's degree in Clinical Analysis and Public Health and a Master's in Hydrobiology from the Faculty of Sciences, UP. She is a doctoral student in Gerontology at the Institute of Biomedical Sciences Abel Salazar (ICBAS), UP, Portugal.

Vanessa Amorim is a Business and Economics Ph.D. student at the University of Aveiro - Portugal. She has a master's in Organizational Management - Specialization: Business Management and a Post-Graduation in Management Tools for Business Competitiveness from the Institute Polytechnic of Porto - Portugal. Her main research interests are Innovation, Entrepreneurship, Marketing, and Business Management.

Orlando Lima Rua holds a Habilitation and a Ph.D. in Management. He is an Adjunct Professor of Management at the Porto Accounting and Business School (ISCAP) of the Polytechnic of Porto (Portugal). He is a researcher at the Center for Organizational and Social Studies (CEOS.PP) (Polytechnic of Porto – ISCAP), the Research Center of Business Sciences (NECE) of the University of Beira Interior (UBI), and the Management Applied Research Unit (UNIAG) of the Association of Polytechnic Institutes of Northern Portugal (APNOR). His major research subjects are entrepreneurship, innovation, and strategy, and his papers have been published in several relevant international journals and scientific conferences (JCR/Web of Science and Scopus).

* * *

John Burgess is Professor of Management. Previous professorial appointments were at the University of Newcastle, Curtin University, and RMIT University. Research has included contingent employment arrangements, transitional labor markets; equity and diversity workforce practices; technological change and skills development; and gig working. He has co-edited several books on workforce developments in the Asia Pacific and co-edited special issues in such journals as the International Journal of Human Resource Management and Personnel Review.

Abeni El-Amin, Ph.D., Ed.D., D.PC., MPsy - I/O, LSSMBB, has nearly two decades of experience and education in Management as an educator and practitioner. Further, as a higher education professor, she has designed and developed curriculum and training programs in business administration, educational leadership, legal studies, political science, psychology, and health sciences. She is a globally recognized thought leader on diversity, equity, inclusion, and belonging. She helps organizations develop a culture of belongingness through innovative and thought-provoking training. Dr. El-Amin is an author, international university lecturer, trainer, and speaker. Dr. El-Amin is the editor of Implementing Diversity, Equity, Inclusion, and Belonging Management in Organizational Change Initiatives and Implementing Diversity, Equity, Inclusion, and Belonging in Educational Management Practices - IGI Global. Dr. El-Amin is co-founder of Titan and Mogul, Inc., a global consultancy that provides lean six sigma and HR consultancy focusing on DEIB to improve organizational culture. She is also the author of, In Search of Servant Leadership.

Nadine E. Franz, Ed.D., is a Graduate Writing Coordinator in the Research and Writing Development Center within the Ed.D., Learning, and Organizational Change Program. Dr. Franz earned a B.A. in Anthropology from Brandeis University, an M.S. in Human Resource Development and Administration from Barry University, and an Ed.D. in Learning and Organizational Change from Baylor University. Dr. Franz's teaching competencies include Professional and Academic Writing Development, Workplace Ageism, Diversity Equity & Inclusion (DEI), Human Resources (HR), Human Resource Management (HRM), Career Management, International Business, and Organizational Leadership. Additionally, Dr. Franz works as a Career Coach, HR Strategist, and Ageism and DEI Consultant. She is a member of the Society for

Human Resource Management (SHRM), the Academy of Management (HR & Organization Development and Change), the Academy of Human Resource Development (AHRD), and the North American Network in Aging Studies (NANAS). Dr. Franz's primary research foci include workplace ageism, DEI, workplace marginalization, and similar topics. She is passionate about creating equitable and inclusive work environments that foster a sense of belonging for underrepresented employees and job seekers. She consults organizations on strategies to develop and sustain inclusive workplaces, mainly through implementing non-biased and non-ageist recruiting, hiring, and retention strategies. Dr. Franz serves on several Boards.

Linda Lambey is a Senior Lecturer in the Faculty of Business and Economics at the University of Sam Ratulangi, Manado, Indonesia. She undertook her Ph.D. in Management at the University of Newcastle, Australia. Her research interests include Management Accounting, Organisational Behaviour, and Human Resource Management.

Raja Saravanan is a Ph.D. student at the University of Aveiro. He is working on a necessary idea to build layers of abstraction and automate tasks to reduce the gap between an organization's business and technology. He is interested in distributed ledger technology, enterprise architecture, and intra-organizational communication. He has a varied background of experience in website administration, business development, digital marketing, and data administration. He likes to give practical solutions to complex and challenging problems and is passionate about his research. He has published two conference papers focused on strategic solutions for technologies for retail business.

Maria Inês Sousa has a Bachelor's degree in Animation and Sociocultural Intervention and is currently doing her Master's in Education and Society at ISCTE- University Institute of Lisbon. Her research interests are related to the areas of gerontology (aging, dementia, etc.) as well as psychology (pathology and special educational needs). She is also certified in Training Trainers and intends to become certified in Portuguese Sign Language and, later, in British Sign Language.

Elni Jeini Usoh is a Senior Lecturer at Universitas Negeri Manado, Indonesia, and is in charge as Secretary of the International Office. She obtained her master's degree in Leadership and Management in Education (Honours) in 2008 and her Ph.D. in Education in 2015 from the University of Newcastle, Australia.

Index

A

Active Aging 45, 49, 55, 58, 68, 70-72, 87, 95, 98, 154
Age Bias 128, 158
Age Discrimination 107-108, 110-116, 118, 122-123, 125-127, 167
Age Prejudice 128
Ageing 15-17, 19, 42-44, 46, 71, 89-90, 104-105, 123, 126-127, 155, 159-160, 173-174
Ageism 107-128, 158
Aging in Place 3, 17
Aging Workforce 1-2, 16, 19-20, 73, 75, 93-94, 100-101, 104, 107-113, 115-118, 121, 126-128, 130, 156, 160-165, 167-170, 172-174
Audition 16, 19

B

Bias 5, 107, 115, 123, 125, 128, 141, 158

C

Career 41, 70, 108-109, 115-116, 121, 126, 129-131, 134-136, 138-140, 143, 145, 147-149, 151-154, 156-157, 160, 170
Career Management 129-131, 134-135, 139-140, 147-149, 151, 154, 156-157, 160
Creativity 93-94, 97-106, 124

D

DEI 121
Dependency Ratio 73-74, 79-83, 85, 87-88, 92
Digital Transformation 105, 170, 174
Discrimination 77, 107-116, 118, 122-123, 125-128, 164-165, 167

E

Economic Development 74, 96, 103, 162-163, 167, 170, 174
Economic Growth 76, 84, 96, 98, 100-101, 106, 134, 161-163
Enterprise Architect 161, 169-170
Enterprise Architecture 161, 164, 167-170, 172, 174

G

Gender Equity Index (GEN) 92
Geriatric 1, 4, 11, 13, 15, 17, 41-42
Gerontology 1-2, 11-12, 15-18, 65-66, 70, 124-125

H

Healthy Aging 21, 73-74, 83, 85, 87
Hearing 12, 16, 19-23, 42, 44, 82
Hiring Practices 109, 111-113, 115, 118-122, 128
Human Capital Index (HCI) 77, 92
Human Development Index (HDI) 77, 91-92

Human Resource (HR) Policies and Procedures 128

I

Impact and Challenges 163
Individual Aging 45, 50-51, 72, 131
Industry 4.0 161, 165-167, 169, 172-175
Informal Employment 13, 74, 77, 81, 92
Informal Sector 75, 77, 79, 82-83, 85, 87-88, 92
Innovation 64, 93-104, 106, 165
Innovative Work Behavior 93, 99, 103-104, 106

K

Knowledge Transfer 106

L

Lifelong Learning 11, 45-46, 50, 60, 66, 70, 72, 75, 125

M

Mental Health 2, 13, 16, 39, 45, 52-53, 55, 71-72

O

Organizations 20, 63, 72, 86, 94, 96-97, 99-102, 109, 111, 120, 124, 129-131, 133, 135, 137, 139, 143, 147, 149-150, 153-154, 156-157, 160, 166, 168-172

P

Pancasli 92
Pharmacodynamics 16-18
Pharmacokinetics 9, 16-18
Productivity 6, 16, 21, 72-73, 77-78, 80, 82-84, 88, 104, 109-110, 120, 127, 149, 163-166, 168, 170-171
Protected Classes 128

Q

Quality of Life (QoL) 3, 18, 72

R

Retirement 1, 14, 46, 54, 74, 77, 79-81, 83, 85-88, 94-95, 101, 113, 126, 128-131, 133, 136-140, 142-143, 146, 149, 151-153, 155-157, 159-160, 162, 164, 166, 170, 174

S

Senior Collaborators 129, 160
Sensory Impairment 19, 44
Sensory Impairment Taste 19
Sensory System 20-21, 42, 44
Skills 6, 20, 54, 60, 63, 66, 74, 77-78, 84, 87, 91, 93-94, 97-98, 106, 109, 112-114, 116-120, 130, 135-136, 150, 165, 168, 171, 173-174
Smell 19, 21, 24, 42-44
Social Development 45-46, 71, 73, 97, 161, 163, 169, 175
Social Responses 46, 56, 59, 66, 72
Sociocultural Animation 45, 59, 63-72
Stereotypes 5, 107, 112-114, 116-119, 121-122, 125-126, 173
Succession Plan 135-137, 149-150, 153, 156, 160

T

Taste 21, 23-24, 42, 44
Telomere Erosion Theory (TET) 8, 18
Touch 21, 23-24, 44
Training 9, 14, 24, 39, 58, 60-61, 64, 70, 73, 77, 81-82, 84, 86-88, 111, 115-117, 119-121, 123, 128, 135, 137, 148, 162, 165-167, 172

U

Untying 129, 160

V

Vision 6, 12, 20-21, 41, 43-44, 155

W

Workforce 1-2, 6, 13-16, 19-20, 25, 28, 30, 32, 37-40, 44, 73-78, 80-82, 84-85, 87-89, 91, 93-94, 99-101, 104-105, 107-121, 123, 126-128, 130, 132, 136, 151, 156-157, 160-165, 167-170, 172-174
Workplace 19-20, 99, 107-108, 110-123, 125-128, 156, 158, 161, 166, 170, 172, 174

www.ingramcontent.com/pod-product-compliance
Lightning Source LLC
LaVergne TN
LVHW061535290926
849162LV00004B/795
* 9 7 8 1 6 6 8 4 6 3 5 1 2 *